THE LAST LINCOLN REPUBLICAN

American Presidential Elections

MICHAEL NELSON

JOHN M. MCCARDELL, JR.

THE LAST LINCOLN REPUBLICAN

THE PRESIDENTIAL ELECTION OF 1880

BENJAMIN T. ARRINGTON

UNIVERSITY PRESS OF KANSAS

Published by the University Press of Kansas (Lawrence, Kansas 66045), which was organized by the Kansas Board of Regents and is operated and funded by Emporia State University, Fort Hays State University, Kansas State University, Pittsburg State University, the University of Kansas, and Wichita State University

© 2020 by the University Press of Kansas
First paperback edition published in 2023.
All rights reserved

Library of Congress Cataloging-in-Publication Data

Names: Arrington, B. T. (Benjamin T.), author.
Title: The last Lincoln Republican : the presidential election of 1880 / Benjamin T. Arrington.
Description: Lawrence : University Press of Kansas, [2020] | Series: American presidential elections | Includes bibliographical references and index.
Identifiers: LCCN 2020006824
 ISBN 9780700629824 (cloth)
 ISBN 9780700636037 (paperback)
 ISBN 9780700629831 (epub)
Subjects: LCSH: Presidents—United States—Election—1880. | Garfield, James A. (James Abram), 1831–1881. | Republican Party (U.S. : 1854–)—History—19th century. | United States—Politics and government—1865–1883. | Hancock, Winfield Scott, 1824–1886. | Presidents—United States—Election—1876. | Hayes, Rutherford B., 1822–1893. | Tilden, Samuel J. (Samuel Jones), 1814–1886.
Classification: LCC E685 .A77 2020 | DDC 324.973/09034—dc23
LC record available at https://lccn.loc.gov/2020006824.

British Library Cataloguing-in-Publication Data is available.

Printed in the United States of America

10 9 8 7 6 5 4 3 2 1

The paper used in this publication is recycled and contains 30 percent postconsumer waste. It is acid free and meets the minimum requirements of the American National Standard for Permanence of Paper for Printed Library Materials Z39.48-1992.

For Kristy, Natalie, and Nicholas

CONTENTS

Editors' Foreword ix

Acknowledgments xi

Introduction 1

1 "Half Way between God and the Devil": The Election of 1876 and Its Aftermath 6

2 "Let Us Not Shrink Now": The Rise of James A. Garfield 29

3 "Antagonisms and Controversies": The 1880 Republican National Convention—Part 1 52

4 "If Any Outsider Is Taken, I Hope It Will Be Garfield": The 1880 Republican National Convention—Part 2 78

5 "The Most Infamous Man in America": Winfield Scott Hancock and the 1880 Democratic National Convention 97

6 "Indefatigable Agitators": Third-Party Candidates in the 1880 Election 118

7 "Those Great Questions of National Well-Being": The 1880 Presidential Campaign 127

8 "The Personal Aspects of the Presidency Are Far from Pleasant": James A. Garfield as President 161

Conclusion 182

Notes 187

Bibliographic Essay 203

Index 207

EDITORS' FOREWORD

It is at once a blessing and a curse that we historians know how the stories we tell turn out. Too often, our omniscience both shapes and skews the narrative—the overused term "antebellum" comes to mind. Things participants in the story could not possibly know or foresee become reminders of an outcome that, because it is known, seems "inevitable" (a word historians ought never use).

It is also a blessing and a curse that, over time, a conventional wisdom about events, individuals, periods, and themes can emerge that allows synthesis and simplicity, on the one hand, and impedes new interpretations and bold insights, on the other. Such is the case with American political history covering the final quarter of the nineteenth century. Google "forgettable presidents," and the names Hayes, Garfield, Arthur, Cleveland, and Harrison pop up. To differentiate these presidents from one another, the most common observation is that some had beards and some did not.

Recently, however, a new generation of scholars has challenged this conventional wisdom and sought to move the narrative out of its deeply beaten interpretative grooves. Of these, Benjamin T. Arrington occupies a conspicuous place. In this volume, he lays to rest the old clichés while summarizing and synthesizing the latest scholarship and drawing from it larger and important themes. To be sure, the reader cannot forget the assassin lurking just offstage. But because of the richness of the election story and the particular promise of the Garfield presidency, that knowledge, in Arrington's skillful hands, adds great meaning to the choice facing the electorate.

According to Arrington, James A. Garfield, improbable Republican nominee for the presidency in 1880, was "the last true 'Lincoln Republican.'" By this he means that the Civil War veteran from Ohio was seriously committed to making good on the promises of emancipation and Reconstruction. An assassin's bullet relegated Garfield to the footnotes of history and thwarted freedmen's opportunity to secure the rights that would elude their grasp for nearly another century.

Might-have-beens, of course, are also both a blessing and a curse. But in the story of Garfield's rise to prominence, the appeal of his candidacy, and his early days in office, readers can discern possibilities never realized, purposes never achieved. All this makes the election of 1880 far more important than historians have realized. Arrington notes that 1880 was the only election that pitted war veterans against each other, and service in the Union cause was a prerequisite for a viable candidacy. Moreover, Garfield prevailed by the narrowest of electoral margins. Yet, as the Democratic Party's dependence on the "solid South" became apparent, the Republicans' overtures to business clearly delineated the differences between the parties—differences that in time would have less to do with race and equality and more to do with managing a dynamic and increasingly complex economy. Jim Crow's strange career had begun.

ACKNOWLEDGMENTS

It is both a cliché and a truism that no nonfiction author writes a book alone, and I am certainly no exception. I owe immense debts of gratitude I will never be able to repay to many people who made this work possible.

I have been fortunate to spend more than twenty years working for the National Park Service, and many supervisors and colleagues have guided my career, allowed me to pursue my graduate education, and inspired me with their dedication to history and the agency's noble mission. Former and current bosses Scott Hartwig, Carol Hegeman, Mark Engler, Sherda Williams, Paul Stoehr, and Craig Kenkel all deserve special recognition. My colleagues at the James A. Garfield National Historic Site live and breathe Garfield every day, and any one of them could have written this book. They include Allison Powell, Mary Lintern, Joan Kapsch, Scott Longert, Alan Gephardt, and many others. Members of the Garfield family in Cleveland and elsewhere have been incredibly supportive and encouraging.

During a well-timed visit to Ohio, my former academic adviser at the University of Nebraska–Lincoln, Professor Emeritus Lloyd E. Ambrosius, encouraged me to pursue this opportunity when it first came to my attention.

Through my job, I have been fortunate to get to know several talented writers and filmmakers who have studied not only Garfield and his era but also other periods of history. All provided great support, friendship, and advice as I wrote. Thank you to Candice Millard, Ken Ackerman, Alexandra Zapruder, Lindsey Fitzharris, Louis Picone, Dan Vermilya, Brian Matthew Jordan, Rob Rapley, and others. The late Dr. Allan Peskin, who wrote the authoritative Garfield biography, is greatly missed. His work on Garfield, which is still wonderful more than four decades after its publication, was a critical source for this book.

Special thanks to David Congdon at the University Press of Kansas for his kindness, his belief in this book, and his patience with me. Thank you as well to Joyce Harrison, editor in chief of the press. Charles Myers, formerly with the University Press of Kansas but now at the University of Chicago Press, first asked me to write this book.

My greatest scholarly debt is to Heather Cox Richardson, the nation's foremost historian of the Republican Party and, I am happy to say, a big

James Garfield fan. I emailed Heather out of the blue more than a decade ago, and she has been a friend and colleague ever since. The University Press of Kansas approached her about writing this book several years ago, and she was kind enough to suggest me instead. She also read the manuscript and provided excellent suggestions for improvement.

I am fortunate to have great support from a loving family as well. My parents, Bill and Carmen Arrington, nurtured my love of history from an early age. I am grateful that they never tried to convince me to change my major.

My wife, Kristy, and our children, Natalie and Nicholas, are constant sources of pride, inspiration, and fun. They have been nothing but encouraging for the past several years as I have spent more time in the nineteenth century than with them in the twenty-first. My wife has been my partner, supporter, and best friend for more than twenty years. Our kids are smart, independent, and accomplished because of her. The three of them have been more patient and understanding than I had any right to expect. I do not deserve them, but I am lucky and glad to have them.

INTRODUCTION

The general public and historians alike tend to view several of the post–Civil War presidents—from Ulysses S. Grant to William McKinley—as interchangeable and mostly unimportant. College history textbooks sometimes misidentify them, showing a photo of James A. Garfield with the caption "Rutherford B. Hayes."[1] In the early twentieth century, Thomas Wolfe reinforced this belief in his short story "From Death to Morning," calling these men "the lost Americans" and noting that "their gravely vacant and bewhiskered faces mixed, melted, swam together. . . . Which had the whiskers, which the sideburns, which was which?"[2]

In many circles, these views persist. When asked what they know about Garfield, people visiting the James A. Garfield National Historic Site in Ohio often give the same three answers: he was president, he had a beard, and he got shot. These things are all true, and visitors cannot really be held accountable for their lack of knowledge when, for decades, even many academic historians have reinforced the idea articulated by Wolfe: that the presidency was just a giant black hole filled with nobodies from the death of Abraham Lincoln until the era of Theodore Roosevelt.

Recently, though, things have started to change. Some skilled writers have turned their attention to Reconstruction and the Gilded Age, taking a second look at American leaders from those eras. The public's renewed interest in and curiosity about America's past leaders may be a response to the increasingly fractured and divisive state of modern American politics. Perhaps the ongoing arguments about racial, social, and economic equality have made Americans hungry for information about elected officials who championed equality and bipartisanship. The post–Civil War period offers a number of examples. Despite decades of minimal interest, recent scholarship has taken a fresh look at several presidents from this era. Ron Chernow's *Grant*, for example, goes to great lengths to show how much President Ulysses S. Grant did to promote and ensure the political freedoms of former slaves in the South—including outlawing the Ku Klux Klan. Candice Millard's *Destiny of the Republic: A Tale of Madness, Medicine and the Murder of a President* is ostensibly about President Garfield's assassination, but the author does a masterful job of demonstrating his qualifications to hold such high office, in large measure because of his dedication to racial equality. For those curious about the origins and transformation of the party of Lincoln, Heather Cox Richardson's *To Make Men Free: A History of the Republican Party* shows that the party began as one dedicated to equal opportunity for all Americans. Richardson argues that the Republicans occasionally lost their way but managed to course-correct through a series of transformative figures who returned the party to its equal opportunity roots: Abraham Lincoln, Theodore Roosevelt, and Dwight D. Eisenhower.

The time seems right for a reexamination of the presidency during the so-called Gilded Age and the elections that brought these leaders to power. For many years, the University Press of Kansas has published books on presidential elections, and this work on the 1880 election is part of that series. The 1880 presidential election pitted Republican James Garfield against Democrat Winfield Scott Hancock, but it also offered the country two very different philosophies and visions from which to choose. Garfield, a nine-term member of the House of Representatives and a US senator-elect from Ohio, was a seasoned politician, but few saw his nomination for president coming. Although there were preconvention whispers about Garfield as a possible nominee, hardly anyone thought much beyond the potential candidacies of former president Grant, Senator James Blaine, and Secretary of the Treasury John Sherman. In fact, Garfield attended the convention in Chicago to nominate his fellow Ohioan Sherman.

On the Democratic side, the real drama was whether Samuel J. Tilden would seek the nomination. Tilden had been the Democratic nominee in 1876, besting Republican Rutherford B. Hayes by more than 250,000 popular votes but ultimately losing the electoral vote in a contentious, disputed election decided by a congressionally appointed commission (of which Garfield was a member). Democrats spent the entirety of Hayes's administration (1877–1881) claiming that Tilden had been robbed and urging him to run again in 1880 and claim the White House to which he had been rightfully elected four years earlier. Once Tilden chose not to run—or, more accurately, wasted his opportunity for renomination by playing coy and waiting for the party to seek him out and nominate him unanimously—General Winfield Scott Hancock emerged as a popular choice.

Hancock was the opposite of Garfield: a political novice with no experience in elected office. A native Pennsylvanian, Hancock was a West Point graduate, career military officer, and Mexican-American War veteran who had been wounded several times fighting for the United States in the Civil War. Hancock was somewhat adept at navigating army politics, but he knew little about national elective politics. However, because of a brief postwar stint commanding the Fifth Military District in New Orleans, Hancock—despite fighting against the Confederacy—was an acceptable choice to Southern white Democrats who were desperate to reestablish white supremacy in the South. Northern Democrats liked that Hancock's status as a bona fide Union war hero and a current active-duty general negated the Republicans' most powerful argument for retaining power: the theory that the Democrats were unfit to govern because their party of rebels had sent thousands of Union soldiers to their graves. This was often called "waving the bloody shirt," and it allowed the Republicans to remind voters of their own loyalty to the Union, their emancipation of the enslaved during the war, and their efforts to ensure black rights after it. Interestingly, as white Democrats desperately sought to reassert power and white supremacy in the South, both major candidates in the 1880 election were Union military veterans. Once the ballots were counted, that election would provide the first evidence of a so-called solid South for those Democrats who had overthrown Reconstruction and hoped to regain legal and societal dominance over black people—some of the very things Garfield had battled during his long service in Congress.

During this era, the candidates' respective political parties did the hard work of running national campaigns. For the most part, presidential candidates were expected to be neither seen nor heard. President Hayes advised Garfield to stay home and say nothing. Garfield, however, broke with tradition to some degree by running the nation's first "front porch" campaign from his home in Mentor, Ohio. Hancock stayed out of the public eye, and for good reason. During one of the few interviews he granted, he made a major misstatement that gave the Republicans ammunition to use against him. Hesitant to be too critical of Hancock because of his long military career and distinguished war record, Republicans took advantage when the Democratic candidate played into their hands and proved himself to be an inexperienced politician—"not quite ready for prime time," as modern Americans might say.

Both parties were determined in 1880: Republicans to hold on to the presidency, and Democrats to capture it. Would the result have been the same had either party nominated someone else? Both parties were in transition in 1880. The Republicans were looking for new alliances with industrialists and financiers—on their way to becoming the party of "big business." The Democrats were trying to straddle the fence between reestablishing white supremacy in the South and garnering enough national appeal to win the presidency.

Despite being a compromise nominee in 1880, Garfield was exactly the right man for that time in the Republicans' history—and the nation's. A fierce opponent of slavery before the Civil War and a Union volunteer during it, Garfield had spent years in Congress fighting for civil rights for black Americans. Although some of the things he said and wrote privately might make us cringe today, he was usually a reliable vote for legislation designed to lift up freed people in the South. Even as many Republicans moved away from civil rights as a major issue, Garfield remained convinced that the government could and should continue to help black people realize the rights to which the Reconstruction Amendments to the Constitution entitled them. Hancock, in contrast, had no national political record for the Democratic Party to publicize or for the voters to examine. Thus, the Democrats' primary argument was that Hancock should be elected to right the electoral wrong done to Samuel Tilden four years earlier.

Garfield was the last true "Lincoln Republican" to occupy the White House. He represented the Republican Party's origins as a party dedicated to equal opportunity for all Americans, and, to some extent, that vision died with him. This compounds the tragedy of his death. Had he lived, he might have been one of those transformative figures Richardson examines in *To Make Men Free*. For that reason, I spend more time on Garfield and the Republicans in the following pages than on Hancock and the Democrats. At least in terms of their written platforms, there was little separating the two parties in 1880 anyway. Ultimately, civil service reform, not civil rights, dominated the Republicans' behind-the-scenes campaign and Garfield's presidency. Then, just a few months into his administration, that same issue led a mentally unstable man to shoot Garfield. However, it seems fair to postulate that, had he lived, Garfield would have continued to press Congress and the American people on civil rights for everyone. After all, he dedicated a significant portion of his inaugural address to this very issue.

I do not devote a significant amount of space to third-party movements: just one short chapter examining all of them. The Greenback Party campaign of James B. Weaver was the most significant. Although Weaver won more than 300,000 popular votes, he did not win any electoral votes, and the Greenback Party was all but dissolved before the end of the 1880s. An extended examination of the Greenbackers and other fringe parties would have distracted from my focus on the two main candidates and the two major parties from which the American voters still choose (although party members of the 1880s would likely find the Democratic and Republican Parties of today unrecognizable).

In response to Thomas Wolfe, then: Yes, both Garfield and Hancock mattered in 1880 and still matter today. The two veterans of the Civil War engaged in a political battle between June and November 1880 that, for all they knew, might forever change the direction of American politics and history. All presidential elections and presidential administrations matter, and they all affect us as a nation for years and decades afterward.

I am grateful to the many authors and historians now researching and writing about Reconstruction and the Gilded Age so that we might make sense of our history and better understand how the United States became the nation it is today. I hope readers will come away with a stronger appreciation for not just the people but also the competing political philosophies of 1880. I believe those voters made the correct choice when they elected (albeit very narrowly) James A. Garfield that year, and the American people were denied a potentially strong and effective leader when he died.

1

"HALF WAY BETWEEN GOD AND THE DEVIL" THE ELECTION OF 1876 AND ITS AFTERMATH

The 1880 presidential election actually began four months before the 1876 election. This timing will not seem unusual to twenty-first-century readers or those interested in modern politics, but it was out of the ordinary for the late nineteenth century. During this period, candidates rarely campaigned or appeared in public when seeking the presidency, and the political parties did most of the heavy lifting of presidential campaigns. Before the creation of modern primaries and caucuses, this included selecting candidates at national nominating conventions. Unlike today, voters had no direct voice in choosing their parties' presidential standard-bearers every four years.

The event that set the 1880 election in motion more than four years earlier took place on July 8, 1876, when that year's Republican nominee, Ohio governor Rutherford B. Hayes, issued the customary letter accepting his party's nomination. The Republicans had nominated Hayes and running mate William Wheeler on the seventh ballot at their national convention in Cincinnati in June. President Ulysses S. Grant had considered seeking an unprecedented third term but ultimately chose to adhere to the as-yet-unbroken tradition of presidents limiting themselves to two full terms, following the example of George Washington. From his office in Columbus, Hayes wrote:

> The declaration of principles by the Cincinnati Convention makes no announcement in favor of a single Presidential term. I do not assume to add to that declaration;

but believing that the restoration of the civil service, to the system established by Washington and followed by the early Presidents, can best be accomplished by an Executive who is under no temptation to use the patronage of his office, to promote his own re-election, I desire to perform what I regard as a duty, in stating now my inflexible purpose, if elected, not to be a candidate for election to a second term.[1]

Thus, Republicans knew more than four years before the 1880 election that they would have to select a candidate other than Hayes as their presidential nominee that year. The letter also made it clear that, if elected, Hayes intended to make civil service reform—ending the patronage system of federal job distribution in favor of a merit-based system—a focus of his single term.

Republican congressman James A. Garfield of Ohio, known primarily for his support of civil rights for the formerly enslaved, still told his diary that reformation of the civil service "is needed for every department of the government. The President who will devote a term to that reform and make it sure will stand among the foremost benefactors of his country." Hayes's letter of acceptance pleased Garfield, who called it "a very clear and sensible document."[2] Garfield likely envisioned that a reformed civil service would provide more federal job opportunities for black men.

Not all Republicans agreed with Hayes and Garfield on the necessity of civil service reform. Many elected officials of both major parties remained firmly dedicated to the patronage system, which allowed them to dole out government positions to friends, relatives, and cronies as the spoils of electoral victory. Shrewd politicians understood that patronage gave them the means to build and expand their bases of power by placing loyalists in important positions at nearly all levels of government. Few were eager to voluntarily abandon this system. Powerful Republicans, including President Grant and Senators Roscoe Conkling of New York and John Logan of Illinois, scoffed at or took offense to Hayes's letter. Grant believed that Hayes's pledge to serve a single term was a veiled criticism of him, and Conkling and Logan, both Grant loyalists and masters of patronage, rejected the idea of civil service reform. Logan called the letter "damned stuff," and Conkling, somewhat ominously, said nothing.[3]

Candidate Hayes also addressed Reconstruction and the civil rights of black Americans in his acceptance letter. By 1876, all but three Southern states—South Carolina, Florida, and Louisiana—had been "redeemed" from Republican rule by Democrats who sought to reassert white social and political supremacy. Hayes, a decorated Civil War veteran, assured white Southerners that he would treat them fairly, but he emphasized, "There can be no enduring peace, if the constitutional rights of any portion of the people are habitually disregarded. . . . All parts of the Constitution are sacred, and must be sacredly observed the parts that are new no less than the parts that are old."[4] The rule of law, he wrote, was paramount and would be enforced in all sections of the country. Yet Hayes also included a statement about bringing the South "the blessings of honest and capable self-government." Historian Eric Foner writes that these were "code words . . . for an end to Reconstruction."[5] Although ending Reconstruction as a whole was of interest to white Southerners, black voting rights were of paramount concern.

Hayes's emphasis on civil service reform and civil rights for black people was in accordance with the platform the Republicans approved at their Cincinnati convention. The first three of the platform's eighteen planks referred to civil rights (without offering any specific plans or steps to ensure them), stating that until all Americans received equal treatment, "the work of the Republican party is unfinished." In its one statement on the federal civil service, the platform did not use the word "reform"; it opined that jobs should "be filled by persons selected with sole reference to the efficiency of the public service and the right of citizens to share in the honor of rendering faithful service to their country."[6] Despite Hayes's reputation as a reformer of sorts while governor of Ohio and his expressed desire to reform the civil service, many took this statement as support for, not opposition to, the patronage system.

The platform's lack of specificity on civil rights and its veiled intimation about ending Reconstruction troubled some, including orator, abolitionist, and civil rights advocate Frederick Douglass. In a speech to the Republican National Convention on June 14, 1876—the day before the platform was officially adopted—Douglass challenged the party of Lincoln: "What does it amount to, if the black man, after having been made free by the letter of your law, is unable to exercise that freedom; and after having been freed from the slaveholder's lash he is to be subject to the slaveholder's shotgun?" During the campaign, the Republicans argued about whether they should focus on the general theme of reform or "the danger of giving the Rebels the government," as Hayes called it. This prompted Douglass to write to Republican chairman Zachariah Chandler: "It is the same old conflict: Liberty, union and civilization on the one hand and Slavery disunion and barbarism on the other."[7]

While the Republicans sought desperately to hold on to the presidency in

Rutherford B. Hayes, nineteenth president of the United States. (Courtesy of Library of Congress)

1876, they knew that eight years of scandals and bad press during the Grant administration made their sixteen-year grip on the White House tenuous. Most of the South's return to the control of Democratic "redeemers" also complicated Republicans' path to victory in the nation's centennial year.

Republicans knew they could not run or win on the record of the Grant administration. Though few doubted that Grant was personally honest, he had often surrounded himself with men less interested in doing the country's business than in lining their own pockets. Therefore, Republicans in 1876 resurrected the tried-and-true argument linking all Democrats to treason, rebellion, and the slaughter of Union soldiers—"waving the bloody shirt"—which had worked so well in the previous two elections. Robert Ingersoll of Illinois, who initially backed James Blaine for the Republican nomination but campaigned heartily for Hayes, told a meeting of Union veterans during the campaign: "Every man that endeavored to tear the old flag from the heaven that it enriches was a Democrat. Every man that tried to destroy this nation was a Democrat.... The man that assassinated Abraham Lincoln was a Democrat. Soldiers, every scar you have on your heroic bodies was given you by a Democrat."[8]

Despite this strategy, Democrats smelled blood in the water. They knew that New York's thirty-five electoral votes were the biggest prize, and their candidate had to carry the nation's most populous state if they were to have any chance of winning. This made New York governor Samuel J. Tilden an early front-runner for the Democratic nomination. Many New Yorkers revered Tilden for his prosecution of the infamous Tweed Ring, which had ruled New York City's Democratic Party and political patronage system for years until Tilden brought it down. That achievement had won him New York's governorship in 1874, and many correctly suspected that Tilden had his eye on the White House. He and Indiana governor Thomas Hendricks were considered the favorites for the 1876 Democratic nomination as the party prepared to convene that summer in St. Louis. Tilden, a millionaire several times over and a brilliant campaign organizer, worked harder for his own nomination and spent more of his own money to secure it than any previous presidential nominee of either party. One letter writer to the *Cincinnati Enquirer* described Tilden's pursuit of the nomination: "He treats the nomination as a matter of business, to be made successful by management, as patent medicine is by liberal advertising."[9]

Besides Tilden and Hendricks, a smattering of other prominent Democrats had some support for the nomination. Pennsylvanian Winfield Scott Hancock, one of the Union's ablest and most decorated commanders during the Civil War, was a lifelong Democrat known to harbor presidential ambitions despite never having held elective office. Still on active duty, General Hancock was viewed as palatable to the South because of his time as commander of the Texas-Louisiana military district during Reconstruction. Senator Thomas Bayard of Delaware was the first choice of many northeastern Democrats who were not pledged to Tilden. He was also preferred by many white Southerners, and this alone made him unacceptable to others. Republicans would have little trouble waving the bloody shirt in the face of a Democratic nominee favored by former Confederates. Bayard himself recognized this drawback and willingly stepped aside for Tilden.

Senator Allen G. Thurman of Ohio had supporters as well, but it was uncertain that he could win even his own state's support for the nomination. Hayes called Thurman "the ablest and best man of his party in Ohio" and deemed Democrats who did not support Thurman "howling idiots."[10]

Tilden's claim to the nomination was not absolute. Many Democrats, especially in the Midwest, supported Indiana's Thomas Hendricks and his "soft money" policies. Hendricks favored expanding the currency supply with paper money (known as "greenbacks"), which would cause inflation, raise prices on agricultural goods, and help those in debt pay their bills. Many farmers fell into that category and favored policies and candidates that sought to expand the use of greenbacks. Tilden, in contrast, was a "hard money" man who supported the gold standard.

Despite fierce opposition from Tammany-allied delegates from his own state, Tilden prevailed and received the Democratic nomination on the second ballot. To provide geographic balance and harmony between soft- and hard-money advocates, Hendricks received the vice-presidential nomination. The convention approved a platform that invoked and repeated the phrase "Reform is necessary . . . " in plank after plank. Historian Michael F. Holt writes that the Democratic platform was "far more coherent, comprehensive, and compelling" than that of the Republicans.[11]

The Democrats sought to remove the bloody shirt argument from the Republicans' rhetorical arsenal, criticizing "the false issue by which they seek to light anew the dying embers of sectional hate between kindred peoples once unnaturally estranged but now reunited in one indivisible republic, and a common destiny." The Democrats agreed that "the soldiers and sailors of the Republic, and the widows and orphans of those who have fallen in battle, have a just claim upon the care, protection and gratitude of their fellow-citizens."[12]

A violent racial confrontation in Hamburg, South Carolina, in July left six black men dead, somewhat derailing the Democratic strategy before it was launched. Republicans immediately linked the so-called Hamburg Massacre to the lingering racial hatred and white supremacism of the old Confederacy, and Hayes quietly told Republicans stumping for him to stress that "a Democratic victory will bring the Rebellion to power."[13] South Carolina was one of the three unredeemed Southern states still administered by Northern Republican officials, so it was an important factor in achieving Hayes's goal of an Electoral College victory. "The cry of the bloody shirt . . . has been after all the piece de resistance of the Republicans in this canvass," noted a prominent Democrat.[14]

Democrats did not completely give up on winning black votes, however. They knew that some Southern blacks had grown frustrated with the Republicans' slowness to enforce civil rights in the South and to grant patronage jobs to black men. Bemoaning the "carpet-bag despotism" of the Republican Party, the Democrats appealed to Southern black voters by stating that black suffrage "of itself was not wrong, but was made an instrument by designing politicians" whose unscrupulous administration of the South led to the rise of the Ku Klux Klan and the collapse of the Freedman's Savings Bank, intended to educate former slaves about saving money.[15] The *Cincinnati Enquirer,* which had a history of publishing editorials in support of white supremacy, now lectured Republicans that "it is bad enough to steal from a white man, but to rob a poor negro is the quintessence of meanness."[16]

Republicans knew that the vote would be far closer in 1876 than in the past two elections when the tarnished hero—but hero nonetheless—U. S. Grant had sat atop their ticket. They worried that their grip on the presidency was slipping away. What would the first elected Democratic president since James Buchanan mean for Reconstruction, the protection of freedmen and -women, fiscal policy, and a host of other issues? "My own discussion of the issues," wrote Garfield, "has given me an exaggerated view of the dangers which may follow if Tilden is elected." Yet the Ohioan still worried "that the good sense and patriotism of this country can allow the destiny of the nation to pass into the control of the rebels." The bloody shirt still waved. "If we lose," Hayes wrote, "the South will be the greatest sufferer. Their misfortune will be far greater than ours. . . . The South will drift toward chaos again."[17]

Eight years of scandals under Grant, black Americans' frustration at unfulfilled or only partially fulfilled Republican promises, legitimate Democratic efforts to win black votes, a wealthy Democratic candidate willing to pour much of his own fortune into his campaign, and the specter of racial intimidation at the polls all led to a tense presidential contest in 1876. Most expected the vote to be close, but no one had any idea just how close—and historic—the election would be.

Republicans scored a strategic victory in the summer of 1876 that ended up playing a critical role in that year's presidential election. On August 1, 1876, Colorado was admitted to statehood. The new Centennial State had a Republican-dominated legislature and was considered likely to vote for Hayes in the fall. As Holt points out, prior to Colorado's admission to the Union, the total number of electoral votes was 366, so 184 votes (one more than half) were needed to win the Electoral College. Colorado's three electoral votes brought the total to 369, making the wining number 185.[18]

Nearly nine million American voters went to the polls on November 7, 1876, to cast their ballots in the Hayes-Tilden contest and the various state races. Democrats' assessment that New York would be critical proved prescient, and Tilden easily carried his home state by 32,000 votes. Most of the South seemed to be in Tilden's column as well. Newspapers began printing their November 8 editions carrying the news that Samuel J. Tilden would be the next president, having won "a very considerable majority of the electoral vote."[19] Rutherford B. Hayes went to bed on election night assuming he had lost. "I don't care for myself," he wrote, "and the party, yes, and the country, too, can stand it, but I do care for the poor colored men of the South. . . . The result will be that the Southern people will practically treat the constitutional amendments as nullities and then the colored man's fate will be worse than when he was in slavery."[20]

But Election Day provided no clear answer on which candidate would be the next president. Many believed, as Hayes did, that Tilden had won. But extremely tight races in Oregon and in the three unredeemed Southern states—Florida, Louisiana, and South Carolina—created doubt on both sides. Predictably, Republicans and Democrats both claimed victory. "Hayes is elected if we have carried South Carolina, Florida, and Louisiana. Can you hold your State?" Republican operative William Chandler telegraphed to prominent Republicans in those states.[21] Democratic National Committee chair Abram Hewitt dispatched lieutenants to the contested states to observe the work of the local returning boards as they counted the votes, and the Republicans soon followed suit. Hayes continued to believe he had lost. "I think we are defeated," he said. "I am of the opinion that the Democrats have carried the country and elected Tilden, as it now seems necessary for the Republicans to carry all the States now set down as doubtful to secure even a majority of one."[22] Days after the election, the tally stood at 184 electoral votes for Tilden and 166 for Hayes—with at least 185 needed to win.

Meanwhile, Congressman Garfield returned to Washington from Ohio. Upon arriving at his home in the capital on the night of November 10, he found a dispatch, dated that afternoon, from President Grant: "I would be gratified if you would go to New Orleans to remain until the vote of Louisiana is counted. Governor Kellogg requests that reliable witnesses be sent to see that the canvass of the vote is a fair one. Answer."[23] Garfield expressed some doubt about going but ultimately decided to heed the president's call "to ascertain who is elected and see that he is so declared." When he departed the following day, he was thinking about his wife, Lucretia: "This is the 18th anniversary of our marriage and I was in hopes I could spend the day quietly at home."[24] Instead, he boarded a train and headed south to Louisiana.

Democrats were both furious and nervous. Tilden had clearly carried the nation's popular vote, and to many, this justified their violent rallying cry of "Tilden or blood!" Some urged the party to take the presidency by force, if necessary. To his credit, the normally reserved Tilden opposed these threats of violence, and many Democrats privately fumed that he seemed unwilling to press his own case. Tilden ally John Bigelow told his diary: "Another civil war may be the consequence of this state of things and we may enter upon the next century under a diff[erent] form of gov[ernment] from that of which for nearly a century we have been boasting." Tilden, however, struck a reassuring and conciliatory tone: "Be satisfied with the reflection that the people are too patriotic, too intelligent, too self-poised to allow anything perilous to be done—anything that may disturb or destroy our peculiar form of government. Don't be alarmed."[25]

All the same, Hewitt sent operatives to the contested states to observe the vote counting. This became more urgent for Democrats when President Grant put the army on alert, ready to intervene in the Southern states in the event of violence. Democrats saw this as a not-so-veiled threat to use federal troops to ensure Hayes's victory. Grant's statement that "no man worthy of the office of President should be willing to hold it if counted in or placed there by fraud" did little to ease the minds of Tilden supporters.[26] Shrewdly, among the Democrats Hewitt dispatched to Louisiana were a number of former Republicans who had abandoned that party during the Grant years: George W. Julian of Indiana, Andrew Curtin of Pennsylvania, and Lyman Trumbull of Illinois. Many of "Hewitt's men," Hayes wrote to his friend and supporter Carl Schurz, "are . . . ex-Republicans, and of course bitterly prejudiced against their late associates."[27]

Both sides claimed victory in Louisiana, South Carolina, and Florida. There was also a legal question about the status of one elector in Oregon. Hayes may have been correct when he wrote to Schurz, "I believe that with a fair election in the South, our electoral vote would reach two hundred and that we should have a larger popular majority."[28] Republicans and Democrats alike surely participated in voter fraud in 1876: Republicans controlled the election returning boards in all three contested Southern states, and there is no question that some white Democrats intimidated, threatened, or otherwise prevented black voters from casting their ballots in those states. Senator Oliver P. Morton, Republican of Indiana, argued that the Democrats could carry the Southern states only "by a bloody revolution which no more deserves the name of election than the murder of the Christians by the Turks." Garfield agreed, adding that the Democratic Party represented "secession, disunion, slavery and all that went to make disunion and slavery horrible in the eyes of men and in the eyes of God." Republicanism, however, meant "an indivisible Union, [and] the principles of freedom and equal rights to all men without regard to race or property."[29]

As the Democratic and Republican "visiting statesmen" poured into the disputed Southern states, both sides immediately proclaimed victory and looked for ways to fulfill those prophecies. In Louisiana, Democrat Francis T. Nicholls had been elected governor, succeeding Republican William P. Kellogg. The Democratic contingent, led by John M. Palmer, interviewed Kellogg and all four Republican members of the state's election returning board. One of the board members, Gadane Casenave, was an African American whom Palmer described as "an honest man from his standpoint" but ultimately an unreliable source of information about the electoral dispute because "he thought the interests of the colored race demanded the election of Hayes to the presidency, and blinded by prejudice he was incapable of doing justice to the subject or of a decision according to law."[30]

Republicans were just as determined to declare their side victorious in Louisiana. Less than a day after arriving in New Orleans, and before interviewing anyone or looking at a single piece of paper, Garfield predicted that "the lawful vote" of that state would go to Hayes.[31] Garfield helped work out an arrangement allowing five Democrats and five Republicans to attend and observe the meetings of the election returning board as it canvassed the state's popular votes and tried to determine whether Tilden or Hayes should receive its electoral votes. Louisiana law required a five-member returning board, but during the 1876 election crisis it consisted of only four, and all were Republicans. The board's sole Democrat had resigned in 1874 and never been replaced. Democrats had tried to get a new member of their party appointed to the board eight different times, without success. Therefore, the Louisiana returning board was in violation of state law, being one member short and composed entirely of Republicans.[32]

There were rumors that at least a few members of this all-Republican returning board might be willing to sell their loyalty to the highest bidder, and strong evidence suggests that one of them, J. Madison Wells, offered to throw the vote to Tilden for $1 million, but there were no takers.

The Louisiana board met, discussed, debated, and attempted to resolve the electoral dilemma. On December 5, 1876, the board announced that it had discarded all the votes of two large parishes and rejected some individual ballots from twenty-two others. In total, the board discounted about 15,000 votes—13,000 of them Democratic. Despite an approximately 6,000-vote majority for Tilden, the Louisiana returning board declared Hayes the rightful winner of the state's electoral votes.[33]

Many of the "visiting statesmen" of both parties, having observed the work of the returning board and labored behind the scenes to ensure their own side's victory, had already departed Louisiana by the time the board publicly announced its decision. Garfield arrived back in Washington late on the evening of December 5, and on December 6 he wrote in his diary that he had "called on the President . . . in company with other gentlemen who went to New Orleans, and delivered our report. In the partisan fashion of this period I have no doubt it will be bitterly assailed. Doubtless we ourselves are partisan in making it, but we have sought to exhibit the truth."[34]

Disputes raged in Florida and South Carolina as well. Former Union general (and future author of *Ben-Hur*) Lew Wallace was one of the Republican observers in Florida and was disheartened by what he saw there. "It is terrible to see the extent to which all classes go in their determination to win," he wrote to his wife. "Conscience offers no restraint. Nothing is so common as the resort to perjury, unless it is violence. . . . If we win, our methods are subject to impeachment for possible fraud. If the enemy win, it is the same thing exactly."[35] The vote for Hayes was more solid in South Carolina than in the other two states, and attention there soon turned toward the governorship and other state offices. With both sides claiming victory, the people of South Carolina suddenly found themselves with two state legislatures—one Republican, one Democratic—each claiming to have been legitimately elected.

Through all this, Tilden remained nearly silent. His continued reluctance to advocate on his own behalf baffled Democrats and made their efforts to secure his victory seem indecisive and inconsistent. One Southerner pointedly urged Tilden to get into the fight: "The entire democracy of the south feel more than ever that they are leaning on a bag of mush when they look for aid & comfort from the north."[36] Tilden's perceived lack of interest in promoting his own case ceded the initiative to the Republicans and allowed a number of internal disagreements to cause rifts in the Democratic Party that would affect it far beyond 1876. Still, many Democrats assumed that they would come out on top because their party controlled the US House

Samuel J. Tilden, governor of New York and 1876 Democratic presidential nominee. (Courtesy of Library of Congress)

of Representatives, which, according to the Constitution, would decide a disputed election. "If the House stands firm, all will come out right," one Democrat told Tilden. "The democrats in the House have the power, if they have the nerve, to control the election," said another.[37] Those assessments would be put to the test: Louisiana, South Carolina, Florida, and Oregon all sent two sets of electoral tallies—one Republican, one Democratic—to Washington to be counted.

Almost as soon as it became clear that the election would be disputed, Congress began working on a solution. Under the Constitution, if no candidate receives a majority of votes or if the Electoral College is deadlocked, the House of Representatives decides. However, the Constitution did not anticipate a case in which states sent in two different sets of election returns. On December 7, 1876, a month after the election, Republican representative George W. McCrary of Iowa introduced a resolution calling for the creation of a special commission to resolve the crisis. Democrats and Republicans argued over this proposal for much of the next two months. Many counterproposals were offered and debated before the two sides finally approved a commission in late January. Both Tilden and Hayes were wary of this solution to the constitutional crisis and had to be convinced not to speak out against it. When Tilden expressed his disappointment that Senate Democrats had spoken in favor of the bill without consulting him, Democratic National Committee chair Hewitt tersely replied, "They do not consult you. They are public men and have their own duties and responsibilities. I consult you."[38]

The plan to which both sides agreed and that President Grant signed into law on January 29, 1877, created a fifteen-member commission: five members from the House of Representatives, five from the Senate, and five Supreme Court justices. The House and Senate were permitted to pick their own members to serve on the commission. Four of the Supreme Court justices were specifically named in the law and were automatically appointed to the commission; those justices were responsible for choosing the fifth justice. The commission was supposed to consist of seven Republicans, seven Democrats, and one independent (with the independent coming from the Supreme Court). Their task was to examine both sets of electoral votes from the disputed states and determine which votes to accept and which to discard. This commission was fully empowered to determine whether Tilden or Hayes would be inaugurated on March 4.

Garfield did not believe a commission was the best way to solve the crisis, and he spoke against it for more than an hour on the House floor in late January 1877. He argued that the commission was unconstitutional because it involved Congress in the process of choosing a president in a situation that was not specifically enumerated in the Constitution. Instead, Garfield hoped for an unspecified "responsible, constitutional" solution.[39] Nor did Garfield believe that the Democrats were wholly united behind Tilden. He wrote to Hayes on January 19, 1877: "The Democratic businessmen of the country are more anxious for quiet than for Tilden." However, he wrote in his diary the same day that business and corporate interests "are clamorously in favor of [the Electoral Commission]" and "care more for results than for methods."[40] But Garfield also suggested to Hayes that "it would be a great help if, in some discreet way, those Southern men who are dissatisfied with Tilden . . . could know that the South was going to be treated with kind consideration by you."[41] Was Garfield one of the architects of the eventual "deal" (as some historians have described it) that handed the presidency to Hayes?

Despite Garfield's vocal "nay" when the House voted to create the commission, House Republicans selected him as one of their members on it. Garfield briefly considered refusing to serve on the grounds that he believed the commission to be unconstitutional. He also believed it was a bad political compromise for the Republicans, telling Hayes, "A compromise like this is singularly attractive to that type of men who think that the truth is always half way between God and the Devil and not to split the difference would be partisanship."[42]

Two things convinced Garfield to accept the assignment, despite his misgivings. The first was simple party loyalty and his firm belief that, without white intimidation of black voters, Hayes easily would have won Louisiana and the other disputed Southern states. The second was the knowledge that many Democrats did not want him to serve on the commission. On January 29, the same day President Grant signed the electoral commission bill, Garfield was visited by Jeremiah Black, a Democrat who had served as both attorney general and (briefly) secretary of state during the James Buchanan administration. More recently, Black was one of the lawyers representing Tilden in the election dispute. Black told Garfield that many Democrats opposed his appointment because of his stated opinion that the commission was unconstitutional and because of his service as a Republican observer in Louisiana immediately after the election. The Ohioan had, in their view, already committed himself on the question of which candidate should receive Louisiana's electoral votes. Black advised Garfield that removing himself would "avoid a serious collision with the Democratic Party" and added that Garfield "would be embarrassed by sitting as a member of the Committee," as the congressman reported to his diary that evening.[43]

Garfield eventually decided that while a collision with the Democrats would not bother him, upsetting members of his own party would, so he agreed to serve. The other House Republican on the commission was George F. Hoar of Massachusetts. Republican commissioners from the Senate were George F. Edmunds (Vermont), Frederick Freylinghuysen (New Jersey), and Oliver P. Morton (Indiana). Two Republican Supreme Court justices—Lincoln appointee Samuel F. Miller (Iowa) and William Strong (Pennsylvania), nominated by Grant—served on the commission as well.

Seven Democrats sat on the commission. The three Democrats from the House of Representatives were Josiah G. Abbott (Massachusetts); Eppa Hunton (Virginia), a former Confederate brigadier general; and Henry B. Payne (Ohio). Democratic senators Thomas F. Bayard (Delaware) and Allen G. Thurman (Ohio) joined them, along with Democratic Supreme Court justices Nathan Clifford of Maine, appointed by Buchanan, and Stephen J. Field of California, nominated by Lincoln.

Supreme Court justice David Davis of Illinois, nominated by Lincoln in 1862, was to be the commission's lone independent. Just before the commission began its meetings, however, the Illinois legislature elected Davis to the US Senate as a Democrat—with the hearty support of the state and national Democratic Parties. They reasoned that, to acknowledge their support, Davis would automatically side with Tilden and make the New Yorker president. But they underestimated Davis's integrity and were shocked when the newly elected senator declined to join the commission precisely because of his indebtedness to the Democratic Party and his desire to avoid a conflict of interest. The remaining Supreme Court justices replaced Davis with Republican Joseph P. Bradley of New Jersey, a Grant appointee who was viewed as being the most politically neutral justice. However, Bradley's appointment gave the Republicans an eight-to-seven advantage on the commission, which began its meetings in the Supreme Court chamber on February 1, 1877.

The commission met in early February to review documents, talk to witnesses, and look at evidence and electoral votes from the disputed states. The commissioners took up the case of Florida first, and on February 9 they voted eight to seven—strictly along party lines—to accept the Hayes electors from that state. Members of both parties could see the partisan writing on the wall, and Black raged, "God damn them, they will beat us and elect Hayes, but we shall give them all the trouble we can."[44] Black was correct: Justice Bradley voted with his fellow Republicans each time to accept the Hayes electors from the disputed states and disallow Tilden's. When it came to giving the Republicans "trouble," Garfield told his diary, "It is manifest that the Democrats intend to delay the decision as long as possible. They vote for the longest time, the longest recesses, and the most frequent adjournments."[45]

As it became clear that Hayes was going to win, Black and other Democrats scrambled to come up with a plan to prevent Hayes's inauguration on March 4. They plotted to stall and filibuster to delay a joint congressional session to count the electoral votes until after March 4. There was even discussion of ordering General Winfield Scott Hancock (a possible Democratic candidate before Tilden won the nomination), to go to Washington with the army and forcibly install Tilden as president. Southern Democrats were especially militant about denying Hayes the election to prevent four more years of Republican control over the South and protection of blacks' civil and political rights. "My poor Southern country is looking to you as their only hope for their constitutional rights," one Virginian wrote to Tilden, calling him the South's "political savior." Leroy Pope Walker of Alabama wrote that Tilden's election represented "resurrection after burial," and if Hayes were illegally installed as president, it would seem like being "resurrected only to be reinterred."[46]

Meanwhile, Hayes was preparing to govern and trying to determine the best policy to pursue in the South. Prominent Republicans such as Grant and Conkling hoped Hayes would remain firm with white Southerners and force them to accept the civil rights and voting rights of freedmen, while others, such as Ohio congressman and former secretary of the interior Jacob D. Cox, counseled moderation and a new policy based on "a hearty & earnest avowal on the part of Southern white men that they will in honorable good faith accept & defend the present constitutional rights of the freedmen." Hayes indicated his intention to pursue the latter course, telling Cox that he fully agreed with his view and, "if called on to write down a policy I could adopt your language." On the subject of using the army in the South, Hayes told Schurz, "There is to be an end of all that, except in emergencies which I do not think of as possible again."[47] Hayes, perhaps harkening back to Garfield's advice to show the South "kind consideration," clearly intended to take national policy in a new direction. He even met with Frederick Douglass and informed him that the Hayes administration would seek "to recognize all Southern people, without regard to past political conduct," while ensuring "a firm assertion and maintenance of the rights of the colored people of the South according to the Thirteenth, Fourteenth, and Fifteenth Amendments."[48] Not everyone was encouraged. One Kansas Republican predicted that "the policy of the new administration will be to conciliate the White men of the South, Carpetbaggers to the rear, and niggers take care of yourselves."[49]

On the evening of February 26, 1877, prominent members of both parties met at Wormley's Hotel in Washington, a popular gathering spot for politicians and, ironically, owned and operated by African American businessman James Wormley. Many of those present had already been speaking privately about what it would take to end the electoral dispute and allow Democrats to claim victory in the state races in South Carolina and Louisiana. Republicans, naturally, wanted the electoral votes of the disputed states to go to Hayes, while Democrats sought assurances that, as president, Hayes would allow Democratic "home rule" in the South. Garfield was one of the Republicans in attendance, and it is clear that he was not involved in the private negotiations that occurred before the meeting. He noted in his diary that the conversation "led me to believe that there had been former consultations, and that a compact of some kind was mediated." Garfield told the group that neither he nor anyone else was authorized to speak for Hayes, but as he wrote in his diary, "I had no doubt that the new administration would deal justly and generously by the South . . . but neither could we afford to do anything that would be or appear to be a political bargain."[50] The Ohioan then exited the meeting, which continued after his departure. Garfield was correct that the framework of an agreement had been discussed beforehand, and that evening, the Republican and Democratic power brokers were there mostly to refine and finalize it.

According to historian C. Vann Woodward and others interpreting his seminal work *Reunion and Reconstruction: The Compromise of 1877 and the End of Reconstruction,* Democrats agreed to accept a Hayes presidency in return for several concessions, including withdrawal of federal troops from statehouse grounds in South Carolina, Louisiana, and Florida; financial assistance for construction of a Texas and Pacific Railroad; appointment of a Southerner to a prominent post in Hayes's cabinet; federal subsidies for Southern reconstruction and rehabilitation; and tacit agreement that the South be permitted to solve its own "racial problems." Historian Allan Peskin has argued that few of these concessions ever came to pass, and a "deal whose major terms are never carried out appears suspiciously like no deal at all."[51] But at the time, both sides believed they had secured the upper hand.

After the February 26 meeting, Democratic support in Congress for continuing to resist the inevitable weakened. Two days later, the final count of electoral votes was concluded, and angry Democrats unaware of the Wormley's Hotel meeting rushed the Speaker of the House's chair, shouting and pounding their fists. Speaker of the House Samuel J. Randall, a Pennsylvania Democrat, stood firm, and at just after four o'clock on the morning

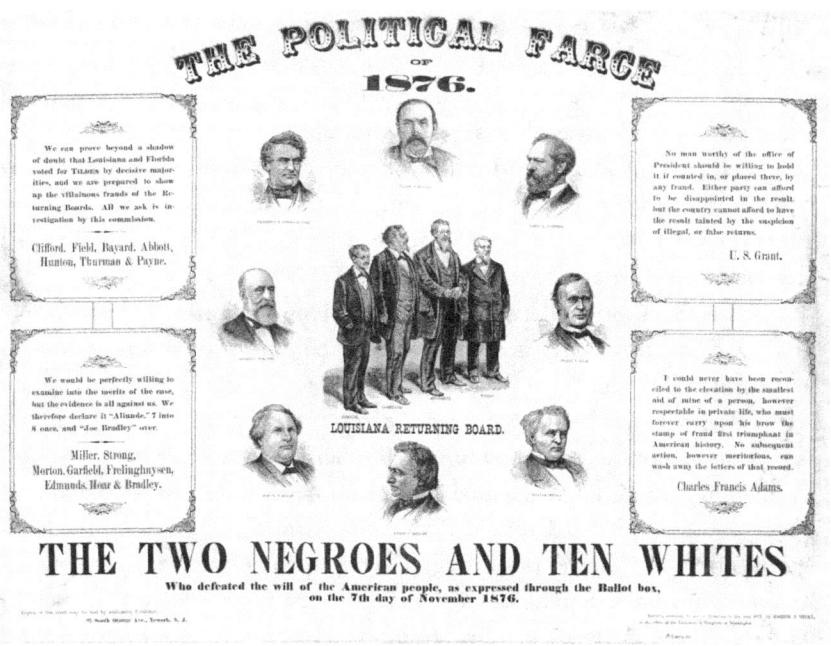

Anti-Republican cartoon depicts James A. Garfield as one of those responsible for "The Political Farce of 1876." (Courtesy of Library of Congress)

of March 1, 1877—three days before Inauguration Day—Congress declared Rutherford B. Hayes the winner of the Electoral College by a count of 185–184. Hayes took the presidential oath privately on Saturday, March 3, and publicly—without incident or protest—on Monday, March 5.[52] Those three electoral votes from Colorado, admitted to statehood just three months before the presidential election, proved to be the difference. Had Colorado not become a state, Tilden would have been the nation's nineteenth president.

As he had in his July 1876 acceptance letter, Hayes addressed both civil rights for black Americans and civil service reform—subjects that would continue to be issues before and after the 1880 campaign—in his inaugural address. He called for "a government which guards the interests of both races carefully and equally" and pledged "a civil policy which will forever wipe out in our political affairs the color line and the differences between North and South, to the end that we may have not merely a united North or a united South, but a unified country." Noting that the founders "meant that public officers should owe their whole service to Government and to the people" rather than to powerful friends, Hayes called for civil service reform "not merely as to certain abuses and practices of so-called official patronage . . . but a change in the system of appointment itself."[53]

President Hayes faced a divided Congress. Democrats had a majority in the House of Representatives, while Republicans controlled the Senate. Democrats also held a majority of state gubernatorial offices, with twenty-three Democratic governors and fifteen Republican. Twelve years after the end of the Civil War, the nation seemed nearly as divided politically as it had been between 1861 and 1865.

Despite the Democratic majority in the House, James Garfield briefly fantasized about becoming Speaker with the support of several Southern Democrats. He even passed up a chance to seek John Sherman's Senate seat once Sherman became Hayes's secretary of the treasury. In fact, the president encouraged Garfield to skip the Senate race and seek the House Speakership; then, after Garfield followed that advice, Hayes casually reversed course and told Garfield that perhaps he should have run for the Senate after all. This episode began a period of estrangement between the two Ohioans. Garfield worried that perhaps it had been a mistake to help Hayes secure the election. He questioned many of Hayes's cabinet choices, including the appointment of former Confederate David M. Key as postmaster general, even though Republicans at the Wormley's Hotel meeting had agreed to naming at least one Southerner to the cabinet. But because the postmaster general had far more patronage positions to hand out than any other official, Key's appointment meant more federal jobs and increased power for white Southern Democrats.

Garfield also disagreed with the manner in which Hayes tackled the issue of civil service reform. In particular, he took issue with Hayes giving patronage jobs to many of his former military cronies while publicly preaching the gospel of reform. "If nobody is to be appointed because he is your friend or my friend," Garfield told fellow Ohioan Jacob D. Cox, "then nobody should be appointed because he is any other man's friend. The President himself should exercise the same self-denial as other officials."[54]

Garfield wanted Congress to pass legislation that would enact wholesale, permanent civil service reform. The Hayes policy relied primarily on executive orders to address some civil service issues but not others. The result was an uneven and piecemeal approach. "The impression is deepening," Garfield wrote to his wife, "that he [Hayes] is not large enough for the place he holds."[55]

Sectional reconciliation, especially in Louisiana and South Carolina, was the other issue that dominated the early days of the Hayes presidency. Republicans of every stripe hoped Hayes would rise to the challenge of protecting the rights and security of former slaves and, perhaps, even turn some Southern whites into Republicans. In the end, most were disappointed when Hayes ordered federal troops in both states back to their barracks instead of forcibly seating Republican governors and legislatures. "The troops are ordered away," Hayes wrote, "and I now hope for peace, and what is equally important, security and prosperity for the colored people." Hayes intended to "get from those States by their governors, legislatures, press, and people pledges that the Thirteenth, Fourteenth, and Fifteenth Amendments shall be faithfully observed; that the colored people shall have equal rights to labor, education, and the privileges of citizenship."[56] To think that white Southerners would allow any of this to happen without the presence of federal troops to enforce the law was naïve at best, and many Republicans criticized the president. The party seemed unmoored as Republicans argued for or against Hayes's Southern policy.

Black Americans naturally felt betrayed by Hayes's tacit approval of the Democratic takeovers in South Carolina and Louisiana. "The whole South—every state in the South—had got into the hands of the very men that held us as slaves," said black Louisianan Henry Adams. "To think that Hayes could go back on us," echoed a freedman in South Carolina, "when we had to wade through blood to help place him where he is now." Many in the national press agreed with these sentiments. "The long controversy over the black man," reported the *Chicago Tribune*, "seems to have reached a finality." The *Nation* added, "The negro will disappear from the field of national politics. Henceforth, the nation, as a nation, will have nothing more to do with him."[57] Knowing that Hayes would serve just one term, black Americans surely wondered who the Republican presidential candidate would be in 1880 and whether he would take their concerns to heart or, as they believed Hayes had done, simply give them lip service to win the election and then promptly betray or ignore them.

Although Ulysses S. Grant moved to scale down Reconstruction in the South late in his presidency, many historians have branded Hayes as the figure most responsible for "ending" Reconstruction. This characterization is not wholly correct. More important than ending Reconstruction was the Hayes administration's passive approach to protecting the rights of black citizens, which represented a noticeable departure from the founding tenets of the Republican Party. That party was built on the idea of equal opportunity—racial, economic, educational—and the federal government's willingness to intervene to ensure it for all citizens. By adopting a hands-off approach to Reconstruction and trusting Southern states to guarantee the civil and political rights of freedmen, Hayes changed the party's direction—and the country's. In less than a decade, the Republicans would be popularly viewed as the party of big business and industrialization. Although some influential Republicans continued to advocate the party's responsibility to ensure the civil rights of African Americans, many others had tired of the "Southern question" and thought the nation had done all it could or should for the freed people. These Republicans began to look for new alliances to increase the party's power and often found allies among wealthy financiers and industrialists.

Southern "Redeemers"—mostly but not exclusively Democrats—were committed to dismantling all remnants of Reconstruction. The Hayes administration's new approach, which allowed for some degree of Southern "home rule," gave them the opportunity to do so. They sought to reduce the political power of black men in the South and reshape the legal system to serve white economic and social supremacy. Foner notes that Redeemers replaced Reconstruction-era state constitutions with new documents that restricted the scope of government and encoded white supremacy. They limited the length of legislative sessions, reduced property taxes, placed strict conditions on states' ability to incur debt, reduced state officials' salaries, repudiated public debts from Reconstruction, and eliminated public aid to corporations and, in some cases, education.[58] Redeemers and Democrats were largely successful in these efforts, and Hayes's hope of creating a foothold for the Republican Party in the South quickly disintegrated. Historian Keith Ian Polakoff argues that "the dream of building a conservative, business-oriented southern Republican party was shattered as soon as the southern Democrats found there was no longer a need to sustain it."[59] James M. Comly visited Louisiana on the president's behalf in May 1877, two months after Hayes took office. "The 'old Whig' sentiment I spoke of," Comly wrote to the president, "petered out before we reached New Orleans. There is nothing to hang an old whig party on. The truth is there does not seem to be anything except the Custom House to hang *anything* on."[60]

Democrats in Washington and elsewhere began to look toward the 1878 midterms and the 1880 presidential election, when they hoped to take their revenge on Republicans for stealing the presidency from Tilden. In the spring of 1878, congressional Democrats led by New York's Clarkson N. Potter launched an investigation into the 1876 election, seeking to link Hayes and the Republicans with fraud. Some Democrats were happy merely to keep doubt about Hayes's legitimacy alive in the public's mind, while others sincerely sought a legal basis on which to challenge his claim to the White House. The investigation backfired on Democrats, producing relative unity in a Republican Party that had been beset by squabbling and disagreement over Hayes's new Southern policy. Even Democratic congressman Alexander Stephens of Georgia—the former vice president of the Confederacy—called the Potter committee's work "most unwise, most unfortunate, and most mischievous." It did not seem to cause Hayes or his allies much concern. "As to the Potter investigation," said Secretary of the Treasury John Sherman in June 1878, "the general impression here is that it is fizzling out."[61]

Ultimately, the Potter investigation was far more damaging to Democrats than Republicans. Hayes was firm in both his claim to the presidency and his actions as the nation's chief executive, and public opinion was mostly in his favor. In October 1878—just a month before the midterm elections—the *New York Tribune* confounded Democrats even more by obtaining, deciphering, and publishing coded messages originating from Samuel Tilden's home during the 1876 election crisis. The messages revealed that the Tilden campaign, in the person of the candidate's nephew, Colonel William T. Pelton, had offered bribes to the election canvassing boards in Florida and South Carolina. Pelton was called to testify before the Potter committee and admitted his offenses. Tilden, who hoped to win the Democratic presidential nomination again in 1880, also appeared before the committee and all but admitted knowing about his nephew's actions. The Potter investigation, designed in part to make the presidency the Democrats' to lose in 1880, instead did irreparable damage to Tilden, the man best positioned to run.

The public's general support of Hayes's claim to the presidency and its disapproval of or indifference to the Potter investigation did not translate to Republican victory at the polls in the 1878 midterm elections. In fact, both parties lost seats in the House of Representatives that year. The Greenback Party, formed during the Civil War to promote the permanent use of paper money, won thirteen seats, primarily in Northern and western states. In the South, only Alabama, North Carolina, and Texas elected Greenbackers to the House—one each. The Republicans lost four House seats in this midterm election, and Garfield emerged as the minority leader. Democrats lost nine seats but managed to maintain control of the House and reelect Samuel Randall of Pennsylvania as Speaker of the House.

Reflecting disaffection with Hayes and the success of black voter suppression efforts in the South, Democrats gained control of the US Senate in

1878 for the first time since before the Civil War, gaining six seats for a total of forty-two. The Republicans lost seven seats, taking their number down to thirty-one. Hayes, already viewed with contempt by most congressional Democrats because of the election controversy that had placed him in office, now faced the prospect of complete political isolation for the last two years of his presidency. He was understandably disheartened by this prospect, especially when reports of continued intimidation of black voters in the South reached him. Republican congressman Joseph H. Rainey, a black South Carolinian, told Hayes, "The Whites are resorting to intimidation and violence to prevent the colored people from organising for the elections." Federal marshals in South Carolina arrested twenty-two whites for intimidating or attacking black voters, but all-white juries acquitted them. In Texas, the *Galveston News* reported that Democrats had "bulldozed the usual Republican majority of the county," and newly elected Democrats were protected by "an armed mob that garrisons the town." A frustrated Hayes acknowledged to the *Washington National Republican* that his conciliatory policy toward the South had not worked: "I am reluctantly forced to admit that the experiment was a failure."[62]

The issues of black voter intimidation and North-South relations would come to a head in early 1879 when congressional Democrats adopted a novel tactic to prevent Republicans from using the army and federal marshals to monitor polling places: refusing to appropriate funds to operate the federal government. One of the Republicans who responded by launching a blistering attack on the Democratic Party was James A. Garfield. By the time the controversy ended, many believed the Ohioan might have a larger political future than previously thought.

2
"LET US NOT SHRINK NOW"
THE RISE OF JAMES A. GARFIELD

Congressman James A. Garfield began 1879 in Chicago, unaware that he would return to the city in the summer of 1880 for the Republican National Convention. He was in Chicago to make a speech celebrating the resumption of specie payments, a cause championed by his fellow Ohioan John Sherman, then serving as secretary of the treasury. Garfield took a brief side trip to Racine, Wisconsin, and noted the brutal winter weather in his diary, including an incredible 56-degree temperature change between Chicago (28 degrees) and Racine (–28 degrees). "It is," he wrote, "the coldest weather I have ever seen."[1]

If temperatures in the Midwest were cold in the literal sense, they were not much better in the metaphorical sense when Garfield returned to Washington. A combination of hard economic times and discontent with President Hayes had led to a Democratic sweep in 1878 in both the House of Representatives and the Senate. Garfield, a close Hayes ally in the House, became the Republican minority leader and, for the most part, handled his duties with skill and agility.

Events in 1879 led some Republicans to consider Garfield a potential presidential candidate in 1880. Although Garfield had certainly thought about running for president sometime in the future, he appeared to have little interest in doing so at this point. In fact, when President Hayes advised him to seek the governorship of Ohio in 1879 and thus position himself for a future presidential run, Garfield declined. Garfield's profile would rise noticeably in 1879, making his seemingly meteoric rise in 1880 possible.

James Abram Garfield was forty-seven years old when the calendar turned from 1878 to 1879. He was born in Orange Township, Ohio, on November 19, 1831. This area, near Cleveland, was known as the Western Reserve due to its status as part of the western lands granted to Connecticut under a royal charter from King Charles I in 1636. Connecticut relinquished claims to much of this land after the American Revolution but retained ownership of the area that is now northeastern Ohio, eventually selling it to land speculators and settlers. When Garfield was born in 1831, the area was still primarily wilderness, and the residents were mostly small farmers.

James Garfield was the youngest child of Abram and Eliza Garfield, New Englanders who had moved from New Hampshire to the Western Reserve in around 1820. Ohio had been officially created by the Northwest Ordinance of 1787, which not only designated several new territories but also declared slavery illegal there. Although northern Ohio was mostly antislavery, many settlers in the southern part of the state came from slaveholding Kentucky and brought proslavery attitudes with them. As a result, significant areas of southern Ohio would express Confederate sympathies during the Civil War.

Abram Garfield died at age thirty-three, when James was only about eighteen months old. After fighting a wildfire that threatened his family's home, Abram became ill and succumbed, probably from a combination of smoke inhalation and something akin to the flu. His widow, Eliza, was left to raise their four children. She was outwardly affectionate to her children, and James grew up to be very close to his mother.

Eliza convinced James to take up a scholarly life after a brief and disastrous stint working on the Ohio and Erie Canal in 1848. He attended the Free Will Baptist Geauga Seminary in Chester (equivalent to a modern high school) and the Western Reserve Eclectic Institute in Hiram (akin to a modern junior college). There, he crossed paths with his future wife, Lucretia Rudolph, a fellow member of the Disciples of Christ. In fact, Lucretia's father, Zeb Rudolph, was one of the founders of the Disciples-affiliated Eclectic Institute. The Disciples of Christ was a homegrown American Protestant sect that sought to eradicate man-made practices and embraced "only the plain commandments of the Bible and the primitive purity of Apostolic days."[2]

Garfield was a natural student and often studied nearly twenty hours a day to fulfill a pledge to himself that no one would outwork him. He gained acceptance to several colleges, and many assumed he would go to Bethany College in Virginia because of its Disciples affiliation. Instead, he chose Williams College in Williamstown, Massachusetts. With impressive self-awareness, Garfield realized that he needed to expand his boundaries beyond the Western Reserve "for the sake of liberalizing my mind."[3] Leaving fiancée Lucretia behind, he departed Hiram in the summer of 1854 and made his way to Williamstown.

Garfield was a devout Disciple of Christ, and as such, he believed that involvement in politics was unbecoming of a true Christian. But the "liberalizing" atmosphere at Williams soon changed his views. "I have been instructed tonight on the political condition of our country," he told his diary on the evening of November 2, 1855. He had attended a speech about the Kansas Territory, recoiling at the tales of proslavery settlers and the evils of human bondage (within months, the conflict there would become known as "Bleeding Kansas"). "At such hours as this I feel like throwing the whole current of my life into the work of opposing this giant Evil," he wrote. "I don't know but the religion of Christ demands some such action."[4] Garfield soon came to understand and accept that participation in the political process was necessary to defeat the "giant Evil" of slavery. He was still a committed Disciple and would be for the rest of his life, but he had started to entertain serious doubts about the literal truth of the Bible. Many, including Garfield, had thought he might take up a career in the ministry, but in June 1856 he wrote to Lucretia, "I think I shall not become a preacher now, if I ever do."[5] After graduating from Williams on August 7, 1856, Garfield returned to the Eclectic Institute as a teacher and, soon thereafter, became its president.

James and Lucretia were married on November 11, 1858. He left the planning and details of the wedding to her, saying at one point, "I don't want much parade about our marriage. Arrange that as you think best." He was so uninvolved, in fact, that Lucretia mailed him an invitation to his own wedding.[6] This pattern would continue for several years and caused much tension in their marriage. Perhaps Garfield's selfishness was a product of his close relationship with his mother, who attended to his every need. This may have given him the idea that his wife should do the same. Lucretia's parents had been much more reserved, and she came into the marriage with very different ideas about the nature of a husband-wife relationship.

By August 1859, local Republicans were courting Garfield, encouraging him to run for the state senate. After exacting a promise that he would not have to campaign, Garfield agreed to stand for election. He won with relative ease on October 11, 1859, and traveled to Columbus to take his seat in the statehouse at the end of the year. Sectional tensions between North and

James A. Garfield as a teenager. (Courtesy of Western Reserve Historical Society)

South were high as Garfield embarked on his political career, and even in the Ohio senate, members debated whether war was inevitable. Early in his term, Garfield vocally opposed a bill, favored by conservatives, promising that no antislavery raids would originate in Ohio. He resented the implication that Ohio was plotting against other states, but he also saw the bill as an affront to the memory of John Brown, whose raid on the federal arsenal at Harpers Ferry, Virginia, was still fresh in people's minds.[7]

In Columbus, Garfield met many fellow Ohioans who would become lifelong friends or political allies. These included Salmon P. Chase, then serving as the state's governor but soon to be secretary of the treasury under Lincoln, and Jacob Dolson Cox, a new senator from the district adjoining Garfield's. In fact, Garfield and Cox ended up as roommates at the home

A young Lucretia Rudolph Garfield. (Courtesy of Library of Congress)

of William Bascom, chairman of the Ohio Central Republican Committee. Cox would later be a Union general during the Civil War and secretary of the interior under President Ulysses S. Grant. Garfield, for his part, developed a reputation as a fine speaker in the state senate.

When James and Lucretia's first child—a daughter they named Eliza Arabella, after their mothers—was born on July 3, 1860, Garfield was barely present. He was off to Ravenna, Ohio, the very next day to deliver a Fourth of July oration. Years later, when Garfield had become more comfortable with and fond of his role as a family man, Lucretia would refer to their early marriage, when her husband was both physically and emotionally absent much of the time, as the "dark years."

The Republicans had run Garfield as a strong antislavery candidate in

1859, and his speeches both in the statehouse and around his district did not disappoint constituents who felt strongly about this issue. He stated publicly his belief that secession was nearly impossible from both a legal and a constitutional standpoint, and he spoke at more than forty meetings in favor of Republican presidential candidate Abraham Lincoln in 1860. One sympathetic paper called Garfield Ohio's "leading orator of freedom," while another christened him "a rising man."[8] Those efforts paid off when Lincoln won Garfield's district by almost 3,000 votes. "God be praised!" the young Ohioan exclaimed to his diary on Election Day.[9]

A few months later, when the president-elect stopped in Columbus on his way to Washington, DC, and addressed the Ohio legislature, Garfield got his first look at Lincoln. "But through all his awkward homeliness," he wrote to his wife, "there is a look of transparent, genuine goodness, which at once reaches your heart and makes you trust and love him. . . . He has the tone and bearing of a fearless, firm man, and I have great hope for the government."[10] Garfield's optimism about the Lincoln administration would be largely unfulfilled, and over the next several years, he grew more and more frustrated with Lincoln until, in the words of one historian, his opinion festered into "cold contempt."[11] Garfield thought Lincoln waited too long to issue the Emancipation Proclamation. He believed the war was being fought over the issue of slavery and that abolition of the "peculiar institution" should have been part of the Union's war effort from the beginning.

Lincoln's election was not warmly received below the Mason-Dixon Line, and within six weeks, South Carolina became the first state to secede from the Union. "To make the concessions demanded by the South would by hypocritical and sinful," Garfield told a friend on January 15, 1861, by which time Mississippi, Florida, and Alabama had joined South Carolina. "I am inclined to believe that the sin of slavery is one of which it may be said that 'without the shedding of blood there is no remission.' All that is left for us as a state or as a company of states is to aim and prepare to defend ourselves and the Federal government."[12] A month later, still apparently thinking of little else but the crisis facing the nation, Garfield told the same friend that Southerners needed to understand "that disunion seals the doom of slavery—that if the South forms a government actually based on the monstrous injustice of human slavery, it will be a Cain among the nations of the earth—the Ishmael of the world."[13]

Like most Northerners, Garfield was incensed when the Confederates fired on Fort Sumter and began the Civil War. Major Robert Anderson, commander of the garrison stationed inside Sumter, held out against rebel shells for about thirty-three hours before surrendering the fort. When the news of his surrender reached Ohio, Garfield continued to vent his frustrations on paper. "I am glad we are defeated at Sumter," he wrote on April 14, 1861, a scant twenty-four hours after Anderson's surrender. "It will rouse the people. I hope we will never stop short of complete subjugation. Better to lose a million men in battle than allow the government to be overthrown." Garfield clearly believed that secession was illegal and ill-advised. But he also understood that slavery was the conflict's root cause: "The war will soon assume the shape of Slavery and Freedom. The world will so understand it, and I believe the final outcome will redound to the good of humanity."[14]

These themes would resurface throughout Garfield's career. To him, Southerners' later attempts to subvert the Constitution by failing to appropriate funds for the government's operations and especially by denying voting rights and equal protection under the law to freed people amounted to little more than continued attempts to overthrow the government. He recognized that Southerners who were desperate to reassert white supremacy did not need cannon or ships to rebel against the federal government. They could use legislation and legal processes as well.

Not content to sit on the sidelines during the greatest crisis the nation had ever faced, Garfield was eager to join the army. "I am big and strong," he told his close friend and fellow state senator Jacob Cox, "and if my relations to the church and college can be broken, I shall have no excuse for not enlisting." He and Cox, neither of whom had any military experience, began devouring military textbooks and histories of the Napoleonic Wars. They even took to practicing drills on the grounds of the state capitol. By August 1861, four months after the attack on Fort Sumter, the principal of the Western Reserve Eclectic Institute and part-time state senator was Lieutenant Colonel Garfield of the Forty-Second Ohio Volunteers.

Service in the army over the next two and a half years only hardened Garfield's feelings about slavery and slave owners. As a regimental and later a brigade commander, he sent men into battle against rebels that he believed were fighting to perpetuate and expand slavery and sunder the nation. "Before God I here record my conviction," he wrote in 1862, "that the spirit of Slavery is the soul of the rebellion and the incarnate devil which must be cast out before we can trust in any peace as lasting and secure."[15] He later called the conflict "an abolition war," noting that Union troops had seen the evils of slavery up close, "and they demand that it be swept away."[16] Garfield grew increasingly frustrated at his inability to free or assist enslaved people while commanding Union troops in the South. "We pass these fine plantations," he wrote, "and see the slaves toiling for masters [sic] sons who are in the rebel army fighting us, and we let them stay at their toil. . . . I could chill your blood with the recital of horrors that have resulted to slaves from their expectation of deliverance and their being abandoned to death at the hands of their overseers."[17]

Garfield rejoiced when, following the September 1862 Union victory at Antietam, President Lincoln issued the preliminary Emancipation Proclamation. Garfield wrote, "The President's proclamation gives great satisfaction among all strong vigorous men. The President's heart is right; God grant that he may have the full strength to stand up to his convictions and carry them out to the full." Still, Garfield's opinion of Lincoln remained relatively low: "Strange that a second-rate Illinois lawyer should be the instrument through which one of the sublimest works of any age is accomplished."[18]

In 1862 Republicans nominated Garfield as their candidate to represent northeastern Ohio's Nineteenth Congressional District in the US House of Representatives. This was not uncommon during this period, when parties, not individuals, held sway over elections in most states and congressional nominations were often rotated among prominent local men. Garfield, who remained in the army and did not campaign, was easily elected, but he was torn between staying in the army and serving in Congress. He certainly would have preferred to go to the House, especially as his frustration with the war's direction grew. He fumed at professional, West Point–educated officers who seemed hesitant to take the war to the Southern populace and insisted that if the North lost the war, "let its obituary be written thus: 'died of West Point.'"[19] He theorized that many of these officers cared little about eradicating slavery. "A command in the army," he speculated, "is a sort of tyranny and in a narrow and ignoble mind engenders a despotic spirit which makes him sympathize with slavery and slave holders."[20]

Even if Congressman-elect Garfield chose to leave the army and enter the House of Representatives, he would not have to do so until late 1863, giving him another year to serve in uniform. After a long sojourn in Washington awaiting an assignment—part of which he spent living with and learning fiscal policy from Secretary of the Treasury Chase—Garfield finally received orders to report to the Army of the Cumberland, commanded

James Garfield, brigadier general of volunteers, during the Civil War. (Courtesy of Library of Congress)

by Major General William S. Rosecrans, to serve as chief of staff. Though Rosecrans was a lifelong Democrat, Garfield enjoyed getting to know his fellow Ohioan. The two often stayed up late into the night discussing the war, religion, and philosophy. It was as Rosecrans's chief of staff that Garfield rendered his most famous Civil War service. During the September 1863 Union defeat at Chickamauga, Rosecrans ordered his army to withdraw, even though Major General George Thomas's corps was still holding down part of the Union line. Garfield voluntarily rode under heavy enemy fire to deliver orders and information to Thomas. The incident went down in history as "Garfield's ride."

Garfield traveled to Washington shortly after Chickamauga, carrying reports and maps of the battle. He was aware that the new Congress would convene on December 5, 1863, but he was still undecided whether to stay in the army or report to the House of Representatives. A conversation with Lincoln convinced him to serve the Union as a politician rather than a soldier. "I have resigned my place in the army and have taken my seat in Congress," he wrote to his friend Mark Hopkins. "I did this with great regret. . . . But the President told me he dared not risk a single vote in the House and he needed men in Congress who were practically acquainted with the wants of the army. I did not feel it right to consult my own preference in such a case."[21]

Garfield entered the House in late 1863, still wearing his army uniform. He was also mourning the death of his daughter, Eliza, who had died of diphtheria just four days before the congressional session opened. His colleagues in the House included luminaries such as Thaddeus Stevens of Pennsylvania, Schuyler Colfax of Indiana, Justin Morrill of Vermont, Henry Dawes of Massachusetts, Henry Winter Davis of Maryland, and Elihu Washburne of Illinois. Across the aisle sat Northern Democrats, many of whom believed the war was a failure and a waste of lives and money. They included New York's Fernando Wood, Ohio's George Pendleton and Samuel "Sunset" Cox, Indiana's Daniel Voorhees and William Holman, and Pennsylvania's Samuel Randall. As he had always done in the past, Garfield threw himself into his work, realizing that this was the best way to make an impression and learn the ways of Congress.

Garfield quickly built a reputation as one of the Republican Party's foremost speakers. He took a hard line on the fate of Confederate generals and politicians after the war: "Set it down at once that the leaders of this rebellion must be executed or banished from the republic. . . . Let the republic drive from its soil the traitors that have conspired against its life, as God and his angels drove Satan and his host from Heaven."[22] He spoke in favor of the Thirteenth Amendment: "To me it is a matter of great surprise that gentlemen on the other side should wish to delay the death of slavery. . . . Has she [slavery] not betrayed and slain men enough? Are they not strewn over a thousand battle-fields? . . . Its best friends know that its final hour is fast approaching. The avenging gods are on its track."[23]

During and after the war, Garfield usually allied himself with the so-called Radical Republicans and was a reliable vote for measures intended to guarantee the civil and political rights and the physical safety of black men and women in the South. He recognized the political and economic power of slavery in the South, stating, "It is well known that the power of slavery rests in large plantations . . . and that the bulk of all the real estate is in the hands of the slaveowners who have plotted the great conspiracy."[24]

On July 4, 1865, Garfield delivered an address entitled "Suffrage and Slavery" in Ravenna, Ohio. Its tone resembled Lincoln's Gettysburg Address, as it challenged the nation to live up to the promises of the Declaration of Independence. Garfield noted that, during the Civil War, Northerners had realized that "we must lose our own freedom or grant it to the slave," and the Emancipation Proclamation had fundamentally changed the nature of the war and the nation's future. But Garfield challenged his audience to consider whether defeating the Confederacy was enough. "Have we given freedom to the black man?" he asked. "What is freedom? Is it mere negation? Is it the bare privilege of not being chained . . . ? If this is all, then freedom is a bitter mockery, a cruel delusion, and it might be questioned whether slavery were not better." Garfield recognized that simply freeing enslaved people was not enough. The government needed to protect their physical safety and ensure that they received equal treatment under the law, had access to economic opportunities, and, when the time came, were free to cast ballots in elections.[25]

Garfield's public and private statements were not always consistent. While he publicly supported the use of black men as soldiers during the Civil War, he was slow to come around to the idea that they should receive the same pay as white troops. His Ravenna address makes it clear that he supported granting African Americans the franchise, yet he told a friend privately that it was not easy to advocate this position because, he wrote, "I could never get myself to fall in love with the creatures."[26] Garfield was far from the only Republican to harbor such feelings. Lincoln himself admitted during the Lincoln-Douglas debates that he did not believe the black man to be the white man's equal. Even so, it is at least a little surprising that someone who fully supported black rights in the public realm could express such thoughts. However, Garfield's public statements and, more important, his votes in the House made him a reliable Radical.

One prominent Garfield biographer wrote, "Once the pressures of wartime were lifted, Garfield's commitment to radicalism began to cool." This author posits that radicalism did not come naturally to Garfield, who, at his core, had a "reflective, essentially passive personality."[27] This explanation is a bit too simple and does not account for another aspect of Garfield's personality: he was an extremely astute politician. Garfield had an uncanny ability to read the public mood, whether that of his constituents in northeastern Ohio, the entire state of Ohio, or the nation, and this would pay him dividends many times over the years (most notably in 1880, when he ran for president). The evidence demonstrates that he was mostly committed to radicalism, yet he was willing to bend his convictions to suit a particular situation. "I am trying to do two things," he told his friend Burke Hinsdale, "viz. be a radical and not be a fool—which, if I am to judge by the exhibitions around me, is a matter of no small difficulty."[28] He was a committed radical—until a particular issue or situation required him not to be.

Evidence strongly suggests that recently freed black families in Charleston, South Carolina, hosted the first local Decoration Day ceremony in May 1865, paying tribute to Unions troops who died in a prisoner of war camp there. But on May 30, 1868, the Grand Army of the Republic, cofounded by Garfield's House colleague John Logan of Illinois, a former Union general, hosted the first national Decoration Day ceremony at Arlington National Cemetery. The forerunner of modern Memorial Day, Decoration Day was intended to honor the soldiers killed defending the Union and freeing the slaves during the Civil War by placing flowers on their graves. Logan chose Garfield, already viewed as a rising star and a powerful speaker among his congressional colleagues, to deliver the keynote address. Garfield did not disappoint, honoring his fallen Union colleagues and reminding everyone of the significance of the location—Arlington House had once been Robert E. Lee's home—and the war's true legacy. "We began the war for the Union alone," Garfield told the crowd, "but we had not gone far into its darkness before a new element was added to the conflict. . . . God had linked to our own, the destiny of an enslaved race." He did not forget that the hallowed ground of Arlington had once been "the home of one who lifted his sword against the life of his country." To Garfield, it was both tragic and ironic that Lee's home, "watered by the tears of slaves," was so close to the nation's capital. He finished by noting that, thanks to the sacrifices of men like those buried at Arlington, "this arena of rebellion and slavery is a scene of violence and crime no longer!"[29]

Garfield's powerful Decoration Day speech came just four days after President Andrew Johnson's acquittal in his impeachment trial in the Senate.

Garfield and Johnson had once been friendly, and Johnson viewed Garfield as a more reasonable Radical than most. He had even hoped to use the Ohioan as a conduit to the Radical Republicans in an effort to keep Southern policy from falling completely into the Radicals' hands. Garfield had no interest in helping Johnson, and Johnson's attempt to use Garfield for this purpose was laughably misguided. During his 1866 campaign for reelection to the House, Garfield had traveled all over Ohio and into several other states to campaign for Republican candidates. Over the course of sixty-five speeches, Garfield honed his message:

> Every Rebel guerrilla and jayhawker, every man who ran to Canada to avoid the draft, every bounty-jumper, every deserter, every cowardly sneak that ran from danger and disgraced his flag, every man who loves slavery and hates liberty, every man who helped massacre loyal negroes at Fort Pillow, or loyal whites at New Orleans, every Knight of the Golden Circle, every incendiary who helped burn Northern steam boats and Northern hotels, and every villain, of whatever name or crime, who loves power more than justice, slavery more than freedom, is a Democrat and indorser of Andrew Johnson.[30]

As early as 1866, Garfield made it clear that he stood for the Union and against Democrats hoping to reassert white supremacy in the postwar South. He would stand up for the Union on several other occasions during his career, including in the 1880 presidential campaign.

When the House impeached Johnson in early 1868, Garfield missed the vote to approve the articles of impeachment. He was away from Washington, working on a legal case. Garfield was sure that Johnson would be removed and wrote to a friend, "Our Impeachment will prove its immortal vigor.... I still think Johnson will be convicted by the end of this week."[31] Ultimately, Johnson avoided conviction by a single vote, helped by several Republican senators who detested Johnson but wondered whether the prosecution had been manipulated to present just one side of the case and by "moderates [who] feared that removing him would obliterate the constitutional system of checks and balances, permitting future Congresses to claim presidential heads over policy disputes."[32] Johnson served out the remainder of what should have been Lincoln's second term. Though he hoped to be the Democrats' nominee in 1868, they recognized that he was toxic and nominated former New York governor Horatio Seymour instead. Seymour went on to lose the general election to Republican Ulysses S. Grant.

Garfield had never been personally close to Grant, and this did not change when Grant became president. In fact, Garfield grew irritated with Grant during the early days of his administration over a trivial issue that would later seem symbolically important: the appointment of a new postmaster in Ravenna, Ohio, a town in Garfield's congressional district. Garfield had made a recommendation for the position, which Grant ignored, giving the post to an old friend of his father's.[33] Such a small patronage position was unimportant in and of itself, but the episode foreshadowed a showdown between Grant and Garfield forces a decade later at the 1880 Republican National Convention. Grant soon mollified Garfield by naming the latter's old friend Jacob D. Cox as secretary of the interior.

During the Grant years, Garfield continued to build his reputation as a vocal advocate of hard money and opponent of greenbacks and inflation. Garfield blamed greenbacks for the rise in speculation and corruption and tried to move the country back to hard money backed by gold. "Inflationists" attacked the national banking system created by Lincoln Republicans during the Civil War as too stringent, preferring to see money backed by national banknotes instead of gold and massive infusions of greenbacks, which were backed by nothing. In 1869 Garfield introduced legislation to reform the banking system by creating additional banknote currency but also withdrawing greenbacks from circulation. He argued that the real issue was not the gold standard but the concentration of banking interests in the Northeast. His bill, he said, would allow new currency to be supplied to banks in the West and South. This would increase the money supply, as demanded by inflationists, but would not rely on greenbacks to do so. "The measure was so complex," notes one historian, "that not even the banking specialists in Congress could agree on whether it would be inflationary or deflationary."[34] The bill went nowhere, but Garfield remained dedicated to hard money and opposed to inflation and greenbacks for the rest of his career.

The ambitious Garfield hoped to be named chairman of one of the House financial committees—preferably Ways and Means—and tried to position himself to run for Speaker of the House as well. He fell short on both measures (although he did chair the Appropriations Committee for four years). Garfield showed little zeal for recasting the civil service from a patronage-based to a merit-based system during the 1870s, in part because, like many of his Republican colleagues, he saw the system's value for building his own power base. Few politicians were willing to voluntarily give up a system that created hordes of loyalists who owed them favors and who turned over a portion of their salaries to the Republican Party. Garfield also regularly rejected the overtures of Republicans who invoked party loyalty and duty to convince him to run for governor of Ohio, at one point remarking, "Any Justice of the Peace in Cleveland has more to do than the Governor of Ohio."[35] Diverting his career away from Washington and toward Columbus was not an option.

Historians have long judged Ulysses S. Grant's presidency a failure due to the numerous scandals that occurred during those years. Recent biographers such as Ron Chernow have concluded that Grant himself was personally honest but often showed poor judgment and misplaced loyalty to friends who did not have his administration's best interests at heart. Chernow also gives Grant relatively high marks for his efforts to protect and help blacks in the South. But scandals did indeed plague the Grant years, and none more prominently than Credit Mobilier. This particular controversy would spread deeply into the Grant administration and into Congress, ensnaring several prominent Republicans—including James A. Garfield.

"This winter would be a delightful one in spite of all the hard work," Garfield wrote in his diary on January 31, 1873, "but for the ugly shadow of Credit Mobilier, which throws a gloom over every social circle."[36] Although the events surrounding the Credit Mobilier scandal had taken place several years earlier, they first came to light in 1872 as Grant's reelection campaign was in full swing. Credit Mobilier was a sham company created by Thomas Durant, vice president of the Union Pacific Railroad, and entrepreneur George Francis Train. On paper, Credit Mobilier was a construction company that had been awarded contracts by the Union Pacific to fund and build its section of the transcontinental railroad. In reality, Credit Mobilier was a scam intended to line the pockets of the company's directors and shareholders.

Congressman Oakes Ames, a Massachusetts Republican who sat on the House Committee on Railroads, sought to obtain political clout for Credit Mobilier. Ames made discounted stock available to several high-ranking politicians, including Vice President Schuyler Colfax, Senator Roscoe Conkling, and Congressman James Garfield. In 1872 the vocally anti-Grant *New York Sun* broke the Credit Mobilier story in what some historians have concluded was a blatant attempt to prevent Grant's reelection. But the ensuing scandal implicated more than thirty members of Congress, eventually leading the House of Representatives to censure Ames and James Brooks, a New York Democrat. Garfield was accused of accepting a paltry $329 in stock dividends, but the charge was never proved. Although Garfield suffered no lasting damage (nor did Grant, who was reelected in 1872), it was stressful enough for him to label 1873 an *anno diaboli:* "It has been a year of ferment; a year of trouble, a year of lessons; and a year that I part without tears."[37]

Despite his own vindication at the polls in 1872, Garfield viewed Grant's second term with trepidation when it came to affairs in the South. Louisiana was particularly troublesome, leading Garfield to believe that Reconstruction had failed to provide sufficient protection for freed people in the South. Louisiana Republicans often employed trickery or fraud to win elections, while white Democrats were more overt and often resorted to intimidation of black voters or outright murder. In Garfield's view, politics there had deteriorated to a contest between "a reckless set of scamps . . . and the armed negro-hating band of murderers." In 1875 federal troops entered the Louisiana statehouse and forced Democrats out of the legislature, allowing Republicans to establish a majority. Even for a partisan Republican like Garfield, this was an ugly development. "I have never given wholly away to despondency," he wrote, but "this is the darkest day for the future of the Republican party I have ever seen. The Louisiana question now appears to be the mill stone that threatens to sink our party out of sight."[38]

Garfield had little fear that this incident would lead to any particular retribution by whites against blacks. After all, white Southerners were already openly hostile to blacks and frequently turned to violence against them. Garfield's real concern was that events in Louisiana would lead to a Northern backlash against Reconstruction. Such a reaction could ultimately lead to the government abandoning African Americans in the South—unless additional civil rights legislation was passed. "God taught us early in this fight," Garfield said on the House floor, "that the fate of our own race was indissolubly linked with that of the black man. . . . Justice to them has always been safety for us. Let us not shrink now."[39] The legislation he was referring to passed both houses and became the Civil Rights Bill of 1875.

As Grant's presidency neared its end (and once he had quashed rumors about seeking an unprecedented third term), numerous Republicans tried to position themselves to succeed him. Garfield was personally close to Senator James Blaine of Maine, and Blaine's presidential ambitions were well known. Senator Roscoe Conkling of New York, Treasury Secretary Benjamin Bristow of Kentucky, and Indiana senator Oliver P. Morton also tested the waters. Garfield was loath to support Conkling or Morton, both of whom were close to Grant and, in Garfield's mind, would equal another term for "Grantism." Though he felt obligated to publicly support his friend Blaine, Garfield privately preferred Bristow, calling him "a higher type of man" and telling his wife that a Bristow presidency "would need no apology."[40]

Garfield put little stock in the rising prospects of Ohio's Republican governor Rutherford B. Hayes. He knew and liked Hayes and encouraged his fellow Ohioan to run, but Garfield thought Hayes was a relatively weak candidate who would have little impact on the field. "I do not find that the mention of his name excites much enthusiasm outside of Ohio," he noted.[41] As it turned out, Blaine's chances faded when several Republican foes, including Conkling, accused him of improperly using his congressional position to benefit a railroad in which he held stock. Then, just days before the Republican National Convention convened in Cincinnati, Blaine fainted in church and spent the next several days nearly comatose. At the convention, Blaine led on the first six ballots, but then his support collapsed, and the party turned to Hayes. Though Hayes was not his first choice, Garfield quickly offered his support.

Hayes emphasized the dangers of turning the federal government over to the Democrats, and Garfield took every opportunity to remind his constituents and others that "this Democratic House is the most inefficient and discordant body I have ever been a member of. It was a good thing for the country that they got into power just enough to show their character." For anyone who might consider voting for the Democratic ticket in 1876, Garfield reminded them that "the Democratic party has been and is now submissive to the despots of the South . . . they are wrong and the Republican party right every time."[42] Garfield clearly feared that the supremacy of the federal government and the rights of freed people were at stake.

On August 2, 1876, Democratic representative L. Q. C. Lamar of Mississippi delivered a speech on the House floor in which he offered a defense of the Democratic Party, thereby hoping to influence the tone of the presidential campaign. Describing conditions in the South, Lamar argued, "These inevitable difficulties were aggravated by the fact that the essential principle of the reconstruction policy of the Republican party was the creation of that very color line which is now represented as the work of Southern malignity." Only granting the former Confederate states the ability to govern themselves would lead to a "true Southern *renaissance,* a real grand reconstruction of the South in all the elements of social order, strength, justice, and equality of all her people."[43]

To Garfield, Lamar's speech was none-too-subtle code for returning the South to the antebellum social order—in other words, white supremacy. The Grant administration had already reduced the number of federal troops in many parts of the South, and only Louisiana, Florida, and South Carolina remained fully under Republican rule. In a long speech two days after Lamar's, Garfield laid out exactly why the Republican Party should be retained in the White House for another four years: "Above all [what] we hoped for and won . . . is the grand, onward movement of the republic, to perpetuate its glory, to save liberty alive, to preserve exact and equal justice to all. . . . And until these great results are accomplished, it is not safe to take one step backward." Indeed, Garfield felt "alarm and apprehension" at the idea of a Tilden presidency.[44]

Once Hayes became president, Garfield immediately recognized that he had two notable policy disputes with the new administration that centered on civil service reform and Reconstruction. Garfield was not opposed to reform of the civil service per se, but he objected to Hayes's piecemeal approach, mandating reform through proclamations rather than the legislative process. Garfield and his old friend Cox agreed that Hayes might not be up to the job of president.

On Reconstruction, Garfield was skeptical of the Hayes approach but wanted to give the new administration a fair shake. Hayes was convinced that appointing former Confederate David M. Key as postmaster general would win him favor with Southern congressmen. Several of them apparently offered to elect Garfield Speaker of the House in return for Key's cabinet post, but Hayes overplayed his hand and embarked on an effort to woo the South and build the Republican Party there. Hayes told Southern audiences that the federal government was done intervening on behalf of black men and women and that federal money would be forthcoming for various infrastructure projects. He also gave more than one-third of Southern patronage jobs to Democrats.

This seemingly disjointed approach bore little fruit for Hayes, and few Southerners relished the idea of Garfield as Speaker of the House. "If General Garfield . . . is counting upon the votes of Southern Democrats to elect him Speaker of the next House," wrote the *New Orleans Democrat*, "he is likely to come to grief." The editorial ended by calling Garfield a "red-mouthed, false-hearted, narrow-minded, unprincipled jobber, hypocrite, and persecutor of the South."[45] Sure enough, every single House Democrat voted for Samuel J. Randall of Pennsylvania as Speaker. Both Hayes and Garfield were a little naïve to think it would go any differently.

Garfield lamented that Hayes's effort to kill the South with kindness—

which he himself had suggested that Hayes do during the electoral crisis—was backfiring. Garfield wrote that Hayes had "offered conciliation everywhere to the South while they have spent their time whetting their knives for every Republican they could find." The overtures to the South were, in Garfield's mind, threatening to split the party asunder. Hayes disagreed. "It seems," Garfield wrote, "to be impossible for a President to see through the atmosphere of praise in which he lives."[46] As House minority leader, Garfield now found himself in the difficult position of trying to keep his fellow Republicans loyal to a president with whom he himself disagreed on many pressing issues. Things did not improve when the economy took a downturn and debates about inflation, specie resumption, and bimetallism consumed the House.

In early 1879 the magazine *North American Review* planned to hold a symposium and publish an issue on black suffrage. The editors asked several members of Congress—Republicans and Democrats alike—to submit articles based on the questions "Ought the Negro to Be Disfranchised?" and "Ought He to Have Been Enfranchised?" Garfield, James G. Blaine, Montgomery Blair, and Wendell Phillips were among the Republicans asked to submit articles. Democrats L. Q. C. Lamar, Alexander Stephens (former Confederate vice president), Thomas A. Hendricks, and Wade Hampton also wrote their opinions. In his piece, Garfield observed that both parties "are influenced by the strongest political motives to maintain at least a profession of friendship for the negro. Political interest will therefore prevent a direct assault upon the constitutional amendments." Here he referred to the three Reconstruction Amendments making slavery illegal, granting African Americans citizenship, and conferring the franchise on black men. Garfield continued:

> To strike the shackles from the negro's limbs, to declare by law that he should not be bought or sold, scourged or branded at the will of his master, and then to leave him with no means of defending his rights before the courts and juries of the country—to arm him with no legal or political weapons of defense—would have been an injustice hardly less cruel to him, and a policy even more dangerous to the public peace, than slavery itself.

Garfield concluded by stating that "the negro ought to have been franchised," and "for the same reasons, strengthened and confirmed by our experience, he ought not to be disfranchised."[47]

Garfield's contribution to the *North American Review* was certainly the most articulate of those written by Republicans. Indeed, it was so good that it almost did not get published. Garfield's friend Blaine, by then a US senator, was in charge of organizing the Republican responses, as well as writing one of his own. When Blaine read Garfield's contribution, he worried that Garfield had made all the best points, leaving Blaine with little to offer. Blaine actually tried to convince the magazine's editor to reject Garfield's article, but he refused to go along with the scheme. Even though Garfield and Blaine were close, Garfield had no illusions about his friend's ambition. This incident merely confirmed that Blaine's faults were "growing rather than decreasing." Garfield speculated that Blaine's "mind is warped by the constant pressure of the presidential idea upon him."[48] Blaine's desire to be president was well known in Washington, and everyone—Garfield included—fully expected the Maine senator to seek the Republican nomination again in 1880.

The ongoing racial problems in the South and the overall failure of Hayes's Southern policy came to a head in the waning days of the Forty-Fifth Congress, scheduled to end on March 4, 1879. There was currently a Democratic majority in the House but a Republican majority in the Senate. That would change with the Forty-Sixth Congress, which would have Democratic majorities in both houses. In early 1879 the House's Democratic majority attached riders to funding bills prohibiting the use of federal marshals and the army to monitor polling places and protect voters and prevent violence at the polls. Democrats had long considered these measures unlawful federal protection for black voters, who voted overwhelmingly for Republican candidates. Naturally, the Republican majority in the Senate opposed these riders and refused to pass them. As a result, Congress failed to pass a bill appropriating $45 million to fund the federal government's operations for the fiscal year beginning July 1, 1879. The nation faced an unprecedented government shutdown.[49]

President Hayes called the new Forty-Sixth Congress into special session on March 19, 1879, to fund the government. He wrote to a friend that Democrats "would stop the wheels . . . of government if I do not yield my convictions in favor of the election laws. It will be a severe, perhaps a long contest. I do not fear it—I do not even dread it. The people will not allow this Revolutionary course to triumph." He condemned the idea that Congress could hold the president and the nation hostage by refusing to pass appropriations bills, calling it "radical, dangerous, and unconstitutional."[50]

He stated, "I object to the [army appropriations] bill because it is an unconstitutional and revolutionary attempt to deprive the Executive of one of his most important prerogatives . . . [and to] coerce him to approve a measure which in fact he does not approve."[51]

As the minority party's leader, Garfield was the Hayes administration's chief lieutenant in the House of Representatives. He rose to speak on March 29 and launched a blistering constitutional attack on the Democratic majority in a lengthy speech later published under the title "Revolution in Congress." He told the House that if the Democratic majority "cannot have its own way in certain matters not connected with appropriations, it will so use or refrain from using its voluntary powers to destroy the government." He invoked the Civil War, reminding his listeners that in 1861 Southern Democrats had threatened to destroy the government if the American people elected Abraham Lincoln to the presidency and then attempted to secede from the Union after Lincoln's election. "Then your leaders . . . were heroic enough to withdraw from their seats and fling down the gauge of mortal battle," Garfield thundered in the House chamber. "We called it rebellion . . . but you say . . . if you cannot coerce an independent branch of this government, not that you will shoot our government to death, as you tried to do before, but that you will starve the government to death" by failing to provide appropriations. Garfield rejected Democrats' opposition to federal marshals at polling places and reminded them that "only six years before the war, your law authorized marshals of the United States to enter all our hamlets and households to hunt for fugitive slaves."[52]

Although the main thrust of his masterful performance was the unconstitutionality of the Democrats' approach, Garfield did not miss the opportunity to bring up the pre–Civil War controversy over the enhanced Fugitive Slave Act and the Democratic Party's role in secession and the war itself. He was covering all bases to rally public support for the stand being taken by congressional Republicans and President Hayes.

Garfield's argument was bolstered when even anti-Hayes Republicans Conkling and Blaine, spoke in the Senate in tones similar to Garfield's speech in the House. Conkling called it "revolutionary" that, unless "another species of legislation [a rider] is agreed to, the money of the people . . . shall not be used to maintain the government." Blaine and Conkling had despised each other for more than fifteen years, but the senator from Maine agreed: "I call it the audacity of revolution for any senator or representative . . . to get together and say, 'We will have this legislation or we will stop . . . the government.' That is revolutionary."[53] Conkling and Blaine both echoed

Garfield's sly use of "revolution," an obvious but effective reminder of the upheaval of the Civil War years that few Americans wanted to repeat.

Ultimately, the tactic worked. Under a deluge of public outcry, Democrats "completely abandoned the main ground which they at first took; and the most sensible among them do not hesitate to admit, privately, that it was wholly untenable," Garfield privately noted. The Democrat-controlled Congress ultimately withheld a token $600,000 of federal appropriations rather than the full $45 million.[54]

Garfield's powerful speech had an electric effect on the Republican Party, and he enjoyed a great deal of positive publicity for the next several months. "I am now experiencing one of the 'ups' of political life," he wrote on July 3, 1879. "The great newspapers and the little have been equally profuse of flatter."[55] Ultimately, the special session of Congress proved to be a victory for the Republican Party and the Hayes administration. "The extra session," Garfield wrote his to friend Burke Hinsdale on July 7, "has united the Republican party more than anything since 1868 and it bids fair to give us 1880."[56]

By "give us 1880," Garfield clearly meant returning the Republicans to majorities in one or even both houses of Congress in the next election. However, he was already looking to his own future as well. Garfield was aware that this was the right time for him to make the leap to the US Senate (once again insisting that he had no interest in running for governor of Ohio). According to biographer Allan Peskin, Garfield decided that "if a senatorship should come his way, he would take it."[57] After nearly sixteen years in the House of Representatives, Garfield had accomplished nearly all he could, short of becoming Speaker. The Senate would offer greater prestige, a slower pace, and a respite from the grind of facing reelection every other year. Though sticking to his resolution never to overtly seek an office but to let the office seek him, Garfield set out to work quietly to convince the Ohio legislature to make him the state's next senator.

However, unbeknownst to all but a few, another possibility was taking shape. Just days after his "Revolution in Congress" speech, a newspaper in Cincinnati wrote, "If the entire North is as completely electrified and aroused as . . . here in Cincinnati, it would not be surprising if you [Garfield] would be called upon to accept the nomination in 1880."[58]

In January 1879, two months before the "Revolution in Congress" speech, Garfield had received a message from political organizer Thomas Nichol in Chicago: "Jerry Rusk was here yesterday, and says we'll put up a job and make you President."[59] Former congressman Jeremiah "Jerry"

Rusk was a friend of Garfield's from both the army and Congress and one of Wisconsin's most influential Republicans. He also planned to be one of his state's delegates to the Republican National Convention in 1880. Rusk was one of those responsible for an early 1879 Garfield-for-president movement that gained at least some followers after the appropriations controversy and Garfield's well-received speech.

For his part, the Ohioan put little stock in any of it and remained focused on getting to the Senate. "I long ago made a resolution," Garfield wrote, "that I would never let the Presidential fever get any lodgement in my brain. I think it is the one office in this nation that for his own peace no man ought to set his heart on." Besides, he concluded, "few men in our history have ever obtained the Presidency by planning to obtain it."[60]

3

"ANTAGONISMS AND CONTROVERSIES" THE 1880 REPUBLICAN NATIONAL CONVENTION—PART 1

The special session of Congress called by President Hayes to address the appropriations controversy ended on July 1, 1879. That evening, Congressman James Garfield had dinner with the prickly and acerbic John Sherman, former Ohio senator and then the sitting secretary of the treasury. Sherman was planning to seek the Republican presidential nomination in 1880. "At half-past five dined with Secretary Sherman," Garfield wrote in his diary that night, "and then drove with him far out in Maryland. He talked very freely of the political situation and his prospects for the Presidency. I think he is deeply committed to hope of being nominated. He said he was not a candidate for the Ohio Senatorship and had no doubt I would be chosen by a large majority in case we carried the Legislature."[1]

Garfield was still riding a wave of popularity after his "Revolution in Congress" speech and his role in defeating the Democrats in the appropriations battle. Sherman recognized that Garfield would easily be elected senator as long as the Republicans held a majority in the Ohio legislature. Both men wanted something: Sherman the Republican presidential nomination, and Garfield the Senate seat. Both were experienced and astute politicians, and although the subject apparently did not come up during this meeting, both had surely considered seeking the other's help to obtain his desired position. And both must have speculated about what that assistance might cost him.

Sherman's claim to the Republican presidential nom-

John Sherman, longtime Ohio senator and, in 1880, President Hayes's secretary of the treasury. (Courtesy of Library of Congress)

ination was by no means absolute, despite his admirable service as secretary of the treasury. Sherman was highly regarded for his work during the Hayes administration, especially his skillful resumption of specie payments (which had caused many conflicts between hard- and soft-money advocates), and the public viewed a possible Sherman nomination as a continuation of the policies of the Hayes years. In modern terms, Sherman would be the "establishment" candidate. But his cool personality—he was nicknamed the "Ohio Icicle"—inspired few to flock to his campaign. Privately, even Garfield conceded that Sherman had little chance to be nominated, and Garfield worried that his own Nineteenth Congressional District heavily favored some other candidate. Garfield did not really care whether Sherman received the nomination, but he was determined to demonstrate loyalty to Sherman's ambitions in order to advance his own. Garfield was uncomfortable when other prominent Ohioans, such as future Supreme Court justice Stanley Matthews, publicly speculated that Garfield was far more popular in Ohio than Sherman.[2] Garfield did not disavow such statements but remained publicly committed to Sherman and to his own election to the Senate.

So-called Stalwart Republicans—those who relished "bloody shirt" rhetoric, were pro-business, and had little interest in civil service reform—sought a different Republican standard-bearer. During the eight years of the Grant administration (1869–1877), three powerful Stalwarts had enjoyed unprecedented access to and influence on the White House: Senators Roscoe Conkling of New York, John Logan of Illinois, and Donald Cameron of Pennsylvania. Known collectively as the "Triumvirate," they hoped to bring Grant out of retirement to seek an unprecedented third term. These senators and their acolytes had stymied Hayes's attempts to reform the federal civil service throughout his four-year term. Conkling, the undisputed king of using patronage appointments to demand loyalty and favors, snidely labeled Hayes's efforts "snivel service reform." Conkling was particularly incensed when Hayes fired one of Conkling's chief lieutenants, Chester Alan Arthur, from the nation's most important and lucrative patronage job—collector of the port of New York—for turning a blind eye to rampant corruption at the customhouse. "When Dr. Johnson defined patriotism as the last refuge of scoundrels," Conkling snarled, "he was unconscious of the then undeveloped capabilities and uses of the word 'Reform.'"[3]

Conkling and his fellow Stalwarts hoped the next president would be either one of their own or, at the very least, a Republican they could manage to their benefit. Conkling himself had flirted with a presidential run in the past, but his prickly personality—which included a nearly pathological aversion to being touched[4]—made him far better suited to the role of kingmaker and behind-the-scenes ruler of New York. He had even turned down President Grant's offer to nominate him to the Supreme Court.

Ulysses S. Grant was the most popular man in America when the Civil War ended and, like Dwight D. Eisenhower nearly a century later, he was courted by both parties to run for president in 1868. Grant was elected that year as a Republican, campaigning on the slogan "Let Us Have Peace," and he was reelected in 1872. Few questioned Grant's personal honesty or dedication to his country, but scandals plagued his eight years in the White House. Although Americans still revered him as the man who won the Civil War, many were glad to see the Grant administration end in early

1877. Stalwart Republicans who were close to Grant had seen their own power and influence grow exponentially during his administration, and they became increasingly frustrated with the party's direction under Hayes. In addition to opposing civil service reform, Stalwarts tended to favor a continued commitment to freedmen's rights in the South, so they rejected Hayes's new policy of granting more local political control to white Southerners. Stalwarts were pleasantly surprised when Hayes took a stand (with help from Garfield and others) against the Democrats during the appropriations controversy, but they still hoped to see a member of their own faction elected president in 1880.

After leaving the White House, Ulysses and Julia Grant embarked on a two-year world tour. While the Grants traveled and spent much of their life savings, the Stalwarts plotted to get Grant nominated for a third term. Conkling and his allies knew the Republicans would need a new candidate in 1880, since Hayes was not running. Grant was still personally popular with the American people, and constitutionally, nothing prevented him from running again. (Not until 1951 would the Twenty-Second Amendment prohibit a president from serving more than two full terms.) Only the desire to follow the two-term tradition begun by George Washington had prevented anyone from seeking a third term. In Conkling's view, Grant and Washington had much in common: both were military men, both were revered for saving the nation (from the Confederacy and the British, respectively), and both had portrayed themselves as accepting the presidency not from any personal ambition but from a strong sense of duty. Who better to break the two-term precedent than Grant, who resembled the preeminent founding father in so many ways?

Grant was not unaware of the movement spearheaded by Conkling, Logan, and Cameron on his behalf, nor was he opposed to it. He missed the power of the presidency,[5] and he was genuinely concerned that freedmen's rights in the South had regressed under Hayes, undoing much of his administration's work. In short, Hayes was too moderate a Republican for Grant's taste. One other factor made Grant willing to return to the White House: his wife very much wanted him to be president again. She had vocally supported the idea of a third consecutive term in 1876 and was distraught when they left Washington after Hayes's inauguration: "I bravely stood looking out," she said of the train ride out of town, "waving my scarf as we glided out of the depot, and when we had passed all our friends I quickly sought out my stateroom and, in an abandonment of grief, flung myself on the lounge and wept. Wept, oh, so bitterly."[6]

The Grants' world tour actually helped their chances of returning to the White House. Reporter John Russell Young of the *New York Herald* traveled with the couple and kept readers at home informed of their visits to numerous international capitals. This kept Grant in the public eye and reminded Americans that he was abroad and uninvolved in the upheavals over Southern policy and civil service reform during the Hayes years. Anecdotes, such as Grant's remark that "Venice would be a pretty city if only it were drained," provided entertainment but also reminded Americans of the humbleness of the man who had saved the Union from rebellion and then occupied its highest office for nearly a decade. As readers enjoyed Young's rich, detailed stories about the Grants' meetings with kings, queens, chancellors, and emperors and their visits to exotic locales such as the Great Pyramids of Egypt and cruising down the Suez to gaze at Mount Sinai, some could not help but be reminded of Henry Adams's description of Hayes as "a third-rate non-entity, whose only recommendation is that he is offensive to no one" and feel nostalgic for Grant.[7] The idea of a third term for Grant began to seem plausible not only to Republican politicians but also to average American voters.

Then, in September 1879, Grant committed a major error: he came home too early. The couple had been traveling for two years and wanted to return home to see their children, even though many of Grant's closest associates in the United States had advised him to stay abroad until just before the June 1880 Republican National Convention in Chicago. His return at that time, they told him, would be a triumphant celebration and carry him to the nomination. "Most every letter I get from the States . . . asks me to remain abroad," he wrote from Rome. "They have designs for me which I do not contemplate for myself."[8] Grant was playing coy here, seeking to publicly disavow any interest in the presidency, as was expected of candidates at the time. Privately, he did not direct anyone to stop mentioning his name as a possible Republican candidate in 1880. His silence was taken as agreement.

The Grants arrived in San Francisco to a hero's welcome in late September 1879, more than eight months before the early June convention. They returned to their home in Galena, Illinois, and then, after a short rest, resumed traveling within the United States and Mexico. Everywhere he went—Texas, Louisiana, Alabama, Pennsylvania—Grant was greeted with cheers and lavish receptions. He was still the most popular and beloved man in the country.

Grant continued to publicly disavow any interest in returning to the

Ulysses S. Grant. (Courtesy of Library of Congress)

presidency, but privately, he did nothing to discourage Conkling, Logan, Cameron, and their minions from pressing his case to Republicans. "I believe that if the nomination were to be made tomorrow, Grant would be the nominee," Illinois Republican George S. Davis stated, "but I don't see anything that is liable to occur between now and the day of the nomination that will decrease his strength."[9] George Jones, editor of the *New York Times,* told readers that he understood from an unnamed friend of Grant's that although the former president would not seek the nomination, he would view it as his "duty" to accept it if the convention chose him.[10] As the June

1880 convention approached, Grant was unquestionably the preferred candidate of the Stalwart Republicans. As 1879 turned to 1880, though, some wondered whether his early return to the United States might hurt his chances to reclaim the White House.

The other serious contender for the Republican presidential nomination in 1880 was Senator James G. Blaine of Maine. Blaine had been in Congress since the Civil War; in fact, he had entered the House of Representatives as a freshman member of the Thirty-Eighth Congress in December 1863 with fellow newcomer James A. Garfield of Ohio, then moved on to the Senate in 1876. Blaine had long been any enemy of Conkling's and was therefore an enemy of many leading Stalwarts. Blaine and Conkling had argued on the House floor in April 1866, and Blaine made himself the New Yorker's nemesis for life when he criticized Conkling's "haughty disdain, his grandiloquent swell, his majestic supereminent, his powering, turkey-gobbler strut."[11] Conkling, whom one historian describes as "a touchy egotist who never forgot a slight," hated Blaine and committed himself to stifling the latter's presidential ambitions.[12] "That attack was made without any provocation by me as against Mr. Blaine," Conkling said years later. "I shall never forget it."[13]

Blaine and Conkling should have been allies. Both were dedicated and skillful advocates of the patronage system and more or less committed to the Republican program of Reconstruction after the Civil War. Both had mocked and opposed President Hayes's efforts at civil service reform but defended the president during the appropriations controversy in 1879. Both had also been accused at various times of abuses of power and corruption. But while Conkling was comfortable in the Senate and in his self-appointed role as kingmaker, Blaine yearned to be president. He had sought the Republican nomination in 1876 and did so again in 1880, not only for himself but also to prevent the possibility of a third term for Grant. This set him up for another conflict with Conkling.

Two particular events made Blaine believe that he had a chance to win the nomination in 1880. The first occurred in 1879, when Blaine rushed home to Maine as a potential revolution festered in the state capital of Augusta. A Democratic "fusion" governor—backed by both the Democrats and the Greenback Party—had been elected in 1878, and a Republican majority had been elected to the state legislature a year later. The fusionists attempted to nullify the 1879 results and toss out nearly forty duly elected

Republicans. Blaine dramatically left the floor of the US Senate and headed home to preserve the Republican legislature for the upcoming 1880 presidential canvass. When he got to Augusta, he found armed fusionists blocking Republicans from entering the statehouse and just as many armed Republicans threatening to take the building by force. Blaine strategized with the state's leading Republicans, and Democratic governor Alonzo Garcelon eventually agreed to a legal settlement that allowed the Republican legislature to be seated. Blaine had managed to avoid bloodshed while exposing the corruption in Maine's Democratic Party, giving his popularity a welcome boost just as Republicans were getting serious about evaluating potential presidential candidates.[14] Republican operative William E. Chandler wrote that he hoped Blaine would "mount the saddle instead of running alongside holding on to Grant's stirrup."[15]

The second event was viewed less favorably. With an eye toward appealing to voters in the West and particularly in California, Blaine enthusiastically supported the Chinese Exclusion Act, passed by the House of Representatives in late January 1879 by a vote of 155–72. "The idea of comparing European immigration with an immigration that has no regard to family," Blaine said on the Senate floor, "that does not recognize the relation of husband and wife, that does not observe the tie of parent and child, that does not have in the slightest degree the ennobling and civilizing influences of hearthstone and fireside! Why when gentlemen talk loosely about emigration from European states as contrasted with that, they are certainly forgetting history and forgetting themselves." Fellow Senate Republican Blanche K. Bruce, an African American and former slave representing Mississippi, countered with a poignant statement against the bill that both supported Chinese immigrants and recalled recent history: "Mr. President, I desire to submit a single remark. Representing as I do a people who but a few years ago were considered essentially disqualified from enjoying the privileges and immunities of American citizenship, and who have since been so successfully introduced into the body-politic, and having large confidence in the assimilative power of our institutions, I shall vote against the pending bill."[16]

James Garfield opposed the bill in the House. During the debate there, he demanded "an amendment that this bill shall not take effect until due notice has been given to China according to the usages of international law of the termination of the treaty against which it is a palpable and flat violation."[17] On February 23 Garfield noted in his diary that he had received a note from President Hayes asking him to come to the White House that night. Hayes "asked me about the Chinese Bill. . . . I advised him to veto the

James G. Blaine, senator from Maine and a candidate for the Republican presidential nomination in 1880. (Courtesy of Library of Congress)

bill, and point[ed] out, fully, the iniquity of its provision." Secretary of State William Evarts joined the discussion at some point, and Garfield concluded, "I am sure the bill will be vetoed." The following day, Garfield added in his diary, "The sentiment against that bill is growing very strong. I am satisfied that Senator Blaine has made a great mistake in his advocacy of it."[18]

The bill eventually passed both houses of Congress, and, as Garfield predicted, President Hayes vetoed it. His veto message objected to the bill not on the basis of racial discrimination against Chinese immigrants but on the same legal grounds Garfield had raised in his House speech: that the bill violated the 1868 Burlingame Treaty with China.[19] Garfield confessed to his diary, "I am anxious to see some legislation that shall prevent the overflow of Chinese in this country."[20] This diary entry and others demonstrate that Garfield supported curtailing or limiting Chinese immigration, but not at the expense of important international treaties. Garfield's consistent public support for African Americans throughout his political career obviously did not extend to all ethnic minorities. The issue would come up again late in the 1880 presidential campaign, when an anonymous forger tried to demonstrate that Garfield supported unlimited Chinese immigration in an attempt to cost him votes in the western states.

As the Republicans headed toward their 1880 convention, James G. Blaine was clearly the favorite candidate of the so-called Half-Breed faction that opposed a third term for anyone, including the still-popular Ulysses S. Grant. Nearly four years removed from office and increasingly distressed by the Republican Party's direction under President Hayes, Grant was the first choice of the Stalwart faction. Finally, John Sherman was the "establishment" candidate, having served as Hayes's secretary of the treasury.

Many Republicans were sure that Conkling and his allies would try to ram Grant down their throats at the upcoming Chicago convention and recommended an alliance between the Sherman and Blaine forces to prevent this. "Thank Heaven for the agreement between your friends and those of Mr. Blaine," New York Republican A. N. Cole wrote to Sherman after helping to build the alliance. "I am morally certain that if Mr. Blaine becomes convinced that he cannot this time succeed, he will ask his friends to go over to you in a body."[21] Sherman and Blaine might have kept their word to each other at the Chicago convention, but they never got the chance.

During this era, Congress met only from December to March. When he was not in Washington, James Garfield spent much of 1879 crisscrossing Ohio and campaigning for a Republican legislature to be elected that autumn. With his sights set on the US Senate, ensuring that his party controlled the state legislature—which would choose Ohio's next senator—was critical. Garfield had not yet publicly declared himself a candidate for the Senate, but he did all he could behind the scenes to make his election to the upper house possible. This included allying himself with John Sherman and supporting his ambitions for the 1880 presidential nomination. Sherman knew that the first step on the road to the White House was ensuring that Republicans in his home state stood firmly behind him. He wanted Garfield to publicly endorse his candidacy, but Garfield hedged. "My course towards Sherman's candidacy for the presidency," he wrote, "would depend, in part, upon his conduct towards me in the pending [Senate] contest."[22]

Garfield's diary reveals that three considerations led him to seek a Senate seat. "If I were to follow my own preference," he confessed, "I would stay in the House and run for the Speakership when we win, as I think we will next time." Ultimately, though, he feared the workload of the Speakership would take a toll on his health (whereas "a seat in the Senate will delay the catastrophe"). He also knew that other Republicans wanted to run for his House seat, and he feared giving the impression that he chose to stay in the House because he had "a pocket borough (the 19th District) which I could control, but that I feared to risk the chances of a larger field." Finally, he knew that several Republicans from the Cincinnati area, including Alphonso Taft (father of future president William Howard Taft), coveted the Senate seat, and Garfield determined that "I shall therefore be a candidate, preferring to be defeated, rather than not make the race."[23]

Garfield was clearly confident of his chances. "I do not think I shall be defeated," he said. So when several of his closest friends and advisers urged him to head to Columbus to manage his own campaign, he refused. Ever mindful of seeming too eager for office and of a pledge he had made to never seek an office but rather let the office find him, Garfield observed, "A man who is fit to be a U.S. Senator ought to be so well known that his presence is unnecessary." His friend Charles Henry agreed and told Garfield, "To oblige you to be there would be like compelling a virtuous woman to act the part of a street walker." Henry volunteered to travel to the state capital to look out for Garfield's interests. Garfield agreed but instructed Henry not to offer jobs or anything else in return for supporting his candidacy. "If money is to be used," he wrote in his diary, "if the Senatorship is to be bought, I am not a purchaser. But I do not believe it is for sale."[24]

The other Republicans who had hoped to be elected to the Senate realized that their chances were nil when fifty-two of Ohio's ninety legislators were publicly pledged to support Garfield two months before the nominating caucus. Historian Allan Peskin speculates that Garfield likely would have won without Sherman's help, but with it, his election was all but guaranteed.[25] When the caucus took place on January 6, 1880, it was anticlimactic. Garfield was nominated, seconded, and approved in less than thirty minutes. "At 8.30 P.M. [I received] telegrams informing me . . . I was nominated for U.S. Senator by acclamation," Garfield told his diary that night. "The manner of it is more gratifying than the nomination itself."

As he received more details the next day, he added, "I believe the event of last night is without parallel in the history of the state. It leave[s] me untrammelled by any commitments, or complications with any member of the Legislature."[26]

The new senator-elect was not free of all obligations, however. Despite Peskin's view that Garfield could have won without Sherman's help, Garfield was obligated to reciprocate and support Sherman's bid for the presidential nomination. Garfield and his wife attended a party at Sherman's house in Washington on January 17, and although there is no mention in his diary of any conversation about the nomination, one wonders whether the two men spoke about it that night. Eight days later, on January 25, Garfield noted in his diary that someone had asked his opinion on the nomination and he had "expressed the opinion that the State of Ohio ought to support Sherman."[27] Garfield had every intention of honoring his pledge to support the treasury secretary for the presidency at the upcoming convention.

The letter supporting Sherman's nomination, which Garfield surely knew was intended for publication in newspapers, was not the ringing endorsement that many—including Sherman himself—expected. Garfield wrote:

> I have no doubt that a decisive majority of our party in Ohio favors the nomination of John Sherman. He has earned this recognition at their hand by twenty-five years of conspicuous public service—a period which embraces nearly the whole life of the Republican party. He deserves the special recognition of the Nation for the great service he had rendered in making the resumption law a success, and placing the national finances on a better basis. I am aware that some Republicans do not endorse all his opinions. But no man who *has* opinions can expect all universal concurrence of his party in all his views; and no man without opinions is worthy of the support of a great party. I hope the Republicans of Ohio will make no attack on other candidates. They should fairly and generously recognize the merits of all. But I think they ought to present the name of Mr. Sherman to the National Convention and give him their united and cordial support.[28]

Garfield hoped this statement about Sherman would "put to rest the loose talk in the papers, which is connecting my name to the Presidency just enough to embarrass me." But many criticized the endorsement as lukewarm at best. "Your letter is not you at all," a friend told him. "It is the first time I have ever seen in your position the finger of the diplomat and the politician."[29]

Others understood Garfield's feeling of obligation to Sherman and, though not actively seeking to sink the treasury secretary, quietly floated the idea of Garfield as a compromise candidate in the event of a deadlocked convention. "Garfield is the only man we can elect and he will be nominated," said Tom Nichol.[30] Philadelphia financier and power broker Wharton Barker visited Garfield on January 18, 1880, less than two weeks after the Ohio legislature nominated him for the Senate. Barker was a vocal opponent of a third term for Grant and had been one of the earliest to propose Garfield as a potential presidential candidate. Garfield described their meeting that night in his diary: "I told him I would not be a candidate and did not wish my name discussed." This sounded like a firm denial of any interest in running for president. But Garfield continued: "If anything happened to me in that connection, it would only be in case the Convention at Chicago should find they could not nominate either of the candidates [Blaine or Sherman] and I should do nothing to procure such a result; that I was working in good faith for Sherman and should continue to do so." Garfield's denial suddenly became a little softer. He concluded the diary entry by stating: "I should have added that in this connection, that Mr. Sherman said that in case he could not be nominated, he preferred me to any other man and that he would be entirely willing to have his strength transferred to me."[31]

This diary entry makes it clear that Garfield fully intended to do his part for Sherman's campaign, but he was also willing to listen to those who proposed that Garfield himself might have a chance to win the nomination. Like any experienced and skilled politician, he closed the door—but did not slam it. Based on this entry, one can assume that Barker informed Garfield that Sherman would be willing to work for Garfield's nomination if his own chances fizzled. How Barker came by this information is unclear. Perhaps he spoke with Sherman about it; perhaps, sensing that Garfield was interested in the nomination but uneasy about appearing disloyal to Sherman, Barker embellished or simply fabricated Sherman's willingness to support Garfield. Barker was surely confident that Garfield would not discuss the matter with Sherman. Another Garfield confidant, Ohio governor Charles Foster—who was also publicly pledged to Sherman—told Garfield that "when the time comes (if it does come) to support another, then Ohio should wheel into line solidly for him (Garfield)."[32]

John Sherman was understandably viewed by the public and by many

Republicans as the "administration" candidate due to his well-regarded service as Hayes's secretary of the treasury. However, not even Hayes offered Sherman much support or thought his nomination likely. "Barker today visited the President, who says Sherman is in the field to prevent the nomination of Grant or Blaine," Garfield confided to his diary on April 24, 1880. According to Barker, Hayes thought "that Garfield can carry Ohio solid, as Blaine cannot, and in case the other two are broken, Sherman will give way for Garfield." He added to the diary entry: "In short, Barker thinks this is likely to be the outcome. I do not. I should be greatly distressed if I thought otherwise."[33]

What was it about Sherman that made members of his own party so lukewarm toward his candidacy and so desperate to find nearly anyone else—save Grant, of course—to run? First and foremost, the Republicans wanted to win and therefore needed a candidate who was electable. The Republicans were on a presidential winning streak and were not about to concede the nation's highest office to the Democrats, whose party had not elected a president since James Buchanan in 1856. Republicans had come perilously close to losing the presidency during the disputed 1876 election. They knew that a strong Democratic candidate in 1880 would be a formidable opponent and that there were still hard feelings over the outcome of the Hayes-Tilden race. Democrats would surely nominate a candidate with strong national appeal and pull out every stop to elect him, using the memory of the Republican "fraud" in 1876 as a rallying cry. Was John Sherman a strong enough candidate to counter this strategy? Many thought not. Sherman's own cool personality worked against him; he was considered "competent but dull."[34] One of Garfield's old army comrades, Lionel Sheldon, crudely assessed Sherman's lack of appeal: "Herodotus says that some of the Asiatics were in the habit of having connection with dead women. I presume the supporters of Sherman feel a similar enthusiasm."[35]

Sherman asked Senator-elect Garfield to travel to Cleveland in February 1880 to shore up support. He knew that without a united Ohio delegation, he had little chance of being nominated. Garfield made the trip but was unable to sway the Ohioans to present a united front for Sherman. Despite this failure, Sherman insisted that Garfield go to the Chicago convention as a delegate-at-large and floor manager of the Sherman forces. Garfield did not want to go, but he did not want to offend or anger Sherman either. When Garfield asked his friend Burke Hinsdale whether there was any way to honorably decline, Hinsdale replied, "If politics be a sincere affair, I do not see how you can refuse." Wharton Barker, however, told Garfield that

Sherman was being insincere and hoped to derail the quiet "dark horse" momentum building among some Republicans for Garfield. "Sherman evidently believes that if you [Garfield] can be side-tracked, the road will be opened to him," Barker observed. "No honorable man would have sought to take advantage of you in this manner."[36]

Sherman's choice of Garfield to lead his efforts in Chicago was clearly unwise. Sherman had heard the whisperings about Garfield as a potential dark-horse candidate; he had even intimated that he might be willing to throw his support to Garfield if the convention selected his fellow Ohioan. Making his own situation worse, Sherman chose Ohio governor Charles Foster to be a delegate-at-large. Foster was a vocal Blaine supporter who had no presidential ambitions himself but was interested in the vice presidency. Amazingly, Sherman told Foster that if his own campaign faltered, he would support a Blaine-Foster ticket. Peskin notes, "Perhaps Sherman thought he was being clever, but the result was to place his fortunes in the hands of two men [Garfield and Foster] who could succeed only if he failed."[37] Sherman's political tone deafness throughout the period leading up the Chicago convention was astounding, and he was not finished yet: he asked Garfield to place his name in nomination at the convention. Perhaps he wanted to capitalize on Garfield's popularity in their home state, hoping that Garfield's overt support would encourage the rest of the Ohio delegation to back Sherman. Or perhaps Barker was on to something and Sherman wanted to derail any possibility of Garfield's dark-horse candidacy by making him appear unavailable and unwilling because of his support for Sherman.

Garfield's feelings about Sherman's candidacy were lukewarm at best, and he did not believe Sherman had any chance to win the nomination. Personal honor and good political sense compelled him, however, to keep his word and support the treasury secretary, even as Sherman's demands became increasingly aggressive. Garfield was personally close with Blaine and might have been more inclined to support Blaine if not for his quid pro quo with Sherman. Garfield and Blaine chatted on May 23, and the latter "spoke very freely of the political situation. Said he did not much expect the nomination." Blaine yearned to be president, but his heart did not seem to be in it this time. He told Garfield that he "would not have become a candidate but for the belief that he could more effectually prevent the nomination of Gen. Grant than anyone else. On the whole, he thought the nomination of Grant quite probable."[38] Blaine and Garfield both opposed the idea of a third term for Grant.

Two days after his meeting with Blaine and just three days before departing for the Chicago convention, Garfield went to the Treasury Department and asked Sherman "to suggest frankly what he considered the strong points of his public life, that I might present him to the Convention in the strongest light." Garfield was gathering notes for his nominating speech. After considering his response, Sherman "said that he left that wholly to my judgment, but suggested that the chief characteristic of his life, from boyhood up, had been courageous persistence in any course he adopted."[39] Williams College professor Theodore Clarke Smith, whom Garfield's widow later selected as her husband's official biographer, wryly noted: "Garfield made no comment [in his diary] on this observation, but it is likely that to his own mind none was needed, since the one quality he had not been able to discover in Sherman was that very element of courageous persistence. He was in truth left to his own resources."[40]

After spending a few days at his Mentor, Ohio, farm, Congressman and Senator-elect James A. Garfield boarded an evening train for Chicago on May 28, 1880, headed for the Republican National Convention. "I go with much reluctance," he told his diary, "for I dislike the antagonisms and controversies which are likely to blaze out in the convention."[41] This turned out to be a notable understatement.

The political etiquette of the day called for those seeking the presidency or likely to be nominated to stay home rather than attend their party's convention and appear too eager for power. John Sherman and James Blaine stayed in Washington and expected to receive regular updates via telegraph from their allies and managers in Chicago. Ulysses S. Grant remained at his home in Galena, Illinois, less than 170 miles northwest of Chicago. Grant remained publicly stoic about the possibility of being nominated for an unprecedented third term, but privately he was "extremely anxious to receive the nomination," according to author Adam Badeau, a member of the general's Civil War staff and a longtime friend of the Grants. Grant was deeply involved in assessing his own chances, and he "counted the delegates, considered how every movement would affect the result, and was pleased or indignant at the conversion of enemies or the defection of friends."[42]

John Russell Young, the *New York Herald* journalist who had accompanied the Grants on their recent world tour, agreed with Badeau's assessment. He told a reporter from the *Washington Post:* "Grant does not evidence the slightest anxiety . . . he positively refrains from taking any active part in the contest for the nomination. . . . He is as calm as a summer morning." A total of 379 votes were needed to secure the nomination, and Young estimated that Grant would receive at least 410, noting that Grant, "of course, counts the New York, Pennsylvania, and Illinois delegations solid."[43] These were the home states of Senators Conkling, Cameron, and Logan, respectively.

Despite the appearance of a solid Grant foundation—"Nothing but an act of God could prevent Grant's nomination," said Conkling—cracks were beginning to appear. Few Grant supporters spoke publicly about it, but many were wavering in their commitment to the former president due to their opposition to anyone serving a third term. They also worried that Grant was vulnerable to attacks on the ethical lapses of his two earlier terms. Marshall Jewell, Grant's former postmaster general and by 1880 the governor of Connecticut, was the rare exception who spoke openly about abandoning the effort to nominate the former president. "I do not think he ought to be nominated," Jewell told the *Chicago Tribune,* surely aware that his statement would reach Grant in Galena. Jewell refused to attend the Republican National Convention, adding, "I am very glad to be free from the embarrassment which I should feel as a delegate."[44]

Journalist Young actually traveled to Galena and tried to talk Grant into withdrawing from the nomination contest. He spoke respectfully and candidly to Grant, advising him to withdraw because, quite simply, he and countless others were sure that although Grant could secure the Republican nomination, he would be defeated in the general election that fall. The Republicans were already vulnerable: after eight years of Grant, a Democrat, Tilden, had won the popular vote in 1876, and only the partisan electoral commission had made the Hayes presidency a reality. (At this point, many Republicans still feared that the Democrats would run Tilden again in 1880 to avenge his 1876 defeat.) In addition, the Grants' early return from their world tour had given the other candidates time to regroup and counterattack, particularly against the issue of a third term for anyone— even the nation's most revered citizen.

Indeed, word was out that the Triumvirate was trying to enforce the so-called unit rule, which would award all of a state's delegates to the candidate receiving the majority of that state's votes. Many Republicans rightly viewed this as an undemocratic ploy by Conkling and company to stack the deck for Grant, whom most acknowledged was the favorite. Conkling's obsession with controlling patronage appointments in New York was well known, and many feared that a third Grant term would mean nearly unlimited behind-the-scenes power for Conkling and his allies as they were awarded seats in Grant's cabinet and other appointments. The *Chicago Tribune* accused Conkling of trying to be "the King-maker whose power behind the throne will be greater than the occupant." Senator Logan's son pointed out the danger in a letter to his father: "I see that you are rendering your services to Grant. If he is elected he will be under a load of obligation to you, which he cannot possibly discharge."[45]

After talking with Young, Grant may have authored a secret letter—no copy survives—instructing Conkling and Logan to withdraw his name from consideration, if necessary. The letter may have told Grant's managers in Chicago to implore Blaine to withdraw as well, to avoid a party split and allow the nomination of an as-yet-unknown dark horse. Adam Badeau and Julia Grant both reacted strongly when they found out about this letter. Mrs. Grant "told [Young] to tell Senator Cameron to *not* use the letter. . . . If General Grant were not nominated, then let it be so, but he must not withdraw his name—no, never."[46]

The Republican National Convention began on June 2, 1880. As Republicans converged on Chicago, Ulysses S. Grant was considered the favorite for the presidential nomination, but it was by no means a sure thing. If the Triumvirate could enforce the unit rule, though, Grant would surely capture the nomination for the third time. The Republicans had nominated Grant on the first ballot in 1868 and again in 1872, and Conkling, Logan, and Cameron intended to see that it happened again in 1880. Binding the state delegations to the unit rule would all but guarantee Grant's nomination on the first ballot. The Triumvirate arrived in Chicago a week before the convention to lobby members of the Republican National Committee, chaired by Cameron, to accept the unit rule. William E. Chandler, leader of the Blaine contingent, traveled to Chicago at about the same time to encourage committee members to do just the opposite.

James Garfield arrived on May 29 to do his duty for John Sherman. "The city is full of Republicans," Garfield noted in his diary, "and intense activity is seen in all the hostile camps."[47] Garfield did not want to be in Chicago. He had spent just a day or two at his Mentor, Ohio, farm before traveling to the convention, leaving his wife to deal with a major remodeling of their home. After his arrival, Garfield sent her a letter, writing that Chicago was "boiling over with politics" and noting, "the unit rule will be the center of battle and to that I expect to address myself." But he also admitted, "My heart is with you in your struggle to bring order out of our house of your planning, and I would gladly exchange this turmoil for the smaller and sweeter turmoil of the farm."[48]

Despite his preference to be at home in Ohio, Garfield immediately went to work in Chicago coordinating anti–unit rule efforts among the Blaine and Sherman camps. He located the other Ohio delegates-at-large "and before the day was over urged them to take a bold and aggressive stand in favor of District representation, and against the unit rule, and for this purpose that we unite with the friends of all candidates who take this view. The settlement of these principles is more important than the fate of any candidate."[49] Under district representation, votes for the presidential nomination would be awarded from each congressional district rather than in bulk from each state. If the unit rule were not adopted and enforced, the votes of so-called bolters from each state—especially New York, Illinois, and Pennsylvania, the home states of the Triumvirate—would legitimately be counted. An estimated sixty bolters from those three states alone were eager to vote for Blaine, Sherman, or a handful of other potential candidates that included George Edmunds of Vermont, Elihu Washburne of Illinois, and William Windom of Minnesota.

Philosophically, for those opposing Grant, district representation was viewed as the most democratic option. It allowed each man to vote his conscience and support the candidate of his choice. On a practical level, it also offered the best opportunity to stop the Conkling-Logan-Cameron team from bullying the convention into nominating Grant. Among the forty-seven members of the Republican National Committee, anti–third termers were in the majority by a count of twenty-nine to eighteen. However, because Cameron was the committee's chairman, many assumed that the unit rule would prevail. With 756 delegates, a simple majority of 379 was needed to nominate the Republicans' next presidential candidate.

The Grant forces could count on approximately 300 votes before the convention even began. Earlier in 1880 the Triumvirate had muscled and intimidated Republicans at the state conventions where delegates to the national convention were selected. If the unit rule were adopted and enforced by the national committee, those state delegations would have no choice but to support Grant, since Conkling and his allies had ensured the selection of mostly Grant delegates at the state conventions. In this case, the former president would likely be nominated on the convention's first ballot. Without the unit rule, though, delegates were free to break ranks and support the candidate of their choice—as long as they were willing to endure the wrath of Conkling and company. The Triumvirate and their allies craved the predictability of knowing what would happen before it occurred. This was possible only if the Republican National Committee adopted and enforced the unit rule.

The Grant men concocted a relatively simple plan. The Republican National Committee was responsible for electing a "temporary chairman" to preside over the Chicago convention. As chair of the committee, Cameron would preside over this election. He would, quite simply, impose the unit rule on the election of the temporary chairman, ensuring that a pro-Grant, pro–unit rule Republican would be in charge of the convention. This temporary chairman, in turn, would impose the unit rule on all convention votes, including credentialing for delegates and the convention's operating rules.

James Garfield was not a member of the national committee, but he publicly denounced any attempt to force the unit rule on the convention. "It is wholly un-Republican for one man to cast another man's vote," he told the *Chicago Tribune*. He considered defeat of the unit rule "more important than even the choice of a candidate."[50] John Sherman, following the action from his office in Washington, agreed. "Every effort should be made . . . [to] allow each delegate to cast one vote and have it counted," Sherman wrote. "Any other rule is an outrage. Don't compromise this away—or yield it to threats or persuasion."[51]

The Republican National Committee met for most of the day on May 31, two days before the convention began. By then, news of the Triumvirate's plot had leaked, and the meeting was contentious. Cameron refused to say anything about the scheme one way or the other; in fact, he sat in silence for most of the day, confounding everyone and leading at least one committee member to threaten to toss Cameron out the window.[52] When Senator Jerome Chaffee of Colorado offered a resolution opposing the unit rule, Cameron ruled him out of order. The anti-Grant forces pushed through a resolution stating that William E. Chandler, leader of the Blaine contingent in Chicago, would take over as temporary national chairman in the event of Cameron's "death or disability." This not-so-veiled threat led one Grant backer to ask whether Cameron might be assassinated. The answer was not reassuring: Cameron "had the sciatica and might die."[53] At this point, with tempers flaring, the committee adjourned. Garfield attended a large Republican rally that evening, with the question of a temporary chairman still undecided. "I am strongly urged to make a speech against the third term, at mass meeting tonight. I decline," he told his diary. "The fight of delegates should be in the convention. I never fight mock battles."[54]

During the night, both sides realized that a fight in the national committee just one day before the convention started would be disastrous for public relations. They agreed to elect Senator George F. Hoar of Massachusetts as temporary chairman to preside over the convention. Hoar supported his fellow New Englander George Edmunds for the nomination, but Edmunds's support was so minimal that most viewed Hoar as neutral, making him acceptable to all sides. However, this could only be viewed as a defeat for those supporting Grant's nomination. Hoar was unlikely to go along with the unit rule, and although Grant was still considered the favorite, the door was now open for opponents of a third term to try to nominate another candidate.

The 1880 Republican National Convention officially convened at five minutes past noon on June 2 when Donald Cameron banged a wooden gavel supposedly fashioned from a door frame of Abraham Lincoln's Springfield, Illinois, home. An estimated 15,000 delegates and spectators filled Chicago's Interstate Exposition Building, known as the Glass Palace. Cameron addressed the crowd (few of whom could hear him in an age before microphones and speakers), telling them that the convention must nominate "men whose familiarity with other nations will enable them to direct our affairs so that we will take the lead in commerce, as we have in agriculture and manufactures."[55] This was a none-too-subtle endorsement of Grant, who had completed a multiyear world tour just months before. Cameron then placed Hoar's name into nomination as the convention's temporary chair. Hoar was unanimously elected, and the convention began the business of establishing committees. Garfield became head of the Committee on Rules, which would take up the issue of the unit rule.

Friction between the Stalwart and Half-Breed factions of the party was laid bare on the convention's second day—Thursday, June 3. Nothing much could be accomplished until the convention received the reports of the Committee on Credentials and the Committee on Rules. These committees were responsible for deciding who was authorized to be in attendance and in what capacity and determining the procedures by which the convention would operate. When it became clear that the committees were not ready to report, Conkling moved that the convention adjourn until six o'clock that evening. Eugene Hale, a Half-Breed Blaine supporter from Maine, disagreed, arguing that the convention was ready to go to work. "The only work we shall do between now and four or five o'clock," Conkling retorted, "is to sit here idle on uncushioned seats—fortunately with backs, while a vast number of other persons sit in the galleries on benches without cushions or backs."[56] Conkling's motion was defeated, and he and the other Stalwarts were forced to remain in the hot, crowded hall until later that night, even though nothing of consequence could be accomplished until the two committees had reported. Anti-Grant delegates had voted down Conkling's motion simply because Conkling had proposed it.

The only other events of consequence on June 3 came during the convention's evening session. First, Senator Hoar was nominated and approved as the convention's permanent rather than temporary chairman. Second, during a vote on the order in which committees would report, Hoar ruled that individual delegates would cast their own ballots, rather than the state chairman casting the entire state's vote. As historian Stan M. Haynes writes, "With this ruling, the unit rule was dead, unless it could be revived when the Committee on Rules presented its report."[57] To no one's surprise, Conkling and the Grant forces were not willing to simply give up the unit rule without a fight.

On the morning of Friday, June 4, Conkling rose to propose another motion: "Resolved, As the sense of this Convention, that every member of it is bound in honor to support its nominee, whoever that nominee may be; and that no man should hold a seat here who is not ready to so agree." Here, Conkling was attempting to achieve the same result—binding delegates to Grant—but from a different angle, this time, without the unit rule. This move was focused on New Yorkers and Pennsylvanians—from whom Conkling and Cameron, respectively, demanded loyalty and obedience—who were threatening to bolt from Grant and support other candidates if the unit rule failed. Eugene Hale, who was quickly becoming a thorn in Conkling's side, replied, "I take it that a Republican Convention does not need to be instructed that its first and underlying duty, after nominating its candidate, is to elect him over a Democratic candidate." Ultimately, though, when the roll was called, all the Maine delegates, including Hale, voted for the resolution.

In fact, only three delegates, all from West Virginia, voted nay on this resolution. Conkling was incensed and immediately introduced a second resolution calling for these three delegates to be expelled from the convention because they "do not deserve to have, and have forfeited their votes in this Convention." West Virginian Archibald W. Campbell replied that he had fought for Republican principles for twenty years in both Virginia and West Virginia, and if a delegate "to a Republican Convention cannot have a free expression of his opinion, I for one am willing to withdraw from this Convention." A second West Virginia delegate, A. C. Moore, defended his friend: "In the name of God; has it come to this," he asked, "that one who has battled as A. W. Campbell has to my knowledge, in behalf of Republicanism, when it cost something more than it did in the State of New York or in the State of Maine, cannot freely express his opinion in a Republican Convention?"[58]

The convention erupted in chaos, and Wharton Barker saw this as an opportunity for his man Garfield. As he told it many years later, he tried to signal Garfield to speak, but in all the confusion and noise, Garfield missed the signal. Barker's fellow Pennsylvanian Wayne MacVeagh rushed to the platform and implored Hoar to recognize Garfield. Hoar looked toward the Ohio delegation, and Garfield finally seemed to pick up on Barker's effort to get his attention. Garfield stood up, and the chairman recognized him.[59] "I fear this Convention is about to commit a grave error," Garfield began. "Is every delegate here to have his Republicanism inquired into before this Convention will allow him to vote? . . . There never was a Convention, there never can be a Convention, of which I am one delegate, that shall bind my vote against my will on any question whatever. . . . I say [the West Virginians] acted in their right, and not by my vote shall they be deprived of their seats or their freedom." Garfield specifically defended Campbell, "who in the dark days of slavery, and for twenty long years, in the midst of slave-pens and slave-drivers, has stood up for liberty with a clear-sighted courage and a brave heart equal to that of the best Republican that lives on this globe." Garfield concluded by asking Conkling to withdraw his resolution.

After Conkling did so, he sent Garfield a sarcastic note that all but acknowledged what many were whispering and even a few newspapers were speculating: that Garfield was a potential compromise candidate in waiting. "New York requests that Ohio's real candidate and dark horse come forward. We want him in our seats while we prepare our ballots."[60] Shortly after the speech, Barker told Garfield, "Nothing but a blunder on your part can now prevent you from receiving the nomination for President from this Convention."[61] The West Virginians whom Garfield had so eloquently defended told the Ohioan that they hoped "at no distant day [to] have the pleasure of giving you more substantial evidence of our appreciation."[62]

Garfield was secretly flattered and pleased by all the attention and wrote to his wife, "Without any act or word of mine to induce it, there has been growing hourly a current of opinion" that he should be nominated. However, he was still determined to stand by Sherman and "do nothing and ask nothing—far better pleased to have nothing but the knowledge that many desire me." He suspected that, as chairman of the Committee on Rules and a vocal anti–unit rule advocate, he was in for more clashes with Conkling. "If I win that fight, it will be likely to embitter him and his followers against me. If I lose it the convention will lose interest in me. So I am between two fires." Peskin calls this "an odd admission from a man who was insisting that he was not a candidate."[63] Garfield was clearly trying to straddle the fence as long as he could. He was determined to fulfill his obligation to Sherman and give no reason for anyone to question his loyalty or conduct on Sherman's behalf. But he could not help imagining what series of events might lead to his own nomination. He was, in modern terms, keeping his options open, which does not seem the least bit odd for a masterful and ambitious politician like James Garfield.

The convention's next fight centered on the report from the Committee on Credentials. The committee's majority report, in accordance with precedent established at previous Republican conventions, favored seating anti–third term delegates elected at district conventions, while the minority report recommended seating pro-Grant delegates elected at state conventions. Only about fifty seats from six different states were in dispute, but because everyone knew the vote would be close, this was a critical decision for opponents of the unit rule. During speeches from supporters of both viewpoints, the convention hall erupted in cheers and shouting at the mere mention of the names Grant, Blaine, Conkling, Sherman, and others. At one point, each side tried to outshout the other for well over an hour. "Normally sober men stood on tables and chairs," writes Peskin, "cheering and singing innumerable verses of *John Brown's Body*. They waved hats, umbrellas, overcoats and, on the platform, Robert Ingersoll waved a huge red shawl for the greater glory of Blaine."[64]

The convention began to vote on the credentials issue well after midnight on June 5. The first roll call concerned substituting the minority report for the majority report in one Illinois district. Opponents won a slim victory by a tally of 387 to 353. Additional votes were taken on other issues related to credentials, and the results were similar: close votes, but decided rebukes of the Grant forces and the unit rule. Those supporting Grant were losing every battle, and the chance of winning the larger war seemed doubtful when the convention finally adjourned at around 2:30 that morning. It did not look any better when the convention resumed later that day and Garfield's Committee on Rules presented its majority report. The report scrapped the unit rule by allowing any delegate who took issue with the state chairman's announced vote to object, forcing a roll call of that state's delegates. The committee's minority report called for each state chairman to announce the state's vote and for those votes to be accepted without argument or discussion. A voice vote was taken, and the majority report was accepted. The unit rule was dead for the 1880 convention. As it turned out, the unit rule was never again used at any Republican National Convention. Democratic conventions continued to use it well into the twentieth century.[65]

The last committee to report was the Committee on Resolutions, the group responsible for drafting the Republican platform for 1880. Despite all the wrangling among factions supporting Grant, Blaine, Sherman, and other candidates, most Republicans agreed on the majority of issues addressed in the national platform. The most significant differences among Republicans continued to be the need (or not) for civil service reform and, of course, the desirability of Grant running for a third term. Stalwarts and Grant supporters continued to deride the idea of reforming the patronage system. The derisively named Half-Breeds opposed a third term for Grant and favored at least some reformation of the civil service, if for no other reason than to loosen the stranglehold of powerful reform opponents on patronage appointments in their respective states.

The proposed platform had no provision addressing civil service reform. James M. Barker of Massachusetts objected and called for a plank adopting "the declaration of President Hayes, that the reform in the civil service shall be thorough, radical and complete" and that the "tenure of administrative offices . . . shall be made permanent during good behavior, and that the power of removal for cause, with due responsibility for the good conduct of subordinates, shall accompany the power of appointment." Antireform delegate Webster Flanagan of Texas responded:

> Texas has had quite enough of the civil service. During the last four years, sir, out of 1,400 officers appointed by the President of the United States, 140 represented the Republican party. We are not here, sir, for the purpose of providing offices for the Democracy. There is one plank in the Democratic party that I have ever admired, and that is, "To the victors belong the spoils." After we have won the race, as we will, we will give those men who are entitled to positions office. I mean that members of the Republican party are entitled to office, and if we are victorious we will have office.[66]

After some debate, the final approved platform contained no provision addressing civil service reform. This may be viewed as one of the few victories won by the Triumvirate and other Grant backers in Chicago that week.

The platform naturally mentioned the Republican Party's greatness in transforming "4,000,000 human beings from the likeness of things to the rank of citizens" during the Civil War. Republicans also emphasized their transformation of the American economy, including the creation of a strong national currency, the growing miles of railroad tracks, and payment on the national debt. The platform also accused the Democrats of "the habitual sacrifice of patriotism and justice to a supreme and insatiable lust for office and patronage." This was ironic, coming from the party that had produced Roscoe Conkling and his allies. Playing to voters on the West Coast, the Republican platform also called unrestricted Chinese immigration "a matter of grave concernment."[67] This issue in particular would rear its ugly head late in the campaign.

Once the platform was finally written and agreed on, the Republicans in Chicago turned to their primary business: selecting a candidate for president of the United States.

"IF ANY OUTSIDER IS TAKEN, I HOPE IT WILL BE GARFIELD"

THE 1880 REPUBLICAN NATIONAL CONVENTION—PART 2

Throughout the convention, cheers erupted every time some of the nation's most prominent political figures entered the hall. These accolades may have seemed like spontaneous outpourings of admiration for politicians engaged in what was, at the time, the country's most popular spectator sport, but they were often staged. Allies of many important Republicans planted friends (and sometimes paid strangers with fake credentials) in strategic parts of the hall with instructions to cheer whenever certain candidates entered. Wharton Barker positioned allies throughout the Glass Palace and told them to give James Garfield a standing ovation whenever he appeared. Garfield likely knew about this and often entered the hall a little late, thereby calling attention to himself when Barker's group erupted into wild cheers right on cue. "Whenever Garfield entered the hall, arose to speak, or moved about," Barker later recalled, "he was greeted with prolonged applause."[1] This was obviously self-serving on Garfield's part, but he could also claim that the cheers demonstrated support not for him personally but for John Sherman's candidacy. After all, everyone knew that Garfield was there to nominate Sherman. Similarly, applause for Roscoe Conkling and John Logan could be interpreted as enthusiasm for Ulysses S. Grant's candidacy.

Even so, many Sherman supporters suspected that Garfield was more interested in promoting his own interests than Sherman's. "There is treachery over there," one Sherman delegate said while pointing in the direction of the Ohio delegation. Fortunately for Garfield, most Sherman supporters directed their vitriol not at him but at Ohio governor Charles Foster, one of Garfield's fellow delegates-at-large. Foster was hoping to get the vice-presidential nomination if Blaine were nominated, and despite being publicly pledged to Sherman, he spent far more time with Blaine supporters. Fellow Ohioan Warner Bateman told Sherman, "I do not think he [Foster] gave you an hour of honest service during the whole time he was in Chicago."[2] This appearance of disloyalty was exactly what Garfield was desperate to avoid, and he largely succeeded. Although some die-hard Sherman supporters were critical of Garfield's actions in Chicago, few judged him as harshly as Bateman did Governor Foster.

As the Republicans prepared to proceed to nominating and voting on presidential candidates, Garfield and Conkling emerged as two of the convention's key figures. Garfield had already confided to his wife that he expected to have more clashes with Conkling. The two men would soon be colleagues in the Senate, once Garfield took his seat at the beginning of 1881, and both were scheduled to give speeches nominating their respective candidates for the presidency: Garfield for Sherman, and Conkling for Grant. The real drama of the 1880 Republican National Convention was about to begin.

James Gillespie Blaine, US senator from Maine, was the first major candidate to have his name placed in nomination. Four years earlier, in 1876, Robert Ingersoll had given a famous oration nominating Blaine at that year's convention, christening him the "plumed knight." Many Blaine backers hoped for a repeat performance by Ingersoll in 1880. However, William E. Chandler, managing Blaine's efforts on the floor, worried that Ingersoll's avowed atheism would hurt Blaine's chances. It is unclear why no one worried about this in 1876, and perhaps Chandler was guilty of overthinking and micromanaging. In any case, Chandler gave the task of nominating Blaine to millionaire James F. Joy, owner of the Michigan Central Railroad.[3]

Joy's performance was wholly uninspired, and even he seemed to recognize that he was not up to the task. He began his nominating speech by stating: "I shall never cease to regret that circumstances have been such as to impose the duty upon myself to make the nomination of a candidate to this Convention." Joy went on to give a flat recitation of Blaine's career and seemed to mention Grant's name almost as much as Blaine's. At one point, a Mississippi delegate rose and sought "unanimous consent . . . to the gentleman to close his remarks." Garfield implored the convention to allow the Michigander to proceed, and Joy soon closed his remarks, "which have been longer than I intended." Despite the lackluster delivery, the published proceedings of the convention reported "loud and long-continued applause" at the conclusion of Joy's speech.[4]

Delegate F. M. Pixley of California seconded Blaine's nomination, and then William P. Frye of Maine asked for two minutes to address the convention. Frye's speech was by far the most moving of the three, as he compared Maine to a ship and Blaine to its captain, guiding it through the storm of disunion and rebellion. "The good old ship, 'The State of Maine,'" Frye passionately told the crowd, "has just encountered such a tempest. Freighted with the precious principles of this Republic, with the rights of American citizenship, with the privileges guaranteed by the Constitution, she was battling with the waves. . . . A true man was at her helm . . . and his name is James G. Blaine!" Once again, the conference proceedings reported "loud and long-continued applause," this time with "tremendous cheering" as well.[5]

Senator William Windom of Minnesota was the next presidential candidate nominated. Windom had little chance to win the nomination, but his fellow Minnesotans nominated him as a favorite-son candidate in a brief speech by delegate E. F. Drake. "We believe," Drake said, "that the candidate that we present will better unite all the discordant elements of the party [than] any of the distinguished names that will be before this Convention. . . . In his course he has ever sustained the cause of the oppressed and supported the Government loyally."[6]

When the roll call of states reached New York, Roscoe Conkling rose to his full and imposing height of six feet, three inches, and bellowed: "When asked what State he hails from, Our sole reply shall be, He hails from Appomattox, And its famous apple tree." It was an obvious reference to Grant's acceptance of Robert E. Lee's surrender that all but ended the Civil War in 1865, and it sent the Republican crowd into a frenzy of cheers, applause, and shouts. Referring to Grant's heroism on the battlefield and in politics, Conkling continued: "The election before us is the Austerlitz of American politics. It will decide, for many years, whether the country shall be Republican or Cossack. . . . New York is for Ulysses S. Grant. Never defeated—in peace or in war—his name is the most illustrious borne by any living man."

Conkling's speech was much longer than Joy's for Blaine, and Conkling was a skilled and practiced orator. The New Yorker, defeated in his quest to

15—14—13.—THE GREAT PRESIDENTIAL PUZZLE.

Political cartoon depicts Senator Roscoe Conkling trying to solve the Republican "presidential puzzle" of 1880. Note that Garfield's likeness does not appear. (Courtesy of Library of Congress)

impose the unit rule, was determined to give a speech that made it seem unpatriotic to oppose Grant. Referring to Grant's long world tour, he said: "He has studied the needs and the defects of many systems of government; and he has returned a better American than ever." Conkling even posited that Grant, not John Sherman, was the true hero of specie resumption: "When inflation, at the height of its popularity and frenzy, had swept both Houses of Congress, it was the veto of Grant, single and alone, which overthrew expansion and cleared the way for more specie resumption. To him, immeasurably more than to any other man, is due the fact that every paper dollar is at last as good as gold." On civil rights for African Americans, he vowed: "Life, liberty and property will find a safeguard in him. When he said of the colored man, 'Wherever I am, they may come also,' he meant that had he the power, the poor dwellers in the cabins of the South should no longer be driven in terror from the homes of their childhood and the graves of their murdered dead."

Finally, Conkling addressed the delegates' concerns about a third term for Grant and reminded Republicans what, in his view, was truly at stake:

There is no "third term" in the case, and the pretense will die with the political dog days that gendered it. One week after the Democratic convention we shall have heard the last of this rubbish about a "third term." Nobody now is really disquieted about a third term except those hopelessly longing for a first term, and their dupes and coadjutors. Without effort or intrigue on his part, he is the candidate whose friends have never threatened to bolt unless this Convention did as they said. He is a Republican who never wavers. He and his friends stand by the creed and the candidates of the Republican party. They hold the rightful rule of the majority as the very essence of their faith, and they mean to uphold that faith against not only the common enemy, but against the charlatans, jayhawkers, tramps and guerillas who deploy between the lines and forage, now on one side and then on the other. This Convention is master of supreme opportunity. It can name the next President of the United States. It can make sure of his election. It can make sure not only of his election, but of his certain and peaceful inauguration. . . . The purpose of the Democratic party is spoils. Its very hope and existence is a solid South. Its success is a menace to order and prosperity. This Convention can overthrow and disintegrate these hurtful forces. It can dissolve and emancipate a distracted "solid South." It can speed the Nation in a career of grandeur eclipsing all past achievements.[7]

When Conkling finished, the hall erupted in cheers, shouts, and chaos that even Grant's opponents had to admire. One reporter wrote that Conkling's speech contained "the play of sarcasm, the saber-cuts of severity, and all the pageantry of eloquence."[8] Another gleefully reported that many Grant backers "threw away the characteristics of age and became boys once more."[9] Amid the cheering and shouting, a few chants of "Blaine!" could be heard, but had the vote been taken at the conclusion of Conkling's speech, Grant might have carried the nomination on the first ballot. Conkling's "rally the troops" speech was vastly different from and certainly more effective than that delivered by Joy to nominate Blaine.

The roll call continued. Ohio was the next state to offer a candidate for nomination, and Garfield rose to make his speech placing Sherman's name before the convention. Garfield dreaded making the speech, which he had procrastinated in writing. "I have not made the first step in preparation," he wrote to his wife earlier in the week. "It was a frightful mistake not to write [the speech] before I came."[10] Since arriving in Chicago nearly a week earlier, Garfield had had little time to do much of anything other than talk to people, attend meetings, chair a committee, and work to defeat the unit rule. Clearly, Garfield was not truly enthusiastic about Sherman's candidacy, but for a politician as skilled and calculating as Garfield, this lack of preparation was striking. Or perhaps his lack of preparation was the most calculated move he made in Chicago that week. Either way, even though Garfield was as polished and skilled a speaker as Conkling, he made no effort to match the emotion of Conkling's speech. "Conkling's extraordinary speech gave me the idea of carrying the mind of the convention in a different direction," Garfield later wrote.[11]

Like Conkling before him, Garfield eschewed the formal speaker's platform and stood up on a table. Then, one of the best and most highly regarded speakers in the Republican Party surprised the convention by taking a calmer, quieter tone. "As I sat in this seat and witnessed this demonstration, this assemblage seemed to me a human ocean in tempest," he said. "I have seen the sea lashed into fury and tossed into spray, and its grandeur moves the soul of the dullest man; but I remember that it is not the billows, but the calm level of the sea from which all heights are measured."[12] Garfield's nautical theme harked back to Frye's brief speech for Blaine. As a young man, Garfield had dreamed of being a sailor, and he often used the imagery of the ocean in his speeches. He had just told his wife in a letter written the previous day, "Your words from the dear home . . . came to me like a beam of peaceful light shining across evening fields into a tempest tossed sea." (He wrote in the same letter, "Our work here still drags its slow length along through more passion than there was a Chickamauga.")[13] Garfield continued his speech for Sherman:

> Not here, in this brilliant circle where 15,000 . . . are gathered, is the destiny of the Republic to be decreed for the next four years. Not here, where I see the enthusiastic faces of 756 delegates, waiting to cast their lots into the urn and determine the choice of the Republic; but by four millions of Republican firesides, where the thoughtful voters, with wives and children about them, with the calm thoughts inspired by love of home and country, with the history of the past, the hopes of the future, and reverence for the great men who have adorned and blessed our nation in days gone by, burning in their hearts—*there* God prepares the verdict which will determine the wisdom of our work tonight. Not in Chicago, in the heat of June, but at the ballot-boxes of the Republic, in the quiet of November, after the silence of deliberate judgment, will this question be settled. And now, gentlemen of the Convention, what do we want?

A single voice answered this question: "We want Garfield."[14] The speaker may have uttered it as a joke, but it was prescient.

Garfield's speech was not the raucous, energetic one that many were expecting. Whereas Conkling whipped the delegates into a Grant frenzy, Garfield's quieter pro-Sherman presentation made them think. He warned them not to get wrapped up in the heat of the moment (in other words, not to jump on the Grant bandwagon) because the election was still five months away. Garfield reminded everyone:

> Twenty-five years ago, this Republic was bearing and wearing a triple chain of bondage. Long familiarity with traffic in the bodies and souls of men had paralyzed the consciences of a majority of our people . . . and the grasping power of slavery was seizing upon the virgin Territories of the West, and dragging them into the den of eternal bondage. At that crisis the Republican Party was born. . . . The Republican party came to deliver and to save.[15]

Garfield recounted many of the horrors of slavery, the Civil War, and Reconstruction. "The Republican party offers to our brethren of the South the olive branch of Peace, and invites them to renewed brotherhood, on this supreme condition: That it shall be admitted, forever, that in the War for the Union we were right and they were wrong."[16] Garfield was obviously not above "waving the bloody shirt" at Democrats who had tried to destroy the government in 1879, and he did it as masterfully as Conkling. Garfield's words likely meant even more to the delegates who knew they were being addressed by a Union army veteran. Garfield had left his comfortable life as a college president and Ohio state senator behind in mid-1861 to fight for the Union. Although no one doubted Conkling's Republican bona fides, and although his Civil War service in the US House of Representatives had been honorable and important, for many, it was less impressive than the contributions of a former Union officer and combat veteran like Garfield.

For all the effectiveness of this history lesson, though, Garfield had not yet mentioned John Sherman's name. His appeal to party loyalty as the best means to secure Republican victory was an obvious but effective retort to Conkling's harsh words for the anti-Grant men that he considered disloyal. "How shall we accomplish this great work?" Garfield asked. "We cannot do it, my friends, by assailing our Republican brethren . . . we want the vote of every Republican—of every Grant Republican and every anti-Grant Republican in America—of every Blaine man and every anti-Blaine man.

Interior photograph of the 1880 Republican convention. (Courtesy of Library of Congress)

The vote of every follower of every candidate is needed to make success certain."[17] Garfield mentioned the names of Sherman's two main rivals before uttering the name of his own candidate, and this riled some of Sherman's operatives. Finally, in the last sentence of his address, after listing some of the highlights of Sherman's long public career to make the point that he had been integral to all the important events of the past twenty years, Garfield stated: "I nominate John Sherman of Ohio." As the proceedings of the convention describe it, the end of Garfield's speech brought "long-continued applause."[18]

E. C. Winkler of Wisconsin and Robert B. Elliott of South Carolina delivered seconding speeches for Sherman, both of which described Sherman's qualifications for the presidency far better than Garfield's had. Elliott told the hall, "I support the nomination of John Sherman because, a friend to humanity, he has been for a quarter-century the unyielding and consistent champion of human rights everywhere. When were the rights of man ever called into question—when did the claims of humanity need a champion—that the voice of John Sherman was not heard in their defense?"[19] Elliott's words carried weight. He was an African American who had served in the South Carolina legislature and the US House of Representatives and had briefly been South Carolina's attorney general. He had for years resisted and fought the Ku Klux Klan in his state.

Speeches nominating George Edmunds of Vermont and Elihu Washburne of Illinois followed Garfield's address, but those two men were favorite-son candidates that few took seriously. When the convention adjourned at nearly midnight, all the attention was focused on Blaine, Grant, and Sherman. Robert Ingersoll, in the crowd with the Illinois delegation, talked with a reporter from the *Washington Evening Star* on his way out of the convention hall. "If any outsider is taken," he said, "I hope it will be Garfield. If Ohio wants a man, let Ohio ask for her best."[20]

Garfield's quiet, measured, metaphor-laced speech appealed to many, but it was not universally praised. Many die-hard Sherman supporters, both in Chicago and across the country as they read the speech in the newspapers over the next few days, seethed at what they viewed as Garfield's less-than-enthusiastic nomination of their candidate. "The sickly manner in which Garfield presented your name," one correspondent telegraphed to Sherman in Washington, "has disgusted your friends here. [Garfield] has been of no service to you . . . he was extremely lukewarm in your support. He is a Garfield man. If you should be nominated you need be under no obligation to him."[21] Others speculated that Foster, the Ohio governor who hoped to be Blaine's running mate, was scheming with Garfield to convince the Ohio delegation to move toward Blaine. There is no evidence of this, but the fact that Foster and Garfield were staying in adjoining rooms at the Grand Pacific Hotel fed the rumor.

Garfield worried that any appearance of disloyalty to Sherman would hurt him both in the short term, as he kept his options open in Chicago, and in the long term, as he moved up from the House of Representatives to the Senate. Even though Sherman was unlikely to win the nomination, he would remain a powerful and influential force in Ohio politics. It would not serve Garfield's interests to make an enemy of Sherman by being disloyal in Chicago. Garfield was only forty-eight years old and presumably had many years left in politics, and Sherman would be a good and powerful friend to have. Back home in Ohio, Lucretia Garfield recognized this as well. "I begin to be half afraid that the convention will give you the nomination," she wrote to her husband, "and the place would be most unenviable with so many disappointed candidates. I don't want you to have the nomination merely because no one else can get it, I want you to have it when the whole country calls for you as the State of Ohio did last Fall." Even so, he replied two days later, "I think the good opinion of the Convention towards me is not lessening."[22]

Garfield was clearly ambitious and, like nearly every Washington politician, wanted to be president. He did nothing to disavow anyone who mentioned him as a potential compromise candidate. But he was also genuinely concerned about the Republican Party's turn toward business interests and away from the enforcement of civil rights, and he must have believed that other Republicans felt the same way, even if they were too afraid to cross Conkling to admit it. As a Union veteran, a supporter of civil rights for freedmen, and a longtime Republican who had seen the good his party could do when it stayed true to its roots, Garfield must have been excited about the convention's "good opinion" of him. His strong faith as a Disciple of Christ surely led him to see God's hand in the convention's movement toward him.

Balloting for the presidential nomination began shortly after the convention came to order on the morning of Monday, June 7. The winner would need 379 votes to secure the nomination—one more than half of the convention's 756 delegates. First-ballot nominations for a nonincumbent president were not nearly as common as they would later become. Abraham Lincoln, the patron saint of the Republican Party, had not been nominated until the third ballot in 1860; Rutherford B. Hayes, the sitting president, had needed seven ballots to capture it in 1876. Not only which candidate would prevail but also how many ballots it would take to select him were open questions in 1880, not to mention the added intrigue and passions on both sides regarding a possible third term for Grant.

With the unit rule's defeat, each delegate was free to vote for the candidate of his choice without fear of costing any candidate the vote of his entire state delegation. The real drama would come when the roll call reached large states with internal divisions, especially the three home states of the Triumvirate: Roscoe Conkling (New York), John Logan (Illinois), and Don Cameron (Pennsylvania). Even Sherman's home state of Ohio was not solidly behind him, especially considering the Garfield groundswell that had become more pronounced over the past several days.

Sure enough, when the alphabetical roll call reached Illinois, the drama began. Twenty-four Illinois delegates cast their votes for Grant, ten voted for Blaine, and eight selected favorite-son candidate Washburne. When the roll call reached New York, Conkling rose to answer the clerk's call and declared his support for Grant. He also requested—surely in an effort to identify all those who dared to defy him—that the New York delegates announce their votes individually and that the chairman poll the entire delegation. The next three delegates, including Chester A. Arthur, backed Grant. The next two, however, cast their votes for Blaine "amid a roar of applause and hisses."[23] At the end of the New York voting, fifty-one delegates had remained solid for Grant, seventeen had bolted for Blaine, and two had supported Sherman. Twenty-six of the fifty-eight delegates from Pennsylvania supported candidates other than Grant. Ohio delegates cast no votes for Grant, nine for Blaine, thirty-four for Sherman, and one for Edmunds.

The final tally at the conclusion of the first ballot produced no winner. Grant led with 304 votes, followed by Blaine with 284 and Sherman with 93. As Garfield sat with the Ohio delegation during the first ballot, he read a letter he had received that morning from Titas Coan, a fellow Ohioan: "Your friends' thoughts are with you on this day of battle," Coan wrote. "Mine have followed your career for many years, and let me say, now that the balloting begins, what I heard repeated in this club of late—That your name is the one I would soonest see winning the 379 votes and the nomination. So may it be!"[24] While Garfield surely appreciated Coan's sentiment, the race was clearly a three-way struggle among Grant, Blaine, and Sherman, although Sherman's chances seemed dim at this point. Blaine and Sherman, both at work in Washington that day, received telegraph messages updating them on the proceedings in Chicago, and both were disappointed with the results of the first ballot. Blaine left the Senate and went home to await further word. Sherman remained in his treasury office, where his brother, General of the Army William T. Sherman, joined him to await more news.

The second ballot proceeded immediately after the first, and the final tally barely changed. Grant gained one vote to finish with 305, Blaine lost two votes for a total of 282, and Sherman gained one vote to finish at 94. Edmunds, Windom, and Washburne all received a smattering of votes, but perhaps the most significant turn of events on the second ballot was that a lone Pennsylvanian cast his vote for Garfield.

Little changed as the day wore on. Grant consistently polled 305 votes, Blaine fluctuated between 280 and 282 votes, and Sherman maintained 93 or 94 votes. On the sixth ballot, a second delegate—an Alabamian—added his vote to the Garfield column. The Pennsylvanian who had cast his ballot for Garfield on the second ballot continued to do so, bringing Garfield's total to two votes on the sixth ballot. On the eighth ballot, the Alabamian did not vote for Garfield, but a Maryland delegate did, keeping Garfield's total at two votes. Grant received 308 votes on the same ballot, his highest of the day. By the fourteenth ballot, Garfield had completely fallen off the radar. He garnered no votes until the nineteenth ballot, when he reentered the fray with one vote, again from the lone Pennsylvania delegate.

Twenty-eight ballots were taken that day before the convention adjourned at nearly 10:00 p.m. The final tally showed that little had changed over the previous twelve hours. On the day's last ballot, Grant garnered 307 votes, Blaine 279, Sherman 91, Edmunds 31, Windom 10, Washburne 35, and Garfield 2. The convention adjourned until 10:00 a.m. the next day, and most of the delegates surely left scratching their heads and wondering whether the sixth day of the convention would bring any progress toward breaking the deadlock.[25]

The forces of the three major candidates had remained solid throughout the first day of balloting. The only chance for Blaine or Sherman to supplant Grant as the front-runner was for one to transfer his strength to the other. During the night, leaders of the two factions met at the Palmer House in the suite of William E. Chandler, Blaine's top lieutenant in Chicago. Blaine's men were wholly unwilling to transfer their votes to Sherman, who did not even have the solid support of his home state. Why, the Blaine men asked, should their man give his votes to a candidate with nearly 200 fewer votes? "The attempt to transfer [Blaine's] strength to any candidate would nominate Grant at once," Chandler told the room. By the time the meeting ended in the early hours of June 8, no decision or concessions had been reached.[26]

The leaders of the Grant forces had a similar meeting that night. Despite Grant's consistent lead, many worried that if Grant were capable of securing the nomination he would have done so already. Betting in the streets of Chicago was running two-to-one against Grant's winning the nomination. Many in the room floated the idea of putting Conkling's name forward to secure a Stalwart Republican as the nominee, but Conkling would not hear of it. He was too loyal to Grant, and besides, he believed he had far more power as a senator than he would ever have as president. "I am here as the agent of New York to support General Grant to the end," he told them. "Any man who would forsake him under such conditions does not deserve to be elected, and could not be elected."[27] The Grant camp's strategy for the next day remained the same: stay strong and wait for other candidates' supporters to shift their votes to Grant, if for no other reason than the obvious inevitability of his victory—or the desire to simply nominate someone and bring the convention to an end.

The convention's sixth day—Tuesday, June 8—began at 10:00 a.m. with the twenty-ninth ballot. Little had changed overnight. Grant led with 305 votes, Blaine was next with 278, and Sherman jumped to 116. The thirtieth ballot was basically the same, although one delegate from the Wyoming Territory voted for Lieutenant General Philip H. Sheridan. Sheridan was at the convention and immediately rose to speak, thanking the Wyoming delegate but telling the crowd, "There is no way in which I could accept a nomination from this Convention, if it were possible, unless I should be permitted to turn it over to my best friend [Grant]."[28] Sheridan received no votes on subsequent ballots.

The logjam began to break on the thirty-fourth ballot when John B. Cassoday, chairman of the Wisconsin delegation, rose to announce his state's vote: "Wisconsin casts two votes for General Grant, two votes for James G. Blaine and sixteen votes for James A. Garfield!" It is unclear what caused the Wisconsin delegation to suddenly break for Garfield. Wisconsin had been the site of early rumblings about a possible Garfield candidacy in 1880, but it is hard to believe that Badger State's delegates suddenly viewed the thirty-fourth ballot as the right time to make a move for Garfield. According to one unsubstantiated account, the Wisconsin delegation sent a message to the Ohio delegates stating, "If you will not bring out General Garfield, we shall."[29] A more likely explanation is that delegates from many states, including Wisconsin, were hot, tired, and frustrated after the thirty-third ballot produced a count that was basically unchanged from the first. It was clear that none of the three leading candidates was going to win the nomination, and a compromise was needed. Whether that compromise would be a deal that involved the backers of one of the top three candidates throwing their support to another or the convention settling on a previously unmentioned (or little-mentioned) dark-horse candidate remained to be seen. Either way, Garfield received seventeen votes on the thirty-fourth ballot.

Upon hearing Wisconsin's vote, Garfield jumped to his feet to argue a point of order. "I challenge the correctness of the announcement," he told the president of the convention. "The announcement contains votes for me. No man has a right, without the consent of the person voted for, to announce that person's name, and vote for him in this Convention. Such consent I have not given." Senator George F. Hoar, presiding over the convention, replied, "The gentleman from Ohio is not stating a question of order. He will resume his seat."[30] Whether Hoar was truly concerned about parliamentary procedure or just did not want to interrupt the momentum toward a possible Garfield nomination is not known, but he immediately called for another ballot. Hoar later stated that he was "terrified that he [Garfield] would say something that would make his nomination impossible."[31] Whether Garfield and Hoar conspired beforehand is unknown, but it is certainly possible. Garfield clearly knew before this moment that the nomination might come to him, and Hoar clearly supported the idea of Garfield as a compromise candidate.

On the next ballot, Indiana's Benjamin Harrison (who in 1888 would go through a similar process and win the nomination on the eighth ballot) announced twenty-seven of his state's votes for Garfield. Indiana had previously been split primarily between Grant and Blaine, but on this ballot, Grant received just one vote and Blaine only two. Maryland added four votes for Garfield, who also received one each from Mississippi, North Carolina, and Pennsylvania. Wisconsin again announced sixteen votes for Garfield and two each for Grant and Blaine. When the thirty-fifth ballot was complete, Grant was still far ahead with 313, Blaine had 257, Sherman was a distant third with 99, and Garfield had risen to fourth place with 50 votes. Senator Hoar immediately called for the next ballot. The movement toward Garfield was gaining momentum, and many delegates took note.

Before the thirty-sixth ballot began, Warner Bateman of the Sherman camp scribbled off a note to be telegraphed to the treasury secretary in Washington: "Wisconsin and Indiana have voted for Garfield with much enthusiasm. Our vote is restive—Garfield refuses to allow use of his name without effect. This is a new contingency. Give your views." For his part, Garfield, still trying to be loyal to Sherman, told the Ohioans, "If this convention nominates me, it should be done without a vote from Ohio." Meanwhile, Maryland delegate Stephen Elkins passed a note to Garfield: "You can make Blaine President—Don't stand any longer. If Grant is nominated You and Ohio will be responsible. Do yourself and the Rep[ublican] party an act of simple justice."[32]

Like Sherman, Blaine was hearing about the convention's sudden move toward Garfield. Blaine and Garfield had been friendly for many years, and Blaine, who claimed he had entered the race primarily to prevent a third term for Grant, seemed content to encourage his supporters to back Garfield. This would accomplish Blaine's purpose of preventing Grant's nomination, but it also meant that someone Blaine knew and trusted (and perhaps believed he could influence or even control to some degree) would be the party's nominee. Blaine instructed Chandler to pass a note to Garfield at the appropriate moment, telling the Ohioan, "Maine's vote in this moment cast for you goes with my hearty concurrence. I hope it will aid in securing your nomination and assuring victory to the Republican party."[33]

Sherman also saw the writing on the wall, especially after receiving a note from one of his Chicago surrogates telling him, "You cannot be nominated. Give your influence to Garfield and save the Republican Party." Though disappointed that the Ohio delegation had not unified behind him (he maintained in his 1895 memoirs, "It is probable that if I had received the united vote of the Ohio delegation I would have been nominated"), he also saw Garfield's nomination as at least a partial victory because it prevented the possibility of another Grant term. Sherman telegraphed William Dennison of the Ohio delegation: "Whenever the vote of Ohio will be likely to assure the nomination of Garfield, I appeal to every delegate to vote for him. Let Ohio be solid."[34]

In the Grant camp, Conkling was uncharacteristically slow to act and was likely taken completely off guard by the Garfield stampede. Senator John Jones of Nevada, a Grant delegate, implored Conkling to stop the "dark horse" Garfield by throwing all of New York's votes to Blaine. Conkling claimed he lacked the time to organize such an effort.[35] But Conkling never would have done anything to help his enemy Blaine win the nomination.

By this time, the thirty-sixth ballot was under way. Connecticut was the first state to break for Garfield, throwing all but one of its twelve votes to the Ohioan. Grant's adopted home state of Illinois remained mostly loyal to him, giving him twenty-four of its forty-two votes. Seven Illinois votes went to Garfield, as did all twenty-two of Iowa's votes. When Maine's turn came, it followed the will of its favorite son Blaine and cast all fourteen votes for Garfield. Maryland, Massachusetts, and Michigan added heartily to Garfield's total, as did New Hampshire and New Jersey. New York—Conkling's turf—remained mostly loyal to Grant, giving him fifty votes to Garfield's twenty. Garfield garnered all of his home state's votes. When the ballot was concluded, Garfield had received 399 votes, and he became the Republican presidential nominee.[36]

Garfield kept his seat with the Ohio delegation as the convention hall erupted in cheers and delegates crowded around him for a handshake or a celebratory clap on the back. He told a nearby reporter, "I want it plainly understood that I have not sought this nomination and have protested against the use of my name. . . . [Nonetheless] a nomination coming unsought and unexpected like this will be the crowning gratification of my life."[37] Garfield said the right thing here, even though he had known for some time that he might win the nomination if none of the other candidates could secure it.

"The Appomattox of the Third Termers" depicts Ulysses S. Grant symbolically passing the sword of Republican leadership to James A. Garfield. *(Courtesy of Library of Congress)*

Hoar announced that Garfield was the nominee and asked the convention whether the nomination "shall be made unanimous." Conkling and then Logan—two of the Triumvirate—rose to speak in favor of Garfield's nomination. "We will go forward in this contest, sir," said Logan, "not with tied hands, not with sealed lips, not with bridled tongues, but to speak the truth in favor of the grandest party that has ever been organized in this country."[38] After several similar speeches, the convention adjourned until 5:00 p.m., when it reconvened to nominate a vice-presidential candidate.

Despite their show of party unity upon Garfield's nomination, few expected Conkling, Logan, and their followers to make Garfield's candidacy an easy one. Because Garfield had opposed a third term for Grant, he was just another Half-Breed Republican in their eyes. In fact, those Stalwarts later formed a group they called the Three Hundred and Six Guard, after the number of votes Grant had received on the final ballot that nominated Garfield. For many years to come, they would occasionally meet to rehash the 1880 convention and congratulate themselves on their loyalty to Grant's losing effort in Chicago.

Garfield composed a quick telegram to his wife back home in Ohio, telling her of his nomination. "Dear Wife," it read, "if the result meets your approval I shall be content. Love to all the household."[39]

Then it was back to the business at hand: selecting a running mate. Candidates in this era did not always have much say in the choice of running mates. Because the parties, not the candidates, did most of the real work of presidential campaigns, party elders often suggested or even selected vice-presidential candidates, sometimes in an effort to provide geographic balance.[40] The goal of peacemaking between the two rival factions of the Republican Party was another consideration. Thus, if possible, a New York Stalwart should be Garfield's running mate. Aware of this likelihood, Garfield quickly stated his preference for Levi P. Morton, a well-known Wall Street banker and Conkling ally. Morton was interested until he consulted with Conkling, who told him that no true friend of his or Grant's would agree to a place on the ticket. Not wanting to anger his most powerful friend, Morton quietly withdrew from consideration.

Next, the New Yorkers turned to Chester Alan Arthur, a recent widower who had never been elected to any office. Arthur was best known for serving as collector of the port of New York for several years before being fired for corruption by President Hayes. Many viewed Arthur, a Conkling loyalist, as a run-of-the-mill machine politico. When Arthur's name was floated as a possible vice-presidential candidate, most assumed that Conkling was pulling strings to get his lackey on the ticket. In fact, New York Stalwarts had discussed and settled on Arthur without Conkling even being in the room. When Arthur told Conkling that he had been offered the vice-presidential spot, Conkling advised him, "Well, sir, you should drop it as you would a red hot shoe from the forge." Arthur surprised everyone—especially Conkling—by accepting the offer. "The office of the Vice President," he told Conkling, "is a greater honor than I ever dreamed of attaining. . . . I shall accept the nomination and I shall carry with me the majority of the delegation."[41]

Arthur's selection upset many Republicans, but he was nominated for vice president on the first ballot with 486 votes, including all but one of the New York delegation's. Several other candidates received votes for the second spot on the ticket, most significantly Blanche K. Bruce of Mississippi. The eight votes Bruce received marked the first such recognition of an African American by a major political party. Sherman, though seemingly content with the nomination of Garfield, seethed at Arthur's selection. Sherman wrote, "The only reason for his nomination was that he was discharged from an office that he was unfit to fill." Sherman's Department of the Treasury oversaw the New York customhouse from which Arthur had been fired for corruption just two years earlier. Blaine supporter William

JAMES A. GARFIELD
REPUBLICAN CANDIDATE FOR PRESIDENT

CHESTER A. ARTHUR
REPUBLICAN CANDIDATE FOR VICE PRESIDENT

The 1880 Republican ticket: James A. Garfield of Ohio for president and Chester A. Arthur of New York for vice president. (Courtesy of Library of Congress)

Chandler disagreed. "Arthur is able," Chandler wrote, "and the concession, if one was to be made . . . was the best one."[42]

With Arthur's nomination for the vice presidency, the convention's work was done. "What other Convention in all our history can show as much good and as little harm?" wondered President Hayes, who clearly approved of the party's selection of his fellow Ohioan Garfield. Not everyone agreed. One political reporter wrote, "On the day the delegates turned their backs on Chicago and their faces toward home, Garfield was a beaten man." The three main rivals for the nomination the week before all professed to be pleased with the choice of Garfield, but at least two of them were bitter about it. Grant was quoted as saying only that the choice of Garfield was "all right; he was satisfied." Sherman, in an icy letter to Ohio governor Foster two weeks after the convention, wrote, "The nomination of Garfield is entirely satisfactory to me. The only shade that rests on this feeling is the fact that Garfield went there by my selection to represent me and comes from the convention with the honor that I sought." Sherman admitted that he had no evidence that Garfield had worked for his own interests rather than Sherman's, but the treasury secretary was obviously wounded by the lack of unified support from the Ohio delegation. "The . . . opposition to me in Ohio was unreasonable, without cause, either springing from corrupt or bad motives, or from such trivial causes as would scarcely justify the pouting of a school-boy."[43]

Only Blaine, who yearned to be president, seemed genuinely pleased with Garfield's selection, in all likelihood because he and Garfield were close and Blaine liked his chances of being named to an important cabinet post. "The nomination of General Garfield was unexpected but it was not unwelcome. . . . [Garfield] was neither an unknown nor an untried man. No statesman of the times surpassed him in thorough acquaintance with the principles of free government, in knowledge of the legislative and administrative history of our own country, and in intelligent grasp of the great questions still at issue. . . . He represented the liberal and progressive spirit of Republicanism . . . and his nomination was accepted as placing the party on advanced ground."[44]

Republicans departed Chicago with a dark-horse presidential candidate and a vice-presidential candidate seeking his first elected office. As they journeyed to their respective home states to begin planning and organizing the campaign that would take place over the next five months, the nation's attention turned to the Democratic Party's convention in Cincinnati. Democrats and Republicans alike were asking the same question: who would be the Democratic standard-bearers facing off against James Garfield and Chester Arthur in the upcoming election?

5

"THE MOST INFAMOUS MAN IN AMERICA" WINFIELD SCOTT HANCOCK AND THE 1880 DEMOCRATIC NATIONAL CONVENTION

Almost immediately after the 1876 electoral commission ruled that Rutherford B. Hayes would be president, speculation began that Samuel J. Tilden would run again in 1880 to seek his revenge and claim the office he believed he had legitimately won. Tilden was publicly silent about his plans as the 1880 Democratic convention neared, and his supporters fervently hoped he would run. Privately, despite his frail health, Tilden yearned to be nominated again, telling friends that 1880 would be his reelection campaign.

If he chose to run again, Tilden's path to the nomination would not be an easy one. Although many Democrats believed that Tilden was the obvious candidate after the 1876 debacle, Tilden's reputation, like his health, had suffered during those four years. In May 1878, in an effort to embarrass and discredit the Republicans, the Democrats who controlled the House of Representatives created a special committee to investigate the disputed 1876 election and prove that the electoral commission had stolen the presidency from Tilden. The Potter Committee, named for its chairman, Congressman Clarkson Potter of New York, spent several months reviewing documents and hearing testimony from witnesses. Despite the Democrats' hope that the Potter Committee would prove Hayes's election fraudulent and give them a strong advantage heading into the 1880 campaign, the plan backfired.

In early 1877, before the disputed Hayes-Tilden election

was even decided, a Senate committee (led by Republicans) subpoenaed from Western Union copies of communications between the two parties and their operatives in the disputed states of Florida, Louisiana, and South Carolina. Once Hayes was elected, the Senate committee returned the copies to Western Union, and they were subsequently destroyed. Unbeknownst to just about everyone outside that committee, however, the Republicans had kept copies of more than 700 telegrams detailing communications on the Democratic side. Many were written in code and had been sent to and from Tilden's home. They clearly showed that Tilden's nephew William Pelton had attempted to bribe an Oregon elector as well as electors in South Carolina and Florida to vote for Tilden. Responding to newspaper articles about these telegrams, the Republican members of the Potter Committee called Tilden as a witness in February 1879.[1]

Tilden had already issued a public statement claiming to know nothing about the telegrams or any alleged bribes. His appearance before the Potter Committee did little to help his chances of securing a second straight Democratic nomination in 1880. He suffered from permanent paralysis on his left side due to a stroke he had suffered after the 1876 election. He had difficulty walking, and his voice was barely audible. He was never charged with any crime, and his testimony basically ended the matter, but even the staunchest Tilden supporters began to wonder whether he was physically capable of another presidential campaign.[2]

Tilden was down but not completely out. There was enough residual anger about the outcome of the 1876 contest to make a Tilden nomination possible in 1880. Additionally, Tilden's strategy of saying nothing publicly about his intentions created great curiosity as the Democratic convention in Cincinnati approached. Although some Democrats expressed frustration with Tilden's silence, it actually raised his standing and his profile with many. Behind closed doors, however, frustration with Tilden was far more common than admiration among prominent Democrats gearing up for the campaign. Just days before the convention began on June 22, Tilden informed his two operatives Smith M. Weed and Daniel Manning that he would accept the nomination only if it were unanimous. Aware that this was unlikely, Tilden then proceeded to tell Weed and Manning which of the other candidates he preferred. At the same time, Tilden sent a telegram to one of them, Ohio congressman Henry B. Payne, and offered him the vice-presidential spot on a Tilden ticket. Payne accepted.

The personality quirk that had made Tilden unwilling to press his own case during the 1876 election controversy still plagued him four years later.

Drawing of the 1880 Democratic National Convention in Cincinnati. (Courtesy of Library of Congress)

There is little doubt that Tilden was fiercely ambitious and, despite his poor health, very much wanted the nomination in 1880. In fact, he had declined to run for reelection as governor of New York after the 1876 debacle so that he could focus on another presidential run in 1880. Still, he was unwilling to say publicly that he hoped to be nominated in 1880, even as prominent Democrats and party representatives from several states wrote to or visited him and encouraged him to run. Former attorney general and secretary of state Jeremiah Black, who had advocated for Tilden during the 1876 crisis, visited Tilden shortly before the Democratic convention and asked him point-blank whether he was running. "I take no part in the matter," Tilden replied. "I hold myself perfectly free." William C. Whitney, a close Tilden confidant and Henry Payne's son-in-law, noted: "One of the peculiar weaknesses of Mr. Tilden as a political candidate is that he gives his whole confidence to no one . . . he expects his supporters to guess his intention. And if we do not guess correctly he is angry. He lost the Presidential seat by just such methods."[3]

In addition to seeking revenge for the 1876 election, many Democrats wanted Tilden to run because New York would once again be one of the most critical states in the contest. Tilden had won his home state against Hayes in 1876, and everyone believed he could do it again. "It is simple folly and a waste of effort to nominate men who cannot carry New York," the *Atlanta Constitution* editorialized. "We want no booms because we simply want a man who can secure 47 northern votes."[4] As the Atlanta paper realized, with a solidly Democratic South and New York's thirty-five electoral votes, the Democratic candidate would need just twelve more electoral votes to win the presidency. The convention was just a week away when Democratic operative A. C. McGlacklin wired Tilden and implored him to jump into the race because "Cincinnati means defeat without you."[5] But Samuel Tilden was not the only Democrat who wanted to be president in 1880. His indecision frustrated many and emboldened others to throw their hats into the ring.

Senator Thomas Bayard of Delaware came from one of the East's most prominent political families. His father, James A. Bayard Jr., had preceded him in the US Senate; his uncle, Richard A. Bayard, had also been a senator. During the Civil War, Delaware was one of the so-called border states—along with Kentucky, Maryland, and Missouri—that permitted slavery within their boundaries but never seceded and remained part of the Union for the duration of the war. Slaves made up less than 2 percent of Delaware's population by the time the Civil War began.[6]

All the border states contributed troops to both the Union and Confederate war efforts. Thomas Bayard helped organize an independent Union militia company, the Delaware Guard, and received a commission as a first lieutenant. The unit never saw action, however, and was disbanded in 1862 by order of the governor, who suspected many of its members of having Southern sympathies. In the case of Bayard, the governor was correct.

Thomas Bayard and his father both allied with the peace wing of the Democratic Party throughout the Civil War. In fact, the senior Bayard resigned from the Senate in 1862 to protest a new oath of office (later declared unconstitutional) that required senators to swear they had never borne arms against the United States or given aid, comfort, or encouragement to its enemies. The younger Bayard gave a speech at a peace meeting in Dover, Delaware, in June 1861 at which he declared that "with this secession, or revolution, or rebellion, or whatever name it may be called, the State of Delaware has naught to do." It was better, he argued, to find a peaceful solution, even if that meant letting the Southern states secede.[7] Bayard practiced law in Wilmington, Delaware, for the remainder of the Civil War. He expressed pleasure with the Democratic peace platform of 1864 but was unhappy with that year's Democratic presidential candidate, former general George B. McClellan, who considered himself a War Democrat. The country overwhelmingly reelected Abraham Lincoln in 1864, and the Delaware legislature elected Bayard to the Senate in 1869 to replace a senator who had died.

Bayard worked hard for Delaware during his time in Senate, but Republicans and former War Democrats never let him forget his support of the peace platform during the Civil War. Bayard sought the Democratic presidential nomination in 1876 but was soundly defeated by Tilden. He then ended up as one of the fifteen members of the electoral commission forced to decide the Tilden-Hayes contest. Like Tilden, Bayard wanted to try again in 1880; unlike the New Yorker, Bayard was willing to work (albeit behind the scenes, as was the custom during this era) for his own nomination. Many wondered whether Bayard's Peace Democrat past would keep him from winning enough Northern votes in the general election. No one doubted that the Republicans, led by Union army veteran James Garfield as their presidential candidate, would once again "wave the bloody shirt" in an effort to keep the White House for another four years. To many Northern Democrats, nominating a candidate who had expressed support for letting the South secede seemed reckless. Southern Democrats, of course, loved Bayard for his stance on secession in 1861 and for his later vocal opposition to equality for black men and women. But many of these same Southern Democrats recognized that Bayard would have trouble getting votes in the North.

Stephen Johnson Field also sought the Democratic nomination. Field was nearly sixty-four years old in 1880 and had spent most of his adult life in the legal profession. Born in Connecticut and raised in Massachusetts, Field graduated from Williams College—the same college attended by Republican nominee James Garfield—in 1837 (when Garfield was six years old). Field's two brothers also achieved acclaim. David Dudley Field was a prominent New York attorney and a generous donor to the Republican Party. Cyrus West Field was a wealthy businessman and financier, and he was one of the men responsible for the first transatlantic cable. Ironically, Cyrus was also a friend of James and Lucretia Garfield.

Stephen Field traveled west to California around the time of the gold rush. He opened a successful law practice and served a term in the state house of representatives before being elected to the California Supreme Court in 1857. He became that court's chief justice in 1859 after his predecessor killed a US senator in a duel. Field was a Unionist Democrat during the Civil War, and in 1863 Abraham Lincoln nominated him to a seat on the US Supreme Court, seeking to shore up support in the West and among War Democrats. By the time of the 1880 Democratic National Convention, Field had been an associate justice of the nation's highest court for seventeen years. Like Bayard, he had been one of the fifteen members of the electoral commission that decided the Hayes-Tilden contest. As a pro-business Democrat, Field had supported Tilden's claim to the presidency in 1876, but now, four years later, Field hoped to push Tilden aside and capture the presidential nomination himself. Little was known about Field's political opinions, but as a justice of the Supreme Court, he was not expected to comment on the issues of the day.

Thomas Hendricks of Indiana had sought the presidential nomination in 1876. When Tilden won the nomination instead, Hendricks accepted the vice-presidential spot on the ticket. Hendricks was one of the only candidates of either party to support "soft money," or paper greenbacks, rather than "hard money" consisting of coins made from gold and other precious metals. Soft-money policies were popular with farmers in Hendricks's home state and throughout the West, which was surely at least part of the reason he had been chosen to run alongside hard-money advocate Tilden in 1876. Hendricks's presence on the ticket that most Democrats believed had been illegally robbed of election in 1876 made him a logical choice as the front-runner four years later, although many feared his soft-money policies would adversely affect his popularity in the East. Hendricks had not been implicated in the scandal involving deciphered telegrams and alleged bribery that had ensnared Tilden.

Geography might also work in favor of Hendricks. Indiana was a critical state for Democrats to add to their column in 1880, and Hendricks was that state's favorite son. If he could win the nomination and hold his home state, he stood a strong chance of winning the presidency. Of course, his party had to nominate him first.

The names of other favorite-son candidates were thrown around, including Allen Thurman of Ohio and William Morrison of Illinois. However, General Winfield Scott Hancock, an active-duty army officer and commander of the Department of the Atlantic, was the only other major Democratic candidate in 1880. Just as Stephen Field was not the only sitting Supreme Court justice in American history to actively seek the presidency, Hancock was not the only active-duty general to do so. In fact, his namesake General Winfield Scott had been the Whig Party's presidential nominee in 1852, losing to Democrat Franklin Pierce. Hancock's political and presidential ambitions were well known; he too had made a run at the Democratic nomination in 1876 and fallen to Samuel Tilden.

Most of those seeking the Democratic nomination in 1880 were well known across America, but none embodied heroism like Winfield Hancock. Born near Philadelphia in 1824, Hancock graduated from West Point in 1844 and served with distinction in the Mexican-American War, where he was wounded at the Battle of Churubusco and received a brevet promotion to first lieutenant. He was a captain in the army when the Civil War began and rose quickly through the ranks, becoming a brigadier general of volunteers by September 1861. Hancock fought in nearly every battle in which the Army of the Potomac participated. In May 1862 General George B. McClellan unwittingly gave Hancock a nickname when he mentioned in a report on the Battle of Williamsburg that "Hancock was superb today." From that point on, the press dubbed him "Hancock the Superb."[8]

Four months later, Hancock assumed command of a division upon the death of Major General Israel B. Richardson at the Battle of Antietam. He was promoted to major general of volunteers soon after, was wounded at the Battle of Fredericksburg, and assumed command of the Army of the Potomac's second corps when Major General Darius Couch was transferred to another command. Hancock was seriously wounded again during Pickett's Charge at Gettysburg when a bullet passed through his saddle and lodged in his groin. After healing, he returned to the army and was with General Ulysses S. Grant as Union and Confederate forces slugged it out in Virginia during 1864. Lingering difficulties caused by his Gettysburg wound forced Hancock to give up command of the second corps for good in November 1864, and he later supervised the execution of the Lincoln assassination conspirators.

In his personal memoirs, published posthumously in 1886, Grant wrote:

> Hancock stands as the most conspicuous figure of all the general officers who did not exercise a separate command. He commanded a corps longer than any other one, and his name was never mentioned as having committed in battle a blunder for which he was responsible. He was a man of very conspicuous personal appearance. Tall, well-formed and, at

the time of which I now write, young and fresh-looking, he presented an appearance that would attract the attention of an army as he passed. His genial disposition made him friends, and his personal courage and his presence with his command in the thickest of the fight won for him the confidence of troops serving under him. No matter how hard the fight, the 2d corps always felt that their commander was looking after them.[9]

Had Grant managed to capture the Republican nomination in Chicago, he might have faced off against the former subordinate he later complimented so highly.

After the Civil War ended, the US Army turned its attention back to pacification of the Indians on the western plains. In 1866, at the suggestion of now General of the Army Grant, Hancock was promoted to major general in the regular army and assigned command of the Department of the Missouri, which included Missouri, Kansas, New Mexico, and Colorado. Hancock's stay there was brief and unenjoyable. He tried to negotiate with delegations of Cheyenne and Lakota but had little success.

Meanwhile, Andrew Johnson was an embattled president in the summer of 1867. For two years, he had fought tooth and nail with Radical Republicans in Congress for control over Reconstruction. On August 12, 1867, Johnson suspended Secretary of War Edwin Stanton, who had raised the president's ire by working with Congress on Reconstruction policy. Johnson made Grant, then commanding general of the army, acting secretary of war and ordered him to remove General Philip H. Sheridan from command of the Fifth Military District, covering Texas and Louisiana and with headquarters in New Orleans. Sheridan had also crossed the president by working with Radical Republicans and stretching his own authority to force Southerners to accept the presence and rights of freed black men and women. Johnson ordered Grant to appoint General George H. Thomas, the Civil War's "Rock of Chickamauga," to replace Sheridan. Thomas was known to harbor Republican sentiments, but Johnson chose him in an effort to win back some of Sheridan's supporters. However, Thomas's health was poor, and his doctor advised against going to New Orleans. This gave Johnson the opportunity to appoint the man he had wanted all along: Winfield Scott Hancock.

Hancock was known to be a loyal Democrat, but he wrote to Grant that it was "not a desire of mine to go to . . . the South." Hancock seemed to understand that Johnson was sending him to New Orleans precisely because he was a Democrat and would run the Fifth Military District far differently from Sheridan. "I am expected to exercise extreme military authority over these people," he told his wife. "I shall disappoint them [the Radicals in Congress]," he noted. "I have not been educated to overthrow the civil authorities in time of peace. I intend to recognize the fact that the Civil War is at an end, and shall issue my order or proclamation accordingly. I tell you this because I may lose my commission, and I shall do so willingly, rather than retain it at the sacrifice of a lifelong principle."[10] White Southerners, aware of Hancock's political affiliation and preferring anyone over Sheridan, were pleased at the change. "Our people," wrote the *New Orleans Times*, "will be fully satisfied with the rule of General Hancock, believing that he will deal out justice impartially, unbiased by prejudice or partisan feeling."[11]

Hancock surely understood that he was being used by the president, who was losing his battle with congressional Radicals. Johnson had few options left if he hoped to impose his own vision of Southern Reconstruction, which meant returning social and political power to white Democrats. The power to appoint and remove military district commanders was still his, however, and he was not afraid to use it. Johnson was sure that Hancock shared his vision of a new South dominated by conservative white Democrats—in other words, a new South that discriminated against black men and women but stopped short of returning them to slavery. Andrew Johnson had always hated wealthy slave owners, but he also believed that African Americans were inferior and did not deserve to be on an equal social, political, or economic footing with whites.

Johnson's assessment of Hancock was mostly correct. Hancock had been raised by a staunchly Democratic father and had absorbed his thoughts about the rights and political supremacy of the states. Hancock's wife, Almira, had been born and raised among slaveholders in the border state of Missouri. Finally, many of Hancock's closest friends in the pre–Civil War army were Southerners, leading him to sympathize with the white South. In Hancock's view, Reconstruction was mostly unnecessary. The war had been purely about suppressing rebellion, and once that task was successfully completed, the country should return as much as possible to the prewar status quo—including whites' resumption of civil authority in the South. Slavery was dead, but whites in power could still ensure that black men and women were denied the opportunity to succeed or even live peacefully in the South.

Hancock composed a document during his trip to New Orleans that set the tone for his administration of the Fifth Military District. Issued on his first day of command—November 29, 1867—the document has gone down in history as General Orders No. 40. In it, Hancock wrote, "When insurrectionary force has been overthrown and peace established, and the civil authorities are ready and willing to perform their duties, the military power should cease to lead, and the civil administration resume its natural and rightful dominion."[12] The army, in other words, should not protect the physical safety or the civil rights of freed people.

Although Hancock believed this to be the proper course, he clearly understood that turning over civil power to white Southerners would place him in the Radical Republicans' crosshairs. "They will crucify me," he wrote to his wife. "I warned the President of my intentions. . . . I know I shall have his sympathy, but he is powerless to help me."[13] Johnson, of course, suspected Hancock's intentions all along, which was precisely why he wanted Hancock in command of the Fifth Military District. Johnson called the order "manly and statesmanlike" and sent a message to Congress urging a vote of thanks for Hancock. "I am far from saying that General Hancock is the only officer influenced by the example of Washington," the president wrote. "But the distinguished honor belongs to him of being the first officer in high command south of the Potomac, since the close of the Civil War, who has given utterance to these noble sentiments in the form of a military order."[14]

As expected, Republicans in Congress responded immediately to this resurrection of the Southern white Democrat line of thinking and action. Senator John M. Thayer of Nebraska introduced a bill to reduce the number of major generals in the army by eliminating the most junior one—who just happened to be Winfield Scott Hancock. In the House, James A. Garfield of Ohio—Hancock's presidential rival in 1880—introduced a similar bill. Garfield railed against Hancock in a January 17, 1868, speech on the House floor. "We hear him declaring that he finds nothing in the laws of Louisiana and Texas to warrant his interference in the civil administration of those States," Garfield said. "It is not for him to say which should be first, the civil or the military, in that rebel community. . . . It is for him to obey the laws he was sent to execute." The laws Hancock was expected to execute, of course, were those governing Reconstruction according to the Radical Republicans. Garfield was well aware that General Orders No. 40 had some Democrats looking at Hancock as presidential material, so he continued: "It is for him to aid in building up civil governments, rather than preparing himself to be the presidential candidate of that party which gave him no sympathy when he was gallantly fighting the battles of the country." Garfield knew that his bill to reduce the number of major generals was unlikely to go very far; as he told his friend Burke Hinsdale, he pursued it only to demonstrate to the Democrats and Hancock himself just "how completely he was in our hands."[15] Neither Garfield nor Hancock could know that in twelve years they would be facing each other in a presidential election.

Shortly after arriving in Louisiana, Hancock began to countermand the orders of his predecessor Sheridan, including revoking an order concerning the qualifications of jurors. Sheridan's order had encouraged jury service by blacks and barred whites who had supported the Confederacy. "To determine who shall, and shall not be jurors," Hancock wrote, "appertains to the legislative power. . . . It is deemed best to carry out the will of the people as expressed in the last legislative act upon this subject."[16] Under the "last legislative act," only white men could be jurors. White Louisianans and Texans cheered Hancock's decision; Radical Republicans did not. "Andrew Johnson is determined that governments worse than those imposed by Jefferson Davis shall be erected in the South," wrote the *New Orleans Republican*, "through the Generals he is sending to govern it." One Republican who wrote to Garfield called Hancock "the most infamous man in America."[17]

Hancock also found himself at odds with Texas governor Elisha M. Pease, installed by Sheridan before Hancock's arrival in the Fifth Military District. In late December 1868 Pease requested a military tribunal for three accused murderers in west Texas. "At this time," Hancock answered, "the country is in a state of profound peace. The state government of Texas . . . is in the full exercise of all its proper powers. The courts . . . are in existence." In other words, a military commission was unnecessary as long as the state government was operating and administering the legal system. If Governor Pease could not handle the administrative and legal affairs of his state, "it will then become the duty of the commander to remove" him. Pease relented, but he was seething with anger at Hancock. To Hancock, it was clear that that his predecessors had regularly and illegally interfered with the workings of the judiciary in the Fifth District. He issued a new order on New Year's Day 1868, reiterating his policy that "the administration of civil justice appertains to the regular courts," and the rights of those involved in legal cases were to be judged according to the existing laws, not "the views of the general."[18]

Most white Southerners were pleased with Hancock's administration of the Fifth District. Most Radical Republicans, however, were not. "Hancock is avowedly in sympathy with the rebels," one Army of the Potomac veteran wrote to Oliver O. Howard, commissioner of the Freedman's Bureau. "We poor old soldiers who fought with him have no show." Another called Hancock "a great impediment to reconstruction, giving all aid and power to the Rebs."[19]

Hancock took two actions on January 11, 1868, that inflamed Republican disaffection with his administration. First, he appointed Joshua Baker as the new governor of Louisiana to replace Benjamin Franklin Flanders, a Republican and native of New Hampshire who had resided in New Orleans since 1843. Flanders, appointed by Sheridan in June 1867, had resigned over disagreements with Hancock. Baker was a planter, a West Point graduate, and a Unionist, but he was also a conservative who agreed with President Andrew Johnson's vision for Reconstruction. By choosing Baker, "General Hancock has shown great sagacity . . . toward the people of Louisiana," wrote the *New Orleans Commercial Bulletin*. Baker had "always been a warm friend to the colored race. When he owned hundreds of them he was one of the most indulgent and kind masters in St. Mary."[20]

Hancock's second decision on January 11 was to revoke Sheridan's proclamation regarding voter registration in what one historian described as "an obvious sequel to his jury eligibility decree of five weeks earlier."[21] In May 1867 Sheridan had distributed an order to local voter registrars detailing the questions that prospective voters should be asked and the answers that would result in disqualification. Many—including Hancock—viewed it as an attempt to disqualify former Confederates from voting. Hancock's rescinding of Sheridan's order did not remove black voters from the rolls, but it did allow an onslaught of white voter registration by those who would have been ineligible under Sheridan's rule. This action accelerated the rejuvenation of the Democratic Party—and white supremacy—in the states of the Fifth Military District.

In February 1868 an election crisis arose that dated back to 1866. Arthur Gastinel, a young conservative, had been elected district court recorder of the Second District of New Orleans. His opponent sued in court, alleging that, under the law, Gastinel was too young to serve. When this was proved true, Gastinel's victory was overturned, and the position was left vacant. By February 1868, Gastinel had reached the appropriate age, so Hancock moved to install him as the Second District's recorder. When the Board of Aldermen learned of Hancock's intentions, the members called a joint session with the aim of choosing a recorder. Two days later, Hancock removed all the aldermen who had voted to select a recorder other than Gastinel. Seven of the nine aldermen removed were black, and all had been appointed by Sheridan during his command of the Fifth District. All of Hancock's replacement aldermen were white. "That the colored population is not represented in the new board," commented the *New Orleans Daily Picayune*, "is . . . their fault and their misfortune."[22]

Hancock duly wired his boss, General Grant, to let him know what he had done in the case of the New Orleans aldermen. Grant immediately ordered Hancock to suspend the order dismissing the original aldermen, and Hancock asked to be relieved of command of the Fifth District. Grant then relented and told Hancock the removals could remain in effect while Grant gathered more information and determined the best course. The *New Orleans Times* sarcastically noted, "What wonderfully grand and important individuals some half a dozen Aldermen . . . must be, that the whole nation should be convulsed, and the national capital turned upside down, because better men have been found for their places."[23]

Grant ordered the dismissed aldermen reinstated on February 21, although Hancock did not receive the order until six days later. Ever the loyal soldier, Hancock immediately complied with Grant's directive, but he also requested "to be relieved from the command of this Military District, where it is no longer useful or agreeable for me to serve." Grant relieved Hancock on March 16, and President Johnson summoned Hancock to Washington.

Winfield Scott Hancock's administration of the Fifth Military District had been brief but important. White Southerners had learned a great deal about Hancock—and they liked what they saw. For the rest of his career, Hancock would be thought of not as just a general but, more specifically, as a Democratic general. Federal troops remained in Louisiana for another decade, and Radical Republicans continued to try to force white Southerners to accept governments based on the Reconstruction Amendments to the Constitution. Hancock's time in New Orleans would later make him an appealing Democratic presidential candidate precisely because he was palatable to white Southerners. He had, after all, done everything he could to return legal, civil, and political power to them during his tenure commanding the Fifth District.

Hancock was an attractive presidential candidate to many Democrats. Without any real effort or overt signal of interest on his part, he garnered a number of delegates at the party's 1868 convention, but the nomination eventually went to Horatio Seymour of New York. After Grant won the presidency that year, Hancock was shipped off to St. Louis to command the Department of Dakota. In 1872, following the death of the army's senior major general—Hancock's old Army of the Potomac commander George Gordon

Meade—Hancock was transferred to the more prestigious Department of the Atlantic, based on Governor's Island in New York City. He was again considered as a presidential candidate in 1876, when the party eventually turned to Samuel J. Tilden.

Although Hancock never said much publicly, there is no doubt that he very much wanted to be president. He skillfully and properly portrayed himself as nothing more than a loyal soldier, but behind the scenes, he maintained close ties with those who had worked on his behalf at previous Democratic conventions. In 1880 Hancock was fifty-six years old, stood tall at about six feet, two inches, and still looked every bit the soldier he had been since graduating from West Point in 1844. He had gained quite a bit of weight in the years since the Civil War, but with his commanding height and meticulous uniform—not to mention his well-deserved reputation for bravery under fire—he certainly looked the part of a late nineteenth-century president.

Besides looking appropriately presidential, Hancock had a few other assets that made him seem like the right man to carry Democrats to their first presidential election victory since 1856. First, he was clearly popular in the South after his brief but, in the minds of many white Southerners, successful command of the Fifth Military District. Southern Democrats were prominent in the party again, so choosing a candidate who appealed to them and could carry their states was critical.

Second, because he had never held elective office, Hancock had no record to criticize—no embarrassing speeches in his past like Bayard, no controversial votes to defend, no newspaper editorials that could come back to haunt him. Both parties surely remembered the lesson of 1860, when most Republicans had assumed that William Henry Seward would be their presidential nominee—until his radical rhetoric on abolition scared many party members into thinking he could not be elected and led the convention delegates to choose someone else: Abraham Lincoln.

Finally, Hancock's candidacy would, at least in theory, deny the Republicans their greatest weapon against the Democrats: "waving the bloody shirt" and reminding voters that Republicans had fought to save the nation during the Civil War while Democrats had fought to destroy it. The Democrats had never had a successful presidential candidate who had served the Union in uniform during the Civil War. George B. McClellan had been their candidate in 1864, but he lost to Lincoln. Meanwhile, bona fide war heroes and Republicans Ulysses S. Grant and Rutherford B. Hayes had occupied the White House since early 1869. The three Democrats who had

Winfield Scott Hancock, US Army commander of the Department of the Atlantic and 1880 Democratic nominee for president. (Courtesy of Library of Congress)

run against Grant and Hayes—Horatio Seymour in 1868, Horace Greeley in 1872, and Samuel Tilden in 1876—had all spent the Civil War in New York, far from the battlefields of Virginia or Tennessee. Hancock, however, had not just served in the Union army; he had commanded Northern soldiers in some of the war's bloodiest and most significant battles. Hancock had been wounded in action multiple times, including the severe wound he suffered at Gettysburg—arguably the war's most famous battle and one of the North's most important victories. Hancock had fought, bled, and nearly died for the United States. With the exception of Grant, none of the potential Republican candidates had a war record that could compare to Hancock's.

Not everyone was convinced that Hancock was the right candidate to beat the Republicans in 1880. "There is no other candidate for the Democratic nomination," wrote the Republican *Philadelphia Inquirer*, "who possesses so few of the real qualifications of a President as General Hancock, and none who can involve the Democratic party in so much inconsistency." Despite opinions like this, many Democrats were intrigued by the possibility of a Hancock candidacy. He had no strong opinion or position on hard versus soft money, so he could be sold as more than just a regional candidate. Most assumed that he would have strong support from Southern Democrats, but he might also appeal to Northerners in at least a few important states. New Yorkers had voted for their governor, Tilden, in 1876, and Hancock had resided in New York City as commander of the Department of the Atlantic since 1872. Thus, a skillful campaign there could keep New York in the Democrats' column. Pennsylvania, which had gone for the Republican Hayes in 1876, might also be attracted to a ticket led by its native son Hancock. Many Democrats adopted a wait-and-see attitude due to the uncertainty surrounding Tilden's desire to run again in 1880 and the feeling that he should receive the nomination if he wanted it. Hancock, however, was already becoming a strong second choice in many Democrats' minds. As other candidates had proved in the past, including Lincoln in 1860, being a strong second at the beginning of a nominating convention was not a bad place to be.

The Democrats held their annual convention in Cincinnati from June 22 to 24, just two weeks after the Republicans met in Chicago and nominated the James Garfield–Chester Arthur ticket. The first question the Democrats needed to address was the status of Samuel Tilden. Was he running or not? Just before the convention, Tilden had declared that he wanted the nomination only if it were unanimous, and his silence beyond that encouraged other candidates to believe they had a chance.

Tilden gave his staunch supporter Daniel Manning, publisher of the *Albany Argus* and later secretary of the treasury under President Grover Cleveland, a letter to carry to the Cincinnati convention. Dated June 18, the letter was addressed to the New York delegation, and Tilden instructed Manning to read it at the convention. When word of the letter leaked out, delegates hoped it would provide clarity on whether Tilden wanted the nomination. Instead, it clouded the issue even more.

After a lengthy recounting of the disputed 1876 election in which he had won the popular vote but lost the presidency to Hayes, Tilden told the New Yorkers:

> Having now borne faithfully my full share of labor and care in the public service, and wearing the marks of its burdens, I desire nothing so much as an honorable discharge. I wish to lay down the honors and toils of even *quasi* party leadership, and to seek the repose of private life. In renouncing renomination for the Presidency, I do so with no doubt in my mind . . . because I believe that it is a renunciation of re-election to the Presidency.[24]

Although this seemed to be a fairly straightforward refusal to seek the nomination, Tilden's earlier statement about accepting only a unanimous nomination led to confusion about his willingness to run. Some thought the letter was a subtle bid for the nomination, while others took it at face value and declared Tilden out of the running.

The day Tilden's letter was published, Charles A. Dana presciently noted in the pages of the *New York Sun* that Democrats would immediately lose their most compelling argument for victory if Tilden was not nominated. "The Convention may regard Mr. Tilden's wishes and excuse him," Dana wrote, "but it must not be overlooked that with his retirement the most important issue drops out of the canvass." After admitting that only poor health—from which Tilden definitely suffered in 1880—should keep Tilden from the nomination, Dana wryly noted, "The best evidence of Mr. Tilden's strength is the fact that he has already been once elected. This can be said of no other living Democrat."[25]

The uncertainty surrounding Tilden continued when the chairman of the Democratic National Committee, William H. Barnum of Connecticut, formally called the convention to order at 12:38 p.m. on June 22. After the opening prayer, Barnum nominated George Hoadly, a judge of the Cincinnati Superior Court and a Tilden intimate, to be the convention's temporary chairman. The delegates voted unanimously for Hoadly, who then gave a fiery speech reminding the Democrats that they had been robbed of a Tilden presidency in the last election. Referring to President Hayes, Hoadly told the delegates, "In the Executive Department 'government by the people' has ceased since March 4th, 1877," and he railed against "the fraud of the Republican party, of its infidelity to Republican principles, of its willingness to sacrifice the right of popular election that 'vital principle of Republics,' rather than relax its hold on power." The Democrats, in Hoadly's view, were the true loyalists to the rule of law and the will of the people. "For while, if fairly beaten," he continued, "we shall submit—I repeat, we shall submit if fairly beaten, and again wait; but if again successful, no cunning device of dishonest arbitration shall rob us of the fruits of our triumph." This was seen as a swipe at two other Democratic contenders, Bayard of Delaware and Thurman of Ohio—both of whom had served on the electoral commission that ultimately handed the 1876 election to Hayes. Finally, Hoadly acknowledged that the Republicans had chosen not to nominate Grant again and noted, "Since the eighth day of June, 1880, it has been certain that the usurper will not be immediately followed by the monarch. . . . And the real danger is not so much in the third term as in the Republican party, which makes the third term possible." Hoadly also called Samuel Tilden and Thomas Hendricks—the 1876 presidential and vice-presidential nominees—"two of the foremost statesmen of the Nation."[26]

The convention then moved on to establishing committees on organization, credentials, and resolutions. John Kelly, head of the Tammany Hall Democratic machine and an avowed Tilden foe since the governor had taken on that machine in the early 1870s, tried to address the chair but was quickly rebuffed. With this, the convention adjourned for the day.

The following day, the Committee on Credentials named John W. Stevenson of Kentucky the convention's permanent chair. As a roll call for nominations got under way, J. E. McElrath nominated Justice Stephen J. Field of the US Supreme Court. Believing that a Field nomination would "sweep California like the winds that blow through her golden gates," many Democrats were unaware that Field was not on good terms with his own state's Democratic Party. As a justice, Field had defied public sentiment in California, choosing to recognize the constitutional rights of Chinese immigrants rather than curtail Chinese immigration. This decision made the state Democratic Party lukewarm at best toward a Field nomination.[27] Field was also widely regarded as too friendly with big business, making him too much like a Republican for many Democrats.

When the roll call got to Delaware, George Gray rose to place Thomas Bayard's name in nomination, calling the senator a statesman whose name and record were known "where our flag floats, aye, wherever the English tongue is spoken." Should Bayard be nominated, Gray told the crowd, "his very name would be a platform."[28]

Daniel Voorhees of Indiana nominated his fellow Hoosier Thomas A.

Hendricks, the 1876 vice-presidential nominee. "To the South who has been more faithful? To the North who has been truer? To the East who has been . . . more faithful? To the West I need not appeal, for he is our own son."[29] Everyone knew that Indiana, with its fifteen electoral votes, would be crucial in the presidential election, so many assumed that Hendricks might win the nomination just for being an Indianan.

After a smattering of additional nominations of regional candidates, Daniel Dougherty of Pennsylvania rose to speak not on behalf of his state but for himself. Dougherty told the delegates that he wanted them to consider a candidate "who on the field of battle was styled 'the superb.'" Winfield Scott Hancock's nomination would "thrill the land from end to end, crush the last embers of sectional strife and be hailed as the dawning of the long-for day of perpetual brotherhood. . . . If elected he will take his seat." The last statement was a clear reference to 1876, when Tilden won the popular vote but was denied the presidency.

Senator Wade Hampton of South Carolina, a former Confederate general, responded to the cheering for Hancock by telling the convention that the South preferred Bayard simply because he was the strongest man. But he also stated that Southerners "would be safe in his [Hancock's] hands, because we were safe when he had the power." This referred to Hancock's brief but eventful tenure in New Orleans as head of the Fifth Military District.[30]

The convention soon proceeded to the first ballot. Hancock led with 171 votes, but Bayard was close behind at 158½. There were a total of 738 votes up for grabs, and Democratic Party rules required a two-thirds majority—or 492 votes—to win the nomination. The *New York Times* wrote the next morning, "Hancock heads the first and only ballot taken by the Cincinnati convention yesterday, and yet Hancock is about the last man that body is likely to nominate." Notably, the *Times* had also been sure that Grant would be the Republican nominee.[31]

When the convention reconvened on the morning of June 24, Rufus W. Peckham of New York (a future Supreme Court justice) informed the convention of Tilden's letter, which the New York delegation interpreted as a refusal to accept the nomination. Peckham then told the audience that, with Tilden out of the running, New York was giving its second-ballot votes to Samuel J. Randall of Pennsylvania, Speaker of the US House of Representatives. As the roll call of states continued, Bayard's total dropped to 112, while Randall garnered a surprising 128½ votes. Wisconsin voted as a unit for Hancock, and New Jersey immediately did the same. Several other large states then threw their votes to Hancock, and when the roll call ended, Hancock had 705 votes. As historian Herbert J. Clancy writes, "Another 'man on horseback' had captured an American political convention." Recognizing that Indiana would be a critical state, the convention then nominated former congressman William H. English of that state for the vice presidency.[32]

Bayard's most ardent supporters were crushed. They had believed that, with Tilden out of the race, the nomination was theirs for the taking. But as one Bayard supporter put it, the convention had rushed to Hancock as "a wild hurrah, and the men flocked like sheep toward the bell-wether after the first stampede."[33]

Tilden continued to tell anyone who would listen that he could have been nominated but had no desire to embark on "five years of hard, exhausting labor," referring to the campaign and the four-year presidential term. Tilden also believed that had his letter been read aloud to the full convention, the stampede that ended up selecting Hancock would have gone for him instead.

Despite the Democrats' enthusiasm for their candidate, the *New York Times* was not impressed. "Does anybody know what General Hancock thinks about the principles of finance, about the tariff, civil service reform, interstate commerce or free ships?" The *Times* was providing a glimpse into the Republican strategy to defeat Hancock: pointing out his lack of political knowledge and his inexperience as an officeholder. Hancock attempted to counter that criticism by stating that he would simply be guided by the Democratic Party's platform. But the platform was not even chosen until after Hancock and English were selected, so it was really something of an afterthought.

Frankly, the Democrats' platform was not much different from the platform approved just two weeks earlier by the Republicans. The Democrats pledged to remain true to "the constitutional doctrines and tradition of the Democratic party," to subordinate military to civil power, and to restrict Chinese immigration. The third plank called for "home rule; honest money, consisting of gold and silver, and paper convertible into coin on demand; the strict maintenance of the public faith, State and National, and a tariff for revenue only." The desire for "home rule" was not-so-subtle code for Democratic white supremacy. The "tariff for revenue only" statement would cause difficulty during the campaign as the Republicans accused the Democrats of being unwilling to economically protect American industries and workers. And the Democrats could not resist taking one more shot at

The 1880 Democratic ticket: Winfield Scott Hancock of Pennsylvania for president and William H. English of Indiana for vice president. (Courtesy of Library of Congress)

the 1876 election debacle, noting that Tilden had chosen not to run again "for the exalted place to which he was elected by a majority of his countrymen." In fact, three of the platform's fourteen planks attacked the Republican Party for the outcome of the 1876 contest.[34]

To many observers, the two parties did not look much different in 1880. However, they and their presidential candidates offered very different visions for the country. As the Democratic convention closed and the general election campaign began, some Republicans feared their two-decade hold on the presidency was in jeopardy. Even the Republican *New York Times* predicted that Hancock would win the presidency with at least eighteen electoral votes to spare.[35]

6

"INDEFATIGABLE AGITATORS"
THIRD-PARTY CANDIDATES IN THE 1880 ELECTION

Nearly everyone expected either James Garfield or Winfield Scott Hancock to move into the White House in March 1881. The Republican and Democratic Parties were both well established and had large national organizations ready to campaign for their respective candidates. However, Garfield and Hancock were not the only men seeking the presidency in 1880. Those unaffiliated with or uninspired by the two main candidates and their parties had other options. Many voters who felt strongly about a particular issue, such as soft money or temperance, supported candidates who focused specifically on that issue. Although none of these candidates made much headway in the national presidential race, their candidacies and the issues for which they advocated deserve at least a brief examination.

The Greenback Party, formed in 1874, was the most significant third-party movement participating in the 1880 election. Its members advocated the continued use of the paper currency issued during the Civil War, called "greenbacks" due to the green ink used to print it. For the most part, the Republican and Democratic Parties both favored a hard-money system backed by gold. The use of inflationary paper money had been a necessity when the federal government was financing the war at a cost of several million dollars per day. Shortly after the war ended, though, most national figures from both major parties favored a return to hard currency as soon as possible.

The federal government had basically suspended the gold standard in the early days of the Civil War, issuing paper currency backed by the good credit of the federal government rather than gold. Three separate issues of greenbacks took place during the war, and nearly $500 million worth of greenbacks was in circulation by the time the Confederacy surrendered in 1865. The greenbacks had the desired effect of helping the federal government fund the war effort, but when the war ended, the greenbacks' value declined. Bankers and other business leaders began to demand that the government return to the gold standard in order to increase the value of the money they held and had received for the payment of debts. The Contraction Act of 1866 began the process of withdrawing greenbacks from circulation in order to reinstate the gold standard. Greenbacks worth nearly $50 million were pulled from circulation over the next two years.

But not everyone agreed that the United States should wholly return to the gold standard. Men with both wealth and political influence liked the gold standard because it made their money more valuable. Others saw benefits to having a currency with a lower value that increased their buying power. A weaker paper currency gave farmers, small business owners, trade union members, and poor people more power to pay down their debts, and it made the creation of business monopolies more difficult. The Panic of 1873 and the ensuing economic depression convinced many that a return to the large-scale issuance of inflationary paper money was necessary, but President Grant vetoed a bill in April 1874 that would have flooded the market with more than $40 million in greenbacks and raised the permissible amount of currency in circulation unbacked by gold to $400 million.

A lame-duck Republican Congress passed the Specie Resumption Act in January 1875. This law restored the United States to the gold standard by giving the government four years to accumulate gold reserves; it would then redeem greenbacks with that gold beginning January 1, 1879. This was a deflationary rather than inflationary move, which angered farmers and others who favored greenbacks. Republicans, including James Garfield, were by and large in favor of specie resumption. The Democratic Party was still viewed by many as the party of secession and white supremacy, so few who favored inflationary currency considered becoming Democrats. Therefore, the time was ripe for the creation of a new party to emphasize currency reform, and in 1874 a small group of Indiana farmers and activists created what they originally called the Independent Party. A larger meeting was held in Indianapolis that November to formalize the creation of the Greenback Party, which ran its first presidential candidate—Peter Cooper of New York—in 1876. Cooper won just 84,000 popular votes and no electoral votes. Nearly all the Greenback Party's support that year came from farmers.

Between the 1876 and 1880 elections, the Greenback Party continued to grow in popularity among farmers, and it had some success in local elections in certain parts of the country. During these years, Greenbackers contributed to the election of twenty-one members of Congress who were not Republicans or Democrats. The *Chicago Weekly Tribune* wrote that the Greenback Party offered "an opportunity to accomplish something . . . not just for the farmers merely, but for all who live by their industry, as distinguished from those who live by politics, speculations, and class-legislation." The Greenbackers entered the 1880 election cycle determined to have a greater impact on the presidential and state elections than they had managed in 1876.

Like the Republicans, the Greenbackers held their 1880 presidential nominating convention in Chicago. In fact, the Greenback convention began in Exposition Hall on June 9, just one day after the Republicans nominated Garfield and concluded their own convention in the same building. Many assumed that Benjamin Butler of Massachusetts would be that year's Greenback nominee. Butler, a prewar Democrat, had been labeled the "Beast" by Southerners during his controversial Union army service, which included administering occupied New Orleans. He later became a Republican but grew disaffected with that party as well, especially after he received lackluster Republican support for his unsuccessful gubernatorial bid in 1879. Butler had also run for the Massachusetts governorship as an independent in 1878 and had drawn some support from Greenbackers. So Butler was not an unknown quantity among Greenback Party members heading into the 1880 presidential race. However, it soon came to light that Butler was planning to jump ship back to the Democratic Party and was hoping to convince Greenbackers to vote Democratic after he switched.

The temporary chairman of the Greenback convention, Gilbert De La Matyr, informed Butler that the convention was leaning toward him, but the Greenbackers needed to know that Butler would accept the nomination if offered. De La Matyr and other Greenbackers worried that Butler was going to try to convince the Democratic Party to nominate him at its upcoming convention in Cincinnati. When Butler failed to reassure the Greenbackers to their satisfaction, they went in search of another candidate.

Another former Union general soon attracted Greenback attention: James Baird Weaver of Iowa. Weaver was born in Ohio in 1833, but his family moved first to Michigan and then to Iowa. Weaver became a lawyer, and although he was raised in a Democratic family, he opposed slavery and became a Republican. He attended the 1860 Republican convention that nominated Abraham Lincoln for president. Weaver joined the Union army soon after the Civil War began and fought under future president Ulysses S. Grant at Fort Donelson in early 1862. Weaver later saw action at Shiloh, Corinth, and Resaca and on Sherman's famous March to the Sea. When his enlistment expired in May 1864, he returned to his young family in Iowa. He later received a promotion to brevet brigadier general, dated from March 1865.

Weaver returned to Republican politics after the war. He became the editor of a Republican newspaper, the *Weekly Union Guard*, and served as district attorney and federal assessor of internal revenue. He was considered a possible congressional candidate in 1874, but many Republicans were leery of his association with the prohibition movement. Weaver then focused on becoming Iowa's governor in 1875, endorsing temperance but also the stricter regulation of railroads. Weaver lost the gubernatorial nomination to Samuel Kirkwood, a former Iowa governor and a future secretary of the interior.

Weaver soon grew disillusioned with the Republicans because of both his electoral failures and policy differences over currency and a host of social issues. He traveled to Indianapolis in May 1876 to attend the convention that formalized the Greenback Party. In addition to support for paper currency, members of the new party advocated for an eight-hour workday, women's suffrage, factory safety regulations, and an end to child labor. In 1878 Weaver won election to the US House of Representatives as a Greenbacker. When he entered the House in early 1879 to represent Iowa's Sixth Congressional District, he was one of thirteen Greenback Party members in the House. By 1880, Weaver was one of the nation's best-known Greenbackers.

When Benjamin Butler failed to alleviate Greenbackers' fears that he might accept their nomination and then bolt for the Democratic Party, the Greenbackers turned their attention to Weaver. The convention opened on June 9, and presidential nominations began at about 1:00 a.m. on June 11. Five hours later, the Greenback Party announced its ticket: James B. Weaver

Civil War veteran James B. Weaver of Iowa was the Greenback Party's candidate for president in 1880. (Courtesy of Library of Congress)

for president and Barzillai J. Chambers of Texas for vice president. The platform called for all money to be issued by the federal government (rather than by individual banks, which was still common at the time), unlimited coinage of silver, repayment of the national debt in bonds rather than gold, a graduated income tax, an end to child labor, improved working conditions and safety regulations in factories, regulation of interstate commerce, and a vague commitment to "denounce as dangerous, the efforts everywhere manifest to restrict the right of suffrage." The western faction of the party insisted on and eventually got a plank opposing Chinese immigration. The convention adjourned at about 6:45 a.m. on June 11. Despite the anti-Chinese immigration plank, the Greenback platform was by far the most progressive of the 1880 race. As one historian notes, this platform "anticipated by almost fifty years the progressive legislation of the first quarter of the twentieth century.... Weaver's efforts in behalf of economic and industrial reform entitle him to a place in history next in importance to William Jennings Bryan and Theodore Roosevelt."[1] This praise is a bit overblown, but the progressive nature of the Greenback platform—and Weaver's efforts to advance many of the items on it—is noteworthy.

Weaver issued the expected letter of acceptance from his Bloomfield, Iowa, home on July 3. He lauded the Greenback platform as "comprehensive, reasonable, and progressive—containing those elements of economic reform essential to the preservation of the liberty and the prosperity of the whole people." He lamented that economic conditions created by both Republicans and Democrats were "fast swallowing up the profits of labor, and reducing the people to a condition of vassalage and dependence." The greatest challenge facing America, Weaver wrote, was "to bring the producer and consumer together." He discounted the "deplorable spirit of sectional hatred" that, in his mind, both parties had perpetuated for political gain since the end of the Civil War. Finally, he called for "a free ballot, a fair count, and equal rights for all classes" and insisted that Americans seek to reestablish "the old time Democracy of Jefferson and Jackson, and the pure Republicanism of Abraham Lincoln, and Thaddeus Stevens." Until those conditions were met—which seemed unlikely to happen anytime soon—Weaver offered himself and the Greenbackers as an alternative to the two major parties.[2]

In an era in which parties did most of the work of national campaigns and candidates were expected to stay home and say nothing of consequence, the Greenback Party was unique. It expected its candidates to travel and campaign for themselves, and Weaver noted in his letter of acceptance that he planned to do so. His running mate, Chambers of Texas, also intended to travel and speak, but he was injured in a fall from a train in July and was sidelined for the rest of the campaign. Chambers was the only Southerner on any party's presidential ticket in 1880, and the Greenbackers hoped his presence would help them win votes in the South.

Weaver and the Greenback candidates running in local and state elections traveled to various parts of the country to speak and meet with the public. Weaver was fairly active in the South, but his economic message received much less attention there than his plea for racial equality. Most white Southerners were not at all interested in that aspect of the Greenback program, even if they agreed with Weaver on economic policies. Weaver campaigned in the North as well, where he refused several overtures to run on a fusion ticket with Democrats. Had he done so, the Greenback-Democrat ticket may well have defeated Republicans in some Northern states.

Press coverage of the Greenback campaign was spotty, and when major newspapers did pay attention, it was often to criticize or mock Weaver. For example, on the day after the Greenback convention ended, the *New York Times* called it "fitting that this assemblage of lunatics should nominate for President that indefatigable agitator and inflationist" Weaver. The *Times* then misrepresented Weaver's soft-money position as "a return to the primitive system of money under which anything is money which men agree to call by that name."[3]

No one expected Weaver to win the presidency, but both he and his party expected him to do much better in the general election than he did. On Election Day, Weaver garnered 309,000 popular votes (about 3 percent of the national popular vote) but won no votes in the Electoral College. The Greenback Party did best in the South and West. Its highest percentage of the popular vote came in Texas, the home state of Weaver's injured running mate, where Weaver won about 12 percent of the vote. Given the closeness of the 1880 election, even a fraction of those 309,000 popular votes could have swung the election in a different direction for the Republicans and Democrats. Weaver and Chambers increased the Greenback Party's vote total of 84,000 in the 1876 election, but ultimately, the 1880 Greenback campaign was a disappointment.[4]

The Prohibition Party held a nominating convention in Cleveland, Ohio, just a few days after the Greenbackers nominated Weaver in Chicago. Only twelve states sent delegates to that meeting, and the party's platform said little about any of the country's major issues, focusing on banning the sale and consumption of alcohol in the United States.

The Prohibitionists nominated Neal Dow of Maine as their presidential candidate and Ohio's Henry Adams Thompson as their vice-presidential candidate. Dow was a longtime temperance advocate and the former mayor of Portland. While serving in that office in the early 1850s, Dow succeeded in pushing the Maine legislature to ban alcohol in the state, an action that came to be known nationwide as the "Maine law." He vigorously enforced the law in Portland, even ordering the state militia to fire into a crowd of citizens protesting the measure. Dow served the Union cause during the Civil War, enduring both a wound and capture by the Confederates during the siege of Port Hudson in 1863. After being exchanged in 1864, General Dow returned to Maine to work on behalf of the prohibition cause.

Dow did not attend the Cleveland convention and did not participate in the campaign in any meaningful way. He appeared to pay little attention at all to the presidential election. He remained in Maine to care for his ailing wife and put all his energies into trying to get local Prohibition Party candidates elected. On Election Day, Dow and Thompson tallied just over 10,000 votes nationally, less than 1 percent of the ballots cast. Dow was pleased when the Republican Garfield won the election over the "ex-slavedriving rebel element" of the Democratic Party.[5] The prohibition movement continued, resulting nearly four decades later in the Eighteenth Amendment prohibiting the manufacture, sale, and transportation of alcohol.

The last fringe party to nominate a presidential candidate in 1880 was the American Anti-Mason Party, a descendant of the old Anti-Masonic and American Know-Nothing Parties. Like the Prohibitionists, the Anti-Masons were viewed as mostly a one-issue party, even though their platform was more socially progressive and detailed than that of the Prohibitionists. The Anti-Masons' main concern was to "expose, withstand, and remove secret societies, Freemasonry in particular, and other anti-Christian movements, in order to save the churches of Christ from being depraved" and to "redeem the administration of justice from perversion, and our republican government from corruption." The Anti-Masons nominated John W. Phelps of Vermont for president and Samuel C. Pomeroy of Kansas for vice president.

Like Garfield, Hancock, Weaver, and Dow, Phelps had been a Union general during the Civil War. Before that, Phelps had served twenty-three years in the prewar army, seeing action in the Mexican-American War, against American Indians in Florida and on the western frontier, and against the Mormons in Utah. Phelps resigned from the army in 1859, only to return two years later when the Civil War began. He participated in the battles leading to the Union capture of New Orleans in early 1862 but ran afoul of higher-ranking officers (including Benjamin Butler) for his ardent and vocal abolitionism. Butler labeled Phelps "mad as a March Hen on the 'nigger question'" when Phelps organized escaped slaves into companies and asked that they be armed so they could fight against the Confederacy. For these efforts, Confederate president Jefferson Davis labeled Phelps an "outlaw."[6]

None of this did Phelps or the Anti-Mason Party any good in 1880. Phelps and Pomeroy ran on a platform that included banning alcohol, prohibiting secret societies and lodges, granting fair and just treatment to American Indians, requiring all educational institutions to use the Bible as a text, and abolishing the Electoral College. Phelps and Pomeroy garnered just over 1,000 votes in the national election, making them a nonfactor in the final outcome.

Ultimately, none of the parties or candidates examined in this chapter had any legitimate hope of winning the presidency in 1880, although the Greenbackers might have influenced the outcome if some of them had cast their ballots for Garfield or Hancock instead of Weaver. In some cases, these third parties focused on issues that deserved more attention than the Republicans or Democrats gave them, and some of them would finally be addressed decades later. Still, the 1880 presidential election boiled down to a choice between the Republican Garfield and the Democrat Hancock.

7

"THOSE GREAT QUESTIONS OF NATIONAL WELL-BEING" THE 1880 PRESIDENTIAL CAMPAIGN

On June 9, the day after he received his party's presidential nomination, James A. Garfield awoke in his hotel room to a flood of callers, telegrams, requests for statements, and those seeking meetings with him. Garfield had lived in the public eye for nearly two decades, but over the next five months, the level of activity around him and the scrutiny of his past and present would astound both the candidate and his family. His wife, Lucretia, and their five children had sent him off to Chicago with little inkling that he would return as a candidate for president. Garfield, a dedicated diarist for most of his adult life, made no entries in his diary for nearly two months that summer as he adjusted to his new role.

Republican newspapers touted Garfield as an excellent choice to be the party's standard-bearer. "He is one of the ablest men in the country," wrote the *Boston Herald,* "and he represents the liberal and progressive wing of the party." Noting the contentiousness of the convention, the *Chicago Tribune* called Garfield "a balm for all the wounds received in the six days of strife."[1] Democratic papers attacked him just as quickly, resurrecting Garfield's involvement in two scandals from the early 1870s: Credit Mobilier and DeGolyer Pavement. Garfield had been cleared of any wrongdoing in both.

Thousands jammed the train depot in Chicago as Garfield left that city to travel home to Ohio, and the candidate found "a triumphal caravan" along the way. People lined the tracks waving flags, and they cheered for Garfield at well over a dozen stops across Indiana and Ohio. Booming cannons, loud brass bands, and cheering throngs of people greeted him everywhere he went. In Toledo, Ohio, a hundred cannons boomed from a Maumee River bluff, and Governor Charles Foster addressed the crowd: "The great Senator [Conkling] a few days ago said that nothing but an act of God would prevent the nomination of General Grant. The act of God has come, and General Garfield has become your candidate."[2] Thousands of his fellow citizens greeted Garfield when his train finally pulled into Cleveland. On the trip from Cleveland to his farm in Mentor, the hometown hero was treated to trumpet music, more cannon blasts, and even rose petals.[3]

Once he was home, Garfield faced a dilemma. He was renowned as one of the Republican Party's best orators, yet presidential candidates were not expected to campaign for themselves. Doing so was considered beneath the nation's highest office, and the few who had tried it—including Stephen Douglas in 1860 and Horace Greeley in 1872—had been resoundingly defeated. In the Garfield-Hancock race of 1880, the national Republican and Democratic Parties were expected to do the heavy lifting of campaigning, not the candidates themselves. The sitting president, Rutherford B. Hayes, told Garfield to "sit crosslegged and look wise" for the duration of the campaign and write *"no letters to strangers, or to anybody else on politics."*[4] Whitelaw Reid, publisher of the *New York Tribune*, advised Garfield to "not make promises to anybody," and "don't make any journeys or any speeches."[5] For the moment, Garfield agreed to follow this frustrating convention and turn his electoral fate over to his party. He would stay home and say nothing.

"Home" was a farm of nearly 160 acres in the village of Mentor, located on Lake Erie about thirty miles east of Cleveland. James and Lucretia Garfield had taken out a $17,500 mortgage (about $440,000 today) in 1876 to purchase the farm, which included a nine-room house. They had since enlarged the house to fit their family of five children plus Garfield's mother, Eliza. Doing much of the labor himself, Garfield had cleaned up the property and planted oats and barley. Like many Americans of that era, Garfield—harking back to the Jeffersonian ideal of an agrarian nation of small, independent farmers—revered the farmer as the most virtuous of citizens. Garfield seemed to genuinely enjoy manual labor as a respite from the intellectual and political work of serving in Congress. In fact, one of the things that had most appealed to him about the Mentor property was the presence of farmland. "I must find a place to teach my boys to do farm work," he told his diary.[6] The Mentor property was also safely en-

An idyllic representation of James Garfield's Mentor, Ohio, farm and home during the 1880 presidential campaign. (Courtesy of Library of Congress)

sconced within the Nineteenth Congressional District. His original home in Hiram, Ohio, had been drawn out of his district by the gerrymandering Democrats in 1872.

As the home of their party's candidate, the Mentor farm would become a focal point for Republicans during the campaign. Even as they encouraged Garfield to do and say nothing, important members of the party made plans to visit him there. This posed a bit of a problem, as the Garfields did little formal entertaining in Mentor, and all their nicest furniture and china were in their home in Washington, DC. In addition, the Mentor house was still undergoing renovations and improvements that had begun long before the convention in Chicago. On a quick trip to Washington in mid-June to collect some of his papers, Garfield also carried out instructions from his wife to ship some items back to Mentor for use during the busy presidential campaign: dessert plates, a coffee urn, two tables, chairs, and some of her clothes, among other things. "The events of the past week grow to seem more and more unreal," she wrote. "But I suppose I shall grow accustomed to it all after a while. I ought to be now, for I have had to travel fast and think faster ever since I have known you, to keep even within seeing distance."[7]

Because he had actually gone there to nominate someone else, James Garfield was the first presidential candidate to attend the convention that nominated him. Just as candidates were expected to do no campaigning, prospective nominees were expected to stay away from party nominating conventions. Therefore, Winfield Scott Hancock was nowhere near Cincinnati when he received the Democratic nomination on June 24. He was at home on Governor's Island, and as word of his nomination reached New York, well-wishers crowded the house. One Associated Press reporter made his way to Governor's Island and found Hancock on the veranda. When he congratulated the general, the two shook hands but Hancock told him, "I have nothing to say at present, as I have not been officially notified of my nomination. You know, it might all be a mistake."[8]

Most Democrats—and even many Republicans—agreed that Hancock was the best choice the Democrats could have made. When a reporter tracked down William Tecumseh Sherman—the brother of John Sherman, the man Garfield had nominated for president—the general naturally refrained from getting involved in politics. "But if you sit down and write the best thing that can be put in language about General Hancock as an officer and a gentleman," Sherman added, "I will sign it without hesitation."[9] Accolades for Hancock came from former battlefield adversaries as well. "Your nomination makes me much gladder than you," wrote former Confederate general and sitting Virginia congressman Joseph E. Johnston.[10]

Just as Garfield immediately took fire from Democratic newspapers, Hancock endured the same from the Republican press. "[Hancock] was a good soldier," reported the *Philadelphia Press,* "but there his title begins and ends." The *St. Louis Globe Democrat* agreed, noting that Hancock's selection "no more changes the character of the Democracy than a figurehead of the Virgin on Kidd's pirate craft would change it into an honest ship." A few weeks later, *Harper's Weekly* added that while Hancock was an accomplished soldier, "he represents . . . no policy, no principle, no issue, nothing but the party which has nominated him."[11]

Internally, though, as least some Republicans acknowledged that Hancock's long and distinguished military career, and especially his service during the Civil War, would be troublesome. Garfield was a Union veteran too, of course, but his military record could not compare to Hancock's. In-

THE BIRD TO BET ON!

Winfield Scott Hancock was the "Bird to Bet On," according to this 1880 cartoon. (Courtesy of Library of Congress)

deed, the 1880 election would be the first and only presidential contest in which both candidates had fought for the Union. Carl Schurz, the sitting secretary of the interior and a Liberal Republican bolter of 1872, worried that Hancock's nomination all but removed the Southern issue from the Republicans' playbook for 1880.[12] The "Southern issue"—reconstructing the South and ensuring the physical safety and civil rights of freed black men and women—had been the Republicans' bread and butter since the end of the Civil War. Despite the widely held but incorrect assumption that Reconstruction had ended during the Hayes administration, Republicans still eagerly waved the bloody shirt in political campaigns against Democrats. They intended to do so again in the presidential contest of 1880, but the presence of a bona fide Union war hero at the top of the Democratic ticket made it difficult to label all Democrats traitors.

Like the Garfields in Ohio, the Hancocks prepared to host many visitors at their Governor's Island home over the next five months. Reporters, army comrades, and prominent Democrats all rode the steamer out to the island to meet with Hancock. On July 12 William H. English, the vice-presidential nominee, made his first sojourn to Governor's Island to meet General Hancock. Throughout this meeting, unbeknownst to most of the visitors, Hancock's grandson and namesake, Winfield Scott Hancock II, lay deathly ill inside the home. The four-month-old child of the Hancocks' son Russell and his wife died early the next day. Just hours after the child's death, the Democratic Party's official notification committee arrived to formally inform Hancock of his nomination at the Cincinnati convention.

Like Garfield, Hancock was expected to be a spectator to his own campaign. He took this to the extreme when the Democratic National Committee met to elect a chairman. Hancock supported Senator William Wallace of Pennsylvania but refused to say so publicly, and Wallace lost to William H. Barnum of Connecticut. Because Hancock was still the military commander of the Department of the Atlantic, he continued to fulfill those duties as well. He tried in vain to limit his availability to the throngs of well-wishers and those seeking positions in his administration to three hours per day three days per week. When an army friend visited, he asked Hancock, "General, how do you find this thing?" Hancock replied:

> Don't find it at all. There is nothing congenial about this thing. These miserable devils worry me to death. They come here from all parts of the country, even from Arkansas and Texas, to tell me how many votes they can command. Worst of all, they want to exact pledges that I will give them offices for their services. Did you ever see such a hungry crowd? Hungry, hungry, hungry. . . . They take me in the front and rear. They outflank me and, worst of all, they cut off my retreat . . . the locusts of old are as nothing to them."[13]

During Garfield's trip to Washington in mid-June, he had dinner with President and Mrs. Hayes and, for the first time since the drama of the Chicago convention, met with John Sherman. The treasury secretary offered his congratulations and support for Garfield's campaign. The following night, Wednesday, June 16, the National Veterans Club threw a huge outdoor party for Garfield that brought 10,000 people into the streets for speeches and music—including "Hail to the Chief." The next evening, the Army of the Cumberland Society hosted a banquet for the candidate. There, Garfield sat and laughed with General William Tecumseh Sherman.[14]

The first real sign of the trouble with Senator Roscoe Conkling that would plague Garfield for the next year also surfaced during this trip. Garfield came home one evening to find that Conkling had called while he was out. Garfield immediately sent a note to Conkling offering to meet with him any time: "I wish to see you away from the crowd of callers," Garfield wrote. But the senator never responded. He had apparently thrown a tantrum after he saw the nominee sharing a carriage near the White House with Carl Schurz, one of Conkling's bitterest enemies from the "reform" wing of the Republican Party. Conkling interpreted this as a purposeful snub by Garfield. As one historian notes, "Conkling scornfully declined to answer [Garfield], snorting . . . at the thought of holding commerce with a man who would be seen publicly with Schurz; the breach [between Garfield and Conkling] widened."[15]

Like Hancock's, Garfield's party soon held an election for a new national committee chairman. Hancock had stood idly by and let the chips fall where they may. Garfield, a seasoned and skilled politician, took an active (if behind-the-scenes) role in choosing the next head of the Republican Party. The Republican National Committee met in New York City on July 2 to pick its new leadership, and Governor Charles Foster of Ohio attended to represent Garfield's interests. Foster carried with him a list of Garfield's top four choices for the chairmanship: William Chandler of New Hampshire; Eugene Hale of Maine; Richard McCormick, a New Yorker who had served as territorial governor of the Arizona Territory; and Marshall Jewell of Connecticut. Roscoe Conkling and John Logan were there to push their Stalwart choice, Thomas Platt of New York. The committee, desperate to avoid another public squabble after the wrangling at the Chicago convention, assigned the job of finding the next party chairman to a committee of three: William Chandler, representing the Blaine (or Half-Breed) faction; John Logan, a Stalwart; and John Forbes of Massachusetts, who was unaligned with either faction.

Forbes quickly and correctly pointed out that of those on Garfield's list, only Jewell—a former governor of Connecticut and US postmaster general—had actually expressed any interest in the job, and even his willingness to take on the task was lukewarm at best. When Forbes suggested giving the position to Jewell, Logan cried foul because Jewell had been "disloyal" to Grant in Chicago. Logan pushed for Platt, but Forbes and Chandler refused, despite Logan's screaming at them. Forbes then offered a compromise: if the Stalwarts could stomach Jewell as chairman, they could pick the committee's secretary. Logan immediately agreed and selected Stephen W. Dorsey, a Vermont native who had represented Arkansas in the US Senate in the 1870s. Dorsey had fought alongside both Grant and Garfield in the Civil War but was also an acolyte of Conkling and Logan during his time in the Senate. When someone told Forbes that Dorsey had a reputation for selling his vote to the highest bidder, Forbes tried to reverse the selection of Dorsey, but it was too late.[16]

Dorsey was thrilled and threw himself into the job. "I have sense enough to know that if I want anything," such as a future office, "the way to get it is to show myself entitled to it by the management of the canvass." Dorsey did so much work on the campaign that at one point an exasperated Jewell threw his hands up and said, "Dorsey's running it himself, I guess, or all creation's running it, I don't know which." One point on which Dorsey was adamant was that Garfield and Conkling had to meet face-to-face to iron out their differences. Dorsey visited Garfield's home in Ohio in July and suggested a meeting with Conkling in New York.[17]

As much as Garfield hated the idea of catering to Conkling, he knew he needed the support of the Stalwart wing of the party to win the election. As he prepared to write his formal letter accepting the nomination, Garfield consulted party leaders about which issues he should focus on and how best to handle them so as to appeal to the largest number of Republicans and undecided voters. The answers were clear: Chinese immigration and civil service reform. Few suggested that Garfield needed to take a strong stand—or any stand at all—on civil rights issues in the South. Chinese immigration was a huge issue in the western states, where deep bias against Chinese workers ran rampant. Any candidate seeking the White House would have to address that problem if he hoped to win states like California. Garfield had once criticized his friend James Blaine for opposing Chinese immigration to make himself a more attractive presidential candidate. Now Garfield was in the uncomfortable position of doing the same thing.

Civil service reform was on the minds of many Republicans in the summer of 1880. Some historians examining this period in Republican history have tried to demonstrate that civil service reform was a wedge between the Blaine (Half-Breed) and Conkling (Stalwart) factions of the party, but

This Puck cartoon speaks to both major parties' opposition to unlimited Chinese immigration during the 1880 campaign. (Courtesy of Library of Congress)

this is not the case. In fact, the primary issue between those two factions was the prospect of a third term for Ulysses S. Grant: the Blaine faction opposed it, while the Conkling faction supported it. By that rationale, the two sides should have come together after Garfield's selection as the presidential nominee. But the personal hatred between Blaine and Conkling was too deep and had endured for too long to make this possible.

Garfield was friendly with Blaine, he had opposed a third term for Grant, and he had been instrumental in defeating the unit rule at the national convention, but he was not particularly zealous about civil service reform. President Hayes had pushed for civil service reform but had run into a brick wall in the Senate in the form of Conkling. Members of the reform, or "independent," wing of the Republican Party made support for a new civil service system a touchstone for their support in the 1880 election. Although Blaine derided them as "noisy but not numerous, pharisaical but not practical, ambitious but not wise, pretentious but not powerful," they considered Garfield one of their own. Historian Allan Peskin notes that Garfield "had never been wedded to Hayes's particular brand of civil service reform," but he understood that he needed the support of all factions of the party to stand a chance of winning the election. As William Chandler advised the nominee, it was necessary "to stoop a little to conquer much," so Garfield set out to draft a letter of acceptance that would be sufficiently vague to satisfy all party elements.[18]

The other consideration on Garfield's mind was the electoral math. He needed 185 electoral votes to win the presidency—the exact number Hayes had won four year previously. But after the disputed election, Hayes had ultimately won the electoral votes of three Southern states—South Carolina, Florida, and Louisiana—that Garfield expected to lose. The Republicans therefore understood that they needed to pick up a few Northern states that had voted for Tilden in 1876. Of the states that had gone Democratic in 1876, Connecticut (six electoral votes), Indiana (fifteen votes), and New York (thirty-five votes) were the most likely to go Republican in 1880. While a better-known candidate could have entered this race with some degree of confidence, Garfield, a compromise nominee (albeit one with an increased reputation and better name recognition after the 1879 appropriations crisis), had to rely on his party. In other words, "Unless he had the active cooperation of the leaders he had just humiliated in Chicago, he was a beaten man."[19] And alienating any wing of the party in his acceptance letter was no way to begin what already appeared to be an uphill climb to victory.

Ohio Republican George Baker advised Garfield to "not make any statement to irritate the Democracy; [you] must not do any political talking." He also sketched out the electoral situation as he understood it. Baker predicted a solid South of fifteen states—including the four Civil War border states of Kentucky, Maryland, Missouri, and Delaware—totaling 138 electoral votes in Hancock's column. He also named fifteen Northern and western states, totaling 154 electoral votes, that he was certain Garfield would win. The other seven states—California, Connecticut, Indiana, New Jersey, New York, Oregon, and Nevada—he listed as "doubtful." These states represented seventy-seven electoral votes, and Garfield needed at least thirty-one of them to win. Simply winning New York would do it, but picking up Indiana and Connecticut without New York would not be enough. If Hancock and the Democrats held New York—which had gone for its native son Tilden in 1876—they would need only twelve more electoral votes from Baker's seven "doubtful" states to win the White House. New York would be the top prize in the 1880 presidential election.[20]

On Governor's Island, the Hancocks were simultaneously grieving the death of their grandson and adjusting to life after the general's nomination—both difficult tasks in and of themselves. Like Lucretia Garfield in Ohio, Almira Hancock did not relish being the wife of a presidential contender. Lucretia Garfield was a longtime political wife who understood the rigors of a campaign but certainly had not given much thought to the idea of her husband receiving the Republican nomination until the convention itself. Almira Hancock, in contrast, understood that her husband had a realistic chance of receiving the Democratic nomination before the Cincinnati convention, but because he had never held office, she knew nothing of the demands of a campaign or her role in it. So the woman who knew all about campaigning was caught off guard by her husband's nomination, while the woman who expected her husband's nomination knew nothing about campaigning. "Our home was invaded from the beginning to the end," Almira Hancock noted. "All was turmoil, excitement and discomfort of every known kind."[21]

On the Republican side, Garfield had to bring together the Half-Breeds, the Stalwarts, and the independents to support his campaign. The Democrats also had factions in their party, and they needed a formula to bring peace among disaffected Tildenites, the still-powerful Tammany machine Democrats, and those who had favored other candidates, particularly Delaware's Bayard, at the Cincinnati convention. Many Democrats believed the campaign was off to a poor start with the election of William H. Barnum, a dedicated Tilden follower, as Democratic National Committee chairman. He had been chosen at least in part because the Democrats, like the Republicans, recognized the need to win New York. But many important party members saw Barnum's selection as basically handing over the campaign—and Hancock's presidency, if he won—to Tilden's organization.

This feeling only deepened when Hancock wrote to Tilden, seeking suggestions for his letter of acceptance, and then visited Tilden's home in New York City to ask for his advice. Hancock also reached out to Bayard, inviting the Delaware senator to Governor's Island for a meeting. During that meeting, Hancock shared with Bayard some of the hundreds of letters he had received since capturing the nomination, and of course, the majority of them were positive about his candidacy and his chances of winning the election. This unsolicited encouragement from citizens "caused Hancock fairly to exude confidence," in the words of one historian. "He was confident that all who desired a change—Republicans, soldiers, and the men of the new generation, of whom wished to see the war ended 'in discussion as well as in reality'—would settle the question in the coming election."[22] It fell to New York Democrats to secure the Empire State for Hancock.

Was Hancock simply overconfident? Or was he woefully ignorant of the hard work and effective organization it took to win a presidential campaign in a large and important state like New York? Republicans were hesitant to criticize Hancock personally because of his esteemed reputation as a soldier, but they did go after his lack of political knowledge and experience. At one point during the campaign, the Republicans published a pamphlet entitled *A Record of the Statesmanship and Political Achievements of Gen. Winfield Scott Hancock, Regular Democratic Nominee for President of the United States, Compiled from the Records*. It contained only blank pages.

James Garfield issued his letter of acceptance on July 12, 1880. Even then, the traditional letter of acceptance was an antiquated notion, but it allowed the candidate, his party, and the public to continue the pretense that "the office seeks the man," not the other way around. In fact, few times in American history has this cliché been truer than it was with Garfield in 1880. Garfield was no novice or innocent; he was well aware that his name had been on at least a few minds as a possible compromise candidate before the Chicago convention. But he honestly thought nothing would come of it, and despite what many angry Sherman supporters viewed as Garfield's treachery, he had gone to Chicago and done his duty for Sherman and the party and was genuinely surprised when the convention nominated him on the thirty-sixth ballot.

The letter of acceptance was one of the few exceptions to the unofficial "no campaigning" rule for presidential candidates. It allowed the nominee to at least partially set his own course and communicate directly with the voting public. In a normal campaign, it was perhaps the only time a candidate could "talk" directly to the electorate.

In his letter, Garfield nimbly addressed the two most sensitive subjects: Chinese immigration and civil service reform. He noted that the United States welcomed immigrants who were "willing to share the burdens as well as the benefits of our society," but the recent influx of Chinese workers (who were not eligible for citizenship) "is too much like an importation to be welcomed without restriction; too much like an invasion to be looked upon without solicitude. We cannot consent to any form of servile labor to be introduced among us, under the guise of immigration." He offered no solutions but said just enough to establish his anti-Chinese bona fides for western voters.

Garfield was equally vague on civil service reform, noting that "Congress should devise a method that will determine the tenure of office, and greatly reduce the uncertainty which makes that service so uncertain and unsatisfactory. Without depriving any officer of his rights as a citizen, the government should require him to discharge all his official duties with intelligence, efficiency and faithfulness." Again, he offered no real solutions to address the problems with the civil service and how officers were appointed. Suggesting any significant change would have risked alienating Conkling and his Stalwart allies—something Garfield could not afford to do, considering how badly he needed their help in New York. Despite New Yorker Chester Arthur's place on the ticket, Conkling and his closest confidants remained lukewarm about Garfield and continued to nurse bruised egos after losing the nomination fight in Chicago.

Garfield made other statements in his letter that were uncontroversial and reaffirmed his belief in the original principles of the Republican Party: support for public education, which he called "next in importance to freedom and justice . . . and without which neither justice nor freedom can be permanently maintained"; opposition to government aid for religious schools and belief in "the separation of the Church and the State in everything relating to taxation" (which many took as a thinly veiled reminder that Hancock's wife was Catholic); support for protective tariffs to allow

American manufacturers to compete with foreign producers; opposition to "doubtful financial experiments" such as the coinage of silver; and support for improved navigability of the Mississippi River, a nod to the old "internal improvement" projects of the Whigs, forerunners of the Republicans.

The longest paragraph of Garfield's letter, though, addressed post-Reconstruction conditions in the South. Despite Carl Schurz's assertion that the Democrats' nomination of a decorated Union veteran removed the Southern issue from the campaign, Garfield made his feelings known and provided a glimpse into how he might govern as president. He all but acknowledged that he expected a solid South for Hancock, noting that Republicans "reject the pernicious doctrine of State supremacy" that "brought the union very near to destruction." Again reinforcing his commitment to civil rights, Garfield wrote, "The wounds of the war cannot be completely healed, and the spirit of brotherhood cannot fully pervade the whole country, until every citizen, rich or poor, white or black, is secure in the free and equal enjoyment" of life and liberty as promised by the Declaration of Independence and the Constitution. Garfield looked to the future, insisting that "the best thoughts and energies of our people should be directed to those great questions of national well-being in which all have a common interest."[23]

By 1880, many Republicans had moved on from Reconstruction and the need to protect the civil rights of freedmen and -women in the South. When the Hayes administration took office and promised to return at least some local control, Southern whites moved quickly to reinstitute white supremacy in the former Confederate states. By putting his views about civil rights on the public record, Garfield certainly helped solidify the votes of black Americans, Civil War veterans, and older Republicans. But he also put Southerners on notice that he would enforce laws guaranteeing civil rights and equal protection under the law if elected.

Important issues that Garfield did not address included women's rights, widespread labor unrest, and the ongoing conflict against American Indians in the West. As historian Kenneth D. Ackerman notes, Garfield "tried to ruffle no feathers and make no mistakes."[24] Garfield concluded his letter: "If elected, it will be my purpose to enforce strict obedience to the constitution and the laws, and to promote, as best I may, the interest and honor of the whole country, relying for support upon the wisdom of Congress, the intelligence and patriotism of the people and the favor of God."

Many reform-minded Republicans were unhappy with Garfield's letter, feeling that it did not go far enough in addressing important issues—

especially civil service reform. Despite Garfield's opinion that it was better "to run the risk of being stupid than to risk awakening unnecessary controversies," reformers like Schurz and even President Hayes were less than pleased. In the pages of the *Nation*, E. L. Godkin wrote, "The unworthy phrases in which Mr. Garfield's ideas are concealed or his old-time professions recanted betray a want of backbone."[25]

None of them knew about Garfield's private letter to his friend Burke Hinsdale, written just two weeks later, in which he more clearly explained his take on the civil service. He proposed a fixed term of four years for "minor offices" and strict rules about grounds for removing appointees. "This plan," he wrote, "would bring all the reform sentiments of the country to bear upon Congress, and would sooner or later result in a law which would greatly narrow the field of uncertainty. . . . Again, it would be very dangerous . . . to repeal such a law and reintroduce the doctrine of spoils."[26] But he purposely left these details out of his acceptance letter in order to appeal to as many voters—Republicans and undecideds—as possible.

With Garfield's acceptance letter duly published and his fealty to the Republican platform and the Constitution established, the Republican campaign could begin. For the next several months, the tiny village of Mentor, Ohio, would be the center of the Republican universe.

Democrats also expected a letter of acceptance from their candidate. As a career military officer, Hancock had written or dictated thousands of orders, but he had rarely been called on to draft anything that would be so widely read—or could so greatly affect his own future. Even the public orders he had issued during his brief but consequential tenure in New Orleans as head of the Fifth Military District paled in comparison, in terms of both readership and importance, to his letter accepting the Democratic presidential nomination. Although the Democrats were at least superficially more united than the Republicans, Hancock still had to walk a fine line to please Tilden backers, Tammany Democrats, and disaffected Bayard supporters.

Like Garfield, Hancock kept his letter vague, in the hope of alienating no one. But Garfield's letter looked like a detailed policy brief compared to Hancock's. The Democrat's short letter, written on July 29, offered little but platitudes. After stating that the Reconstruction Amendments to the Constitution were "inviolable," he affirmed that, "if called to the Presidency I should deem it my duty to resist with all my power any attempt to impair or evade the full force and effect of the Constitution, which is . . . the supreme law of the land." In a thinly veiled criticism of the Fourteenth Amendment granting the franchise to black men, Reconstruction, and Haye's 1876 election, Hancock noted that "neither fraud nor force must be allowed to subvert the rights of the people. . . . The bayonet is not a fit instrument for collecting the votes of freemen." These statements criticizing the benchmarks of the post–Civil War movement toward equality for black men held great appeal to Southern white Democrats.

Hancock briefly mentioned civil service reform, but like Garfield, he offered no concrete suggestions or policies for actual reform. He reminded readers, "The war for the Union was successfully closed more than fifteen years ago" and, ignoring the actual conditions of black men and women in the South, claimed, "We are in a state of profound peace." The only statement that came close to being any kind of policy was the idea that Americans should "cultivate friendship and not . . . animosity among our fellow citizens."[27]

Simply put, there was not a lot of red meat for the voters in either candidate's letter, but Hancock's was surely the weaker of the two. It opened him up to one of the Republicans' major criticisms: despite his long and honorable military service, he knew nothing about the civilian administration of the federal government. The *New York Times,* for example, wrote just four days after Hancock's letter appeared that the Democratic nominee possessed "the mind of a school-boy, just capable of grasping the conventional generalities of our politics, but utterly devoid of insight and of practical ideas."[28]

Such criticism by a Republican newspaper was expected, but another attack took Hancock by surprise and deeply stung him. His old commander, former general and president Ulysses S. Grant—no fan of Garfield but a loyal Republican—gave an interview in which he incorrectly stated that Hancock had received a single vote for president at the 1864 Democratic convention, while the Civil War was still raging, and from that time forward, "Hancock had the bee [to be president] in his bonnet and shaped everything to gain Democratic and southern favor." In fact, Hancock had received no such vote at that convention. Grant also wrote Hancock off as "ambitious, vain, and weak." Grant recalled trying to work with Hancock before the latter took command of the Fifth Military District in New Orleans, but Hancock had simply repeated again and again, "Well, I'm opposed to nigger domination." Hancock, Grant concluded, "is crazy to be President." This assessment fit with the overall Republican strategy of portraying Hancock as a man long on ambition but short on policy ideas. Republican National

Committee chairman Marshall Jewell told Garfield, "Grant's utterances on Hancock are the most valuable contribution which has been made to the campaign."[29]

Democrats who wanted a more substantive letter of acceptance could read the one submitted by William H. English, Hancock's running mate. English had been out of politics for some time, but he was still more knowledgeable than Hancock. English went after the Republicans for the 1876 election dispute, calling Hayes's administration "procured by disreputable means and held in defiance of the wishes of a majority of the people." Besides, he opined, "twenty years of continuous power is long enough." English addressed Chinese immigration, pledging that he and Hancock would ensure that American citizens "will be protected from the destructive competition of the Chinese." On federal spending, he wrote, "The public credit will be scrupulously maintained and strengthened by rigid economy in public expenditure." The only way to cure the country's ongoing sectional ills was to rid itself of "pestiferous demagogues"—that is, Republicans—and elect the Democratic ticket, which would "make us in fact, as well as in name, one people. The only rivalry then would be in the race for the development of material prosperity, the elevation of labor, the enlargement of human rights, the promotion of education, morality, religion, liberty, order, and all that would tend to make us the foremost nation of the earth in the grand march of human progress."[30] English might have been a more forceful and effective campaigner than Hancock, but his aid to the campaign was limited. He was, after all, the vice-presidential nominee, not the man at the top of the ticket.

Chester A. Arthur, his Republican counterpart, wrote a relatively bland letter of acceptance that also touched on civil service reform. He agreed that "original appointments should be based upon ascertained fitness," and "the tenure of office should be stable." He added that "positions of responsibility should . . . be filled by the promotion of worthy and efficient officers," and "the investigation of all complaints, and the punishment of all official misconduct, should be prompt and thorough." Arthur said all the right things about civil service reform, which is to say he said nothing at all. He was, after all, a Conkling acolyte, and Conkling despised the idea of what he called "snivel service" reform. Like Garfield, Arthur did his best to ruffle no feathers. Just a few years earlier, Arthur had been fired from the New York customhouse by President Hayes, causing Republican editor George William Curtis to chuckle and tell a friend, "Arthur's letter is very amusing to one who knows some of his performances, as I do."[31]

In Ohio, Garfield considered Stephen Dorsey's offer to arrange a meeting with Conkling. Garfield, who could easily see both sides of most major issues, vacillated on whether to agree to the meeting. He definitely needed the help of Conkling, Grant, Logan, and the Stalwarts, as well as the campaign money they generated. But he certainly did not want to be seen as giving in to the demands of a faction—at least not while he needed the votes of all Republicans, especially in New York.

By late July, Dorsey had grown frustrated that little real campaign work had been accomplished. "We are about where we were the day we organized," he complained. "No money has been raised, nor general organization effected."[32] Dorsey took matters into his own hands. As Garfield continued to debate the merits of a meeting with Conkling, Dorsey organized a gathering of the Republican National Committee in New York City on August 5. The committee meeting was, in fact, just a cover to get everyone, especially Garfield, to New York. This would allow Garfield and Conkling to sit down and iron out their differences without anyone appearing to cave in to a rival. "I am very reluctant to go," Garfield told his diary on July 28. "It is an unreasonable demand that so much effort should be made to conciliate one man [Conkling]."[33] The next day, though, Garfield acknowledged that all indications from New York were that he should attend the meeting, so he made plans to do so.

Garfield departed Mentor on August 3 on a special train provided by the Lake Shore Railroad. Two Indianans—John C. New and future president Benjamin Harrison—rode along with him. The train made numerous stops along the way, including in Buffalo, New York, where the largest crowd yet—about 50,000 people—greeted him. "I spoke briefly, and retired," Garfield noted. He arrived in New York City the next evening and wrote that night, "I think no harm has been done."[34]

The Republican National Committee meeting occurred on Thursday, August 5. "Speeches were made by Blaine, Logan, Sherman, and others," Garfield recorded, but there was one glaring absence: Roscoe Conkling. New York's senior senator did not even bother to show up. "The absence of Senator Conkling," wrote Garfield, "gave rise to unpleasant surmises as to his attitude. His friends were embarrassed and indignant. If he intends to take actively hold of the campaign, it is probably best that he does not call on me here. I think his friends are showing zeal and enthusiasm, and will work, whether he does or not."[35] One report indicated that Conkling was in the hotel during the conference but refused to appear, ridiculously claiming he had not been invited.

The next day's *New York Times* tried to put a positive spin on Conkling's absence:

> The Senator has somewhat of a talent for making enemies—a talent which he did not fail to improve at Chicago—and it is but natural that we should carefully avoid any occasion to reopen wounds inflicted on party rivals were it only by his reappearance as the leader of the New York Republicans. This scrupulous regard for the feelings of others augers well for the tact and self-sacrificing efforts which Mr. Conkling is likely to carry into the canvass. Mr. Garfield will doubtless leave New York thoroughly impressed with the magnanimity of our senior Senator.[36]

This biased and unrealistic assessment of Conkling's attitude was not shared by Garfield, who was clearly none too pleased.

On Friday, August 6, Garfield had his photograph taken and visited with such notable personalities as *New York Tribune* editor Whitelaw Reid and railroad magnate and financier Jay Gould. He also talked with eighty-three-year-old Thurlow Weed, a dominant figure in the Whig Party and then the Republican Party. Weed had spent more than three decades as the editor of the *Albany Evening Journal* and was a vocal booster of the political career of another distinguished New Yorker: William Henry Seward. In declining health (he would die about two years later), Weed had spoken quietly and briefly at the previous day's Republican gathering, noting the party's many accomplishments and predicting a Garfield victory in November.

That night, Garfield was serenaded by a group of Civil War veterans. A huge crowd gathered, and the candidate came out on the balcony of Republican headquarters, located at 241 Fifth Avenue. Garfield "spoke about 15 minutes—rather well—getting above the range of ordinary politics."[37] In fact, his words that evening reiterated the theme of the Republicans as the party of union, but it also reminded the crowd of the party's—and the nation's—debts and obligations to black Americans:

> Soon after the great struggle began, we looked behind the army of white rebels, and saw 4,000,000 of black people condemned to toil as slaves for our enemies; and we found that the hearts of these 4,000,000 were God-inspired with the spirit of Liberty, and that they were all our friends.

We have seen white men betray the flag and fight to kill the Union; but in all that long, dreary war we never saw a traitor in a black skin. Our comrades escaping from the starvation of prison, fleeing to our lines by the light of the North star, never feared to enter the black man's cabin and ask for bread. In all that period of suffering and danger, no Union soldier was ever betrayed by a black man or woman. And now that we have made them free, so long as we live we will stand by these black allies. We will stand by them until the sun of liberty, fixed in the firmament of our Constitution, shall shine with equal ray upon every man, black or white, throughout the Union.[38]

By 1880, even some of the most radical former Radical Republicans had decided that the nation had done everything it could and should for black people. Many of them sought new alliances with financiers and industrialists; indeed, this era was the beginning of the Republican Party's long association with big business. But Garfield's words in this speech harked back to the party's origins, calling for equality for all Americans and viewing an active federal government as the best means to achieve it. This speech, more than any other, gives us a glimpse into how Garfield might have governed as president for a full term or two.

Garfield departed New York on August 7, and on the way home, his train made several stops. He "spoke at every station," he noted, "and, I think, made no serious mistake." Garfield was heartened not only by the size of the crowds but also by their makeup: "I noticed that the working men are more markedly interested than they were at the beginning of the trip. I think their sympathy and enthusiasm are being kindled." On August 8, in Chautauqua, New York, Garfield "was waited on by the Fisk Jubilee Singers, and listened to several of their very beautiful songs." The nationally famous group was from Fisk University, an all-black college in Nashville, Tennessee. They presented Garfield with a songbook signed by all the singers and their director. They sang for Garfield again the next day as his train departed for Ohio.

Garfield arrived home the next evening. Even though the main purpose of the New York trip—a meeting with Conkling—had not happened, the candidate considered the trip worthwhile and believed it had gone well. "Very weary," he wrote that night, "but feeling that no serious mistake had been made and probably much good had been done. No trades, no shackles, and as well fitted for defeat or victory as ever."[39]

Even though presidential candidates were expected to play a minimal public role, the campaign demanded much of their time and energy. Greeting party dignitaries and keeping up with a huge volume of correspondence consumed hours each day. James Garfield could devote most of his waking hours to these tasks, but Winfield Scott Hancock was still responsible for the Division of the Atlantic, a demanding task for any army officer, but especially one running for president of the United States. Hancock never requested a leave of absence or any reduction in his official duties, but he spent a good deal of time in the early days of the campaign trying to make his life a little more manageable. He asked to be excused from serving as president of any military courts of inquiry and began to limit his availability to meet with people to three hours per day, three days per week.

While Hancock remained ensconced on Governor's Island, Democratic surrogates went on the attack. Thomas Bayard gave a speech in his home state of Delaware naming Garfield as leader of the faction that had created many acts Democrats found repugnant: force bills, suspension of habeas corpus, and military protection for black voters, among others. In Bayard's view, Garfield and the Republicans had put military power over civilian authority at every turn and purposely stoked the flames of sectional tension. Hancock, in contrast, "although a distinguished soldier, never forgot that his citizenship was a higher distinction."[40] Edward Spencer, an editorial writer for the *Baltimore Sun,* wrote in mid-July that Garfield's convictions were so fluid that one could prove anything and everything in regard to the Republican nominee—"except that he is honest."[41]

Jeremiah S. Black, former US attorney general and secretary of state during the Buchanan administration, prepared a letter to be read at a September meeting at Tammany Hall in New York City. While admitting that Garfield was a great intellect and morally sound, Black argued that these attributes did not guide the Republican candidate's political life. "For his party," Black wrote of Garfield, "he is willing to do any wrong which will promote their interests or play any card howsoever false which will win them power." Attacks like these caused Garfield to note in his diary, "The campaign on the Democratic side has become also one of exclusively personal assault." He accused the Democrats of becoming "alarmed at the progress of the contest on the doctrines of the two parties" and using personal attacks to distract the public.[42]

Another Democratic attack angered Garfield even more. Much as Hancock had bristled at Grant's unfair characterization of him, Garfield was upset when his own former commander, William S. Rosecrans, publicly objected to assumptions that he would support Garfield because of their military service together. Rosecrans, a Democrat, had left the army and was living in California, where he sought a seat in the US House of Representatives in 1880. The two men had become fast friends during the Civil War when Garfield became chief of staff to Rosecrans's Army of the Cumberland. At the September 1863 Battle of Chickamauga, Garfield refused to retreat, knowing that General George H. Thomas (later called the "Rock of Chickamauga") and his men were still in an exposed position and under Confederate assault. Instead, Garfield rode under fire to deliver orders and information to Thomas. It was Garfield's finest moment as a soldier, and "Garfield's ride" had been used to great effect in previous political campaigns. After the battle, President Lincoln unceremoniously reassigned Rosecrans, and over time, the former commander became convinced that Garfield had betrayed him with unflattering reports and letters to Washington. Garfield left the army shortly after Chickamauga to take his seat in the House of Representatives.

In mid-August 1880 the *Daily Alta Californian* ran a short article suggesting that Rosecrans would support Garfield's candidacy because of their friendship during the war. Rosecrans responded to the paper in writing, noting that his previous history with Garfield would not affect his loyalty to the Democratic Party. When this news reached Ohio, Garfield remarked on it during a short speech, and in an autumn interview with the *San Francisco Call*, Rosecrans called Garfield "an unmitigated fraud." Later that year, President-elect Garfield wrote to Rosecrans about the latter's unfair comments. Rosecrans wrote back, telling his former subordinate that he stood by his remarks. This was the last letter that ever passed between the two former friends.[43]

Another Democratic attack came from an unlikely source: the wife of General William Tecumseh Sherman. Ellen Sherman was a staunch Roman Catholic and, like many of her faith, was convinced that the Republicans were an anti-Catholic party. Indeed, some of the party's earliest converts had been former members of the American (Know-Nothing) Party, which was anti-immigrant and anti-Catholic. She recalled that Congressman Garfield had once opposed a bill to provide $25,000 to a Catholic institution known as the Little Sisters of the Poor. "The divorce between church and state ought to be absolute," Garfield said on the House floor on June 22, 1874. On July 20, 1880, a letter from Mrs. Sherman was published in the *Catholic Herald*. She congratulated the newspaper for its anti-Garfield stance and warned that a President Garfield "would do all he could to injure our holy Catholic Church." Of course, many pro-Garfield papers responded, and the *New York Truth* intimated that nothing would be better for the Republican campaign than to be seen as championing Protestantism and opposing Catholicism. Many Democrats—no great supporters of the Catholic faith, despite the large number of Irish immigrants in the party—attacked Garfield for what the *Democratic Campaign Text Book for 1880* conveniently labeled his "Religious Intolerance."[44]

Democrats also sought to influence voters by reminding them of the two scandals touching Garfield's political career—neither of which had done him much harm during his Ohio congressional campaigns. In the early 1870s Washington, DC, started paving the streets in order to "lift itself out of the mud."[45] The DeGolyer McClelland Company, a paving contractor from Chicago, hoped to receive contracts to perform some $700,000 worth of paving work in the nation's capital, and its directors began to throw money at any influential people who might help them land the job. In 1874 it was revealed that about two years earlier, Congressman Garfield had received $5,000 from DeGolyer. Garfield claimed the payment represented legal fees for work he had done for the company. Although the transaction was not illegal, it was certainly not a wise move for a member of the House Committee on Appropriations. However, the incident aroused little public indignation, other than a few nasty comments from some Democratic newspapers. Now, during the 1880 presidential campaign, the Democrats had little success using the scandal against the Republican candidate.

The second Garfield scandal, also dating back to the early 1870s, concerned Credit Mobilier, a shell construction company involved in building part of the transcontinental railroad. Garfield was one of several members of Congress, along with Vice President Schuyler Colfax, accused of accepting illegal discounted stock shares from Credit Mobilier. Many powerful elected officials were investigated for receiving such kickbacks. The scandal cost Colfax his spot on President Grant's reelection ticket in 1872. Grant replaced him with Massachusetts senator Henry Wilson, who was then implicated in illegal Credit Mobilier activities himself. Garfield was eventually found to have received all of $329 related to the Credit Mobilier scandal, and he explained it away as repayment of a loan. It did Garfield little harm then, but the Democrats dredged it up in 1880 and tried to use it against the Republican. They wore "329" lapel buttons and painting that number on buildings, barns, and sidewalks to remind voters of Garfield's part in the scandal.[46]

Republicans, meanwhile, continued to hammer away at Hancock's lack of political experience and understanding of basic issues. "We hold no controversy with General Hancock, for he is a good soldier," stated one Republican pamphlet. "Our only controversy is with the party that nominated him."[47] The one time during the campaign that Hancock tried to speak out on an issue, he ran into trouble. Talking to a New Jersey newspaper reporter in early October, he discussed the tariff and concluded by saying, "The tariff question is a local question . . . one that the general government seldom cares to interfere with."[48] He played right into the Republicans' hands by making himself appear unfamiliar with a critical and intrinsically federal issue and that any president would be required to fully understand. As expected, Republican newspapers shredded him over this gaffe.

In Mentor, Ohio, reporters were camping out on the lawn of the Garfield home, a farmhouse surrounded by nearly 160 acres of property. The reporters nicknamed the site "Lawnfield," and the name stuck. "It has been a delightful day at Lawnfield—as the papers insist on calling our place," Garfield told his diary on August 22.[49]

Reporters were not the only unexpected guests during the presidential campaign. Once Garfield returned from Chicago in mid-June, members of the general public began to show up as well. Some came individually or in small groups, while others arrived in groups that numbered in the hundreds. Businessmen, German immigrants, Civil War veterans, ladies from Cleveland, African American veterans—all made the journey to the tiny village of Mentor. Many of them arrived at the small train stop located at the far northern end of Garfield's land and simply walked up the path to his home. Garfield had always planned to take President Hayes's advice to "sit cross-legged, look wise," and say nothing, but he eventually felt obligated to address these groups. He began to go outside and give short speeches, and the nation's first "front porch" presidential campaign was born.

Garfield's speeches were often tailored to the particular group before him. To the travelers representing various mercantile interests in Indiana who visited on September 3, Garfield said, "Every stroke of the axe, every blow of the hammer, every turn of a wheel, every purchase and sale, in short, every effort of labor, is measured by the standard value fixed and declared by National law." Garfield, a longtime hard-money advocate, added, "Your Government has at last restored to its people the ancient standard of value, and has made it possible for our people everywhere to secure the blessing which bountiful harvests and prosperous times have brought them, by placing

One of the only known images of Garfield on the front porch of his home during the 1880 campaign. Left to right: the candidate's mother, Eliza; James Garfield; daughter Mollie; and wife Lucretia. (Courtesy of Western Reserve Historical Society)

our National finances on the solid basis of specie values." When German residents of Cleveland visited on October 16, he reminded them that "all English-speaking people drew their old traditions from and found their first fatherland in the forests of Germany." He also recited a poem by the German poet Norvalis, speaking to his guests in their native tongue—surely the first time an American presidential candidate had campaigned in a foreign language. On October 25 he asked black Civil War veterans:

> What is freedom without the intelligence to use it wisely? What is freedom without virtue and intelligence combined to make it not a curse,

but a blessing? You were not made free merely to be allowed to vote, but in order to enjoy an equality of opportunity in the race of life, and to stand equal before the law. Permit no man to praise you because you are black, nor wrong you because you are black."[50]

The same evening—October 25—Frederick Douglass spoke to a group of "colored citizens" at Cooper Union in New York City. "James A. Garfield must be our President," he told the crowd. "I know Garfield, colored man; he is right on our questions, take my word for it. . . . He has shown us how man in the humblest of circumstances can grapple with man, rise, and win." Douglass closed by using Garfield's life story and accomplishments as motivation for his audience, telling them that Garfield "has shown us how it is possible for an American to rise. He has built the road over which he has traveled. He has buffeted the billows of adversity, and tonight he swims in safety where Hancock, in despair, is going down."[51]

While the parties sniped at each other in an attempt to gain the upper hand, most understood that the first real barometer of the 1880 campaign—and the best predictor of which party was better positioned to win the presidency—would be the congressional election results in the early voting states of Maine, Ohio, and Indiana. Maine residents cast their ballots in September, while Ohioans and Indianans went to the polls in October. Democrats and Republicans alike threw energy and money into these states, hoping that winning there would either make their presidential candidate's victory in November seem like a foregone conclusion and drive down the opposition's voter turnout or rally their own party's voters and encourage a high turnout in November. Of course, in addition to winning the presidency, both sides hoped to acquire a majority in one or both houses of Congress. "The afternoon mail," Garfield wrote in his diary on September 2, "brought me important letters . . . in answer to which I wrote some strong letters to Jewell, Reid and Dorsey, urging the concentration of all our forces upon Indiana, assuming that Maine is safe. If we carry Indiana the rest will be easy."[52]

Garfield erred in overlooking Maine, and he did so partly because his close associate James Blaine, a Maine senator, had assured him that the Pine Tree State would go Republican. But Blaine misjudged his own state's complexity, which included a fusion between Democrats and Greenbackers. Blaine predicted a Republican majority of around 8,000 votes; instead, the party of Lincoln—and Garfield—lost in Maine. "The result of the Maine election is a surprise and a disappointment to the Republicans, and an encouragement to the Democrats," proclaimed the September 15, 1880, edition of the *Sacramento Daily Union*. Blaine "has saddled and ridden the party for twenty years," one Republican noted, "and now it has thrown him." Blaine tried to blame the loss on the Democrats pouring more than $100,000 into the Maine elections, but Garfield was more concerned with keeping Republican spirits up. "When the case is examine coolly," the *Sacramento Daily Union* argued, "it will be seen that after all nothing in the shape of a 'tidal wave' or a 'revolution' has occurred . . . all that has happened is the perpetuation of the party relations which existed a year ago. . . . Republican strength has remained solid." Even though Garfield himself had predicted that Maine was safe, all was not lost.

Blaine, undaunted by the losses in his own state, advised Garfield to find new issues that would resonate with voters. The Republicans' principal themes thus far had been Garfield's personality and long congressional experience and, of course, the reliable standby of "waving the bloody shirt"—reminding voters of the Democratic Party's role in secession and the Civil War. "The man who attempts to get up a political excitement in this country on the old sectional issues," Garfield had said in 1878, "will find himself without a party and without support." Of course, just a year later, Garfield had stared down congressional Democrats who threatened to withhold appropriations to put an end to Reconstruction. In 1880, fresh off the loss in Maine, Garfield ignored his own 1878 advice (as many Republicans had already done long before the Maine debacle). The candidate told campaign operatives to print and distribute hundreds of thousands of copies of his well-received March 1879 "Revolution in Congress" speech, and he publicly called the South a "bastard civilization, still steeped to the lips with treason and disloyalty." Although many Republican officeholders wished to be done with sectional issues, it was still an effective campaign theme among rank-and-file Republican voters. Highly placed Republicans like Blaine encouraged Garfield and the party to fold up the bloody shirt and put it away forever, but the old sectional issues still resonated with voters. "I think the Blue will triumph over the Gray as it done at Appomattox Court House," one man wrote to Garfield.[53]

Still, Garfield was desperate to get both Grant and Conkling out on the campaign trail. Grant was one of the most revered men in the country, and Conkling was a highly skilled orator. Their support of the Garfield-Arthur ticket was critical. In advance of the Ohio state elections in October, the Re-

An artist's look into Garfield's home during the 1880 campaign. (Courtesy of Library of Congress)

publican Party planned a huge rally in Warren, about fifty miles southeast of Garfield's Mentor home. Garfield was invited but thought it unwise to go, for fear of appearing too eager for the office. Grant and Conkling, however, agreed to appear at the Warren rally, scheduled for September 29. The day before, Garfield received word that Grant and Conkling, as well as John Logan from Illinois, Levi Morton of New York, and others from Cleveland, would all make a brief stop in Mentor on their way to Warren. The group spent about an hour at Garfield's home. "I had no private conversation with the party," Garfield recalled, "but the call was a pleasant and cordial one all around."[54]

The next day, Garfield noted in his diary that "Conkling's speech at Warren was an event of considerable importance." But as he learned more about the speeches delivered by Grant and Conkling, Garfield became increasingly distressed. Grant spoke first to the crowd of about 40,000 and then introduced Conkling. "The senator spoke fully two hours," the *New York Times* reported, "mostly upon the election and census frauds in the South, the attitude of the Democratic party upon the tariff question, and the foolishness of the Democratic demand for a change." But neither the former president nor the sitting senior senator from New York so much as mentioned James Garfield's name. Garfield was peeved at their "manifest effort . . . to avoid mentioning the head of the ticket in any generous way," but he held out hope that their appearance in Ohio would help not only his own chances in the presidential race but also the Republican ticket in the upcoming state elections.[55]

The month of September ended on a high note when the Fisk Jubilee Singers visited Garfield's home. "They sang some of their finest pieces," he wrote later that day, and "at the conclusion I made a few remarks to them." Garfield and his wife invited the singers into the parlor and served light refreshments of coffee and fruit. Garfield's private secretary, Joseph Stanley-Brown, remembered that the candidate listened intently to the singers and then said, "I tell you now, in the closing days of this campaign, that I would rather be with you and defeated than against you and victorious."[56]

Hancock's gaffe about the tariff being a "local issue" continued to hurt the Democrats in the press and with voters. As the Republicans planned their massive rally in Warren, Ohio, for late September, the Democrats planned a similar event at Tammany Hall in New York City for September 23. Hancock approached Thomas Bayard and asked him to speak at the rally and try to explain the complicated tariff issue in a way that would make Hancock's mistake look minor at worst or, if possible, like not a mistake at all. Bayard was also charged with reassuring the businessmen of the country that a President Hancock would be good for their interests. This was especially important, given that many manufacturers were reportedly warning their workers that a Democratic victory would destroy the nation's industries and cost them their jobs.[57]

Between Hancock's misstatement on the tariff and the Democratic Party's platform favoring "a tariff for revenue only," the Republicans had ample economic ammunition. Hancock and others tried to minimize the damage, insisting that "this tariff must necessarily give protection to the manufacturing interests of the country." This statement made it appear that the Republicans and the Democrats endorsed the same protective tariff. Republican functionaries hammered away at Hancock and the Democrats on these economic issues. Garfield mostly stayed above the fray and continued to give his short front-porch speeches at home. Garfield occasionally waved the bloody shirt but rarely got down into the weeds on economics.

Democrats were cautiously optimistic going into the October state elections in Indiana. The Hoosier State had gone for the Tilden in 1876, and Hendricks, one of its favorite sons, had been both Tilden's running mate and a contender for the party's presidential nomination in 1880. Indiana had a Democratic governor and two Democratic senators, and former Indiana congressman English was Hancock's running mate. Ohio was expected to be a tougher sell, especially considering that Garfield sat atop the Republican ticket. Nearly everyone expected the Buckeye State to go Republican.

Voters in Ohio and Indiana went to the polls on October 12, 1880. As expected, Ohio was a clear blowout for the Republicans, who dominated by a margin of about 20,000 votes, an increase from 1876. Indiana was expected to go down to the wire, and it did. Before Election Day, Democrats had predicted that they would carry Indiana by a razor-thin margin of about 2,000 votes. Instead, the Republicans won by about 5,000 votes. The *New York Times* summed it up as "A Democratic Waterloo." Wrote one correspondent: "The result in Indiana is a surprise alike to Democrats and Republicans. The State was conceded to the Democrats by a small majority, and the most sanguine Republicans had no expectation that there would be such a decided reversal of the figures of former years."[58] While Republicans rejoiced in these much-needed victories, Democrats were left to ponder what Charles Dana called "an unexpected and mortifying defeat" that "may prove fatal."[59]

Democrats had a host of explanations for their loss in Indiana. Tammany boss John Kelly blamed it on "imported niggers," while others blamed the tariff issue, third-party candidates, and other causes. The real question was whether the results could be reversed in the presidential election, which was just three weeks away. Hancock thought he could still carry Indiana, given that local issues affecting the October election would not be relevant in the presidential voting, but others were not so sure. Ultimately, the attention of both parties remained solidly on the top prize: New York. For

An 1880 Democratic campaign song dedicated to Winfield Scott Hancock. (Courtesy of Library of Congress)

either candidate, winning the White House without winning New York was nearly impossible.

As the campaign wound down to its final days, Republican and Democratic operatives alike continued to believe that the election would be very close. Someone, however, tried to tip the scales in Hancock's favor with an "October surprise." On October 20, just two weeks before the election, Garfield received a telegram from James W. Simonton of the Associated Press asking whether a letter written by Garfield "on the Chinese question" was genuine. Garfield requested a copy of the letter, which Simonton sent later that day. The letter was dated January 23, 1880, and was printed on US House of Representatives stationery. It was addressed to H. L. Morey of the Employers Union in Lynn, Massachusetts. In it, Garfield allegedly stated that "individuals and companys [sic] have the right to buy labor where they can get it cheapest" and that unlimited Chinese immigration should be allowed to continue "until our great manufacturing and corporate interests are conserved in the matter of labor." If genuine, this letter would be a bombshell. Garfield's support for unlimited Chinese immigration would cost him dearly among voters on the West Coast. After examining the copy sent by Simonton, Garfield proclaimed the letter a forgery. "It is evidently the purpose of the Democracy," Garfield wrote, "in their desperation to seek by this means to take the Pacific Coast from us at the coming election."[60]

The *Truth*, a New York newspaper, ran the letter the next day, along with a statement from an alleged friend of Garfield's that the handwriting was, in fact, his. Democrats smelled blood, so they printed and circulated half a million copies of the letter, posting it to signboards and in store windows all over the country.

Based on Garfield's firm denial that he had authored the so-called Morey letter, the Republican National Committee sent operatives to Lynn, Massachusetts, to talk to H. L. Morey. When they arrived, they could find no trace of anyone by that name who had ever lived there. Similarly, no one had ever heard of the Employers Union. Garfield was not surprised: "I never heard of such a man and the sentiment of the letter is one I never expressed." He wisely covered his bases, though, sending a secretary to Washington to examine his files and ensure that he had never received or replied to such a letter. The secretary found nothing in the files, and Garfield continued to insist that the letter was "not in the handwriting of any person whom I know, but it is a manifestly bungling attempt to copy my hand and signature." At the insistence of the Republican National Committee, Garfield eventually issued a public statement denying authorship of the letter, even though the candidate himself would have preferred not to respond at all. The controversy soon blew over, but the author of the Morey letter was never identified.[61]

November 2, 1880—Election Day—"opened clear and bright with indications here, and in the weather reports, of a fair day throughout the country." Garfield went to the Mentor town hall and voted at around 2:00 p.m. Hancock remained on Governor's Island in New York as more than nine million Americans—about 78 percent of those eligible—went to the polls to cast their ballots for the twentieth president of the United States. Garfield recorded in his diary: "At 6 returns began to come in. . . . Some reporters, and friends from Cleveland came." In New York, Hancock was told to expect to win that state by 25,000 votes, and he was confident enough to go to bed at around 9:30 p.m. "The results so far are very encouraging," he said, "and I hope they will continue to be. . . . I don't care to see any further despatches [sic] or be waked up."[62]

As expected, the South was solidly for the Democrat Hancock, including South Carolina, Louisiana, and Florida—the three states that had ultimately made Hayes president in 1876. Also as expected, the Midwest was solidly for Garfield, including Indiana, which the Democrats could not turn around after losing in the state elections three weeks earlier. As everyone had predicted all along, it came down to New York. With his solid block of electoral votes from the South, a win in New York would make Hancock president.

But New York, which had voted for Tilden in 1876, did not go into the Democrats' column in 1880. Garfield wrote, "By 11 p.m. it became evident that we had carried New York," and with that, Hancock's chances of victory disappeared. Conkling's decision to help Garfield's campaign—despite rarely mentioning the candidate's name in his speeches—paid off in the end. It helped Garfield get elected, but it also gave Conkling the idea that he could manipulate and control the new president.

While the Garfields hosted a large celebratory dinner for family and friends at around midnight, Hancock woke up at 5:00 a.m. on November 3 and asked his wife for the news. "It has been a complete Waterloo for you," she replied somewhat dramatically. "That is all right," her husband replied. "I can stand it."[63]

Ultimately, the 1880 presidential election was agonizingly close. James Garfield won the popular vote by only about 7,400 votes—less than one-tenth of 1 percent of the ballots cast nationwide. When the votes of third parties are considered, Garfield won the presidency with only about 48.3 percent of the popular vote. Republicans controlled the House of Representatives, but by the narrow margin of just twelve seats, and the Senate was evenly split between Republicans and Democrats. Garfield would become president of a politically divided nation in March 1881. Garfield's Electoral College victory was decisive, with the winner claiming 214 electoral votes to Hancock's 155.

Just five months after being the Republicans' compromise presidential nominee, Garfield was president-elect of the United States. The Republican Party's prospects had looked dim in the months leading up to the election, but because he took an active role in his own campaign and avoided any major mistakes, Garfield ended the year putting together a presidential cabinet and writing an inaugural address. "Your real troubles," Carl Schurz warned him, "will now begin."[64]

"THE PERSONAL ASPECTS OF THE PRESIDENCY ARE FAR FROM PLEASANT" JAMES A. GARFIELD AS PRESIDENT

On December 31, 1880, President-elect James A. Garfield sat down to write in his diary:

> I regret that I am too much occupied to review the impressions which the year has brought. In regard to the principal political event of my life, I have to say that my chief gratification arises from the fact that the office came to me without any violation of the law of my life, viz., never to ask for any office. I came to that resolution in October, 1849 . . . and I have followed it ever since, until I have come to believe that should I violate that law, I would fail.
>
> It may be a whim. I would not impose the rule on others: for each shall have and obey his own law of life. I close the year with a sad conviction that I am bidding good-by to the freedom of private life, and to a long series of happy years, which I fear terminate with 1880.[1]

Garfield could not have known how right he was. By next New Year's Eve, he would be three months in his grave. But this passage demonstrates that while Garfield was a politician and viewed his election to the presidency as "the principal political event of my life," he was also a man who craved at least some degree of privacy and time to spend with his family and pursue personal enjoyments—reading and working on his farm among them. He clearly recognized that becoming president would limit his time to do all these things. However, at just forty-nine years old, Garfield surely believed that, whether he served one term or two, he would have many years after his presidency to enjoy life and pursue his interests.

Presidential inaugurations took place on March 4 until the adoption of the Twentieth Amendment in 1933, so President-elect James Garfield had four months between his electoral victory in November 1880 and his inauguration in March 1881. During that time, he had to select cabinet officers, write an inaugural address, and determine a vision and direction for his administration. Putting together a cabinet occupied much of that time, which Garfield spent mostly at home in Mentor. Like most of his predecessors, Garfield wanted to find talented men to serve in his cabinet but also to provide geographic balance. Nearly all sections of the country expected to be represented in the new president's "official family," and Garfield hoped to please the Stalwart faction of his own party as well. Chester Arthur's election as vice president had been a good start, but Garfield correctly feared that this would not be enough for Roscoe Conkling and his allies.

Almost immediately upon his election, Garfield was besieged by office seekers. They showed up at his home and sent thousands of letters seeking positions in his administration. "I wood liuke to be in the Kustim Hous," wrote one unqualified hopeful. People came from all over the country seeking an audience with the president-elect to apply for positions from cabinet secretaries to postmasters and everything in between. His friend John Hay, former private secretary to President Lincoln and future secretary of state, reminded Garfield, "There are fifty million of us. . . . You can't give us all a first rate office. Do what *you* think is right." But Garfield met with as many people as he could and regretted that he could not help them all. "I fear," he wrote, "it remains for me to make my pathway over the wrecks of human hearts."[2] No wonder the civil service became the chief issue of Garfield's brief presidency.

At this period in American history, only seven cabinet positions existed to be filled: attorney general; postmaster general; and the secretaries of state, war, treasury, interior, and navy. Nearly everyone agreed that the top jobs at the State and Treasury Departments were the most important and prestigious posts; they were also the ones that, along with the postmaster, had the most patronage largesse to distribute. Recognizing just how close the popular election had been, Garfield was determined to preserve party unity by achieving both sectional and factional balance in the cabinet. This was especially critical for the large and important states of New York, Penn-

Cartoonist's view of President Hayes leaving civil service reform on President-elect Garfield's doorstep. (Courtesy of Library of Congress)

sylvania, and Illinois—the home states of Stalwart leaders Roscoe Conkling, Don Cameron, and John Logan, respectively.

Not all Republicans agreed, of course. Carl Schurz, the perpetual reformer and interior secretary under President Hayes, urged Garfield to simply choose "the fittest man for each place and then going ahead to make a good business administration." James Blaine, the de facto leader of the Republicans' Half-Breed faction, advised Garfield to make all his cabinet appointments from that faction. Garfield appreciated the advice of Schurz, Blaine, and the countless other Republicans who offered it, but he remained dedicated to creating a balanced administration.[3]

Garfield bandied about names for months. He quickly decided to find a place in his cabinet for Wayne MacVeagh, a Pennsylvanian endorsed by both the reformer Schurz and the Stalwart Cameron. Garfield also warmed to Logan's suggestion of a prominent Illinoisan for a cabinet post: Robert Todd Lincoln, son of President Abraham Lincoln. Convincing Lincoln to serve would be a challenge, though, since Republicans had been begging him to run for office since his father's death. Lincoln, convinced that these men were interested only in his surname and not in his own merits, had always resisted.

The other man Garfield was sure he wanted in his cabinet was James Blaine, but first, he had to make sure that Blaine would not oppose Garfield for the Republican nomination in 1884. On November 27, 1880, during a quick trip to Washington, Garfield had breakfast at Blaine's home. As the president-elect recorded in his diary that evening, he asked the Maine senator if he would be interested in a cabinet post. "And before you answer," Garfield recorded, "please tell me whether you are, or will be, a candidate for the presidency in 1884. I ask this because I do not purpose for myself, nor to allow anyone else to use the next four years as the camping ground for fighting the next presidential battle."[4] Blaine assured Garfield that he would not seek the nomination in 1884, and he told the president-elect that at this point in his career, he believed his only chance of getting the presidential nomination would be if it came to him unsought. Garfield tentatively offered Blaine the position of secretary of state.

As he continued to build his cabinet, Garfield ran into some trouble from the Stalwarts. This was not surprising, as the president-elect knew he had to give New Yorkers a cabinet spot, and Conkling, of course, wanted his home state to have the most powerful appointment: secretary of the treasury. On the same day he got Blaine's assurance that he would not run against him in 1884, Garfield met with the powerful New York Stalwart and Wall Street executive Levi P. Morton, one of the architects of the Republican summit the previous August that Conkling had skipped. The meeting grew icy when Morton referenced an August agreement to give the secretary of the treasury post to a New Yorker—preferably, Morton himself. Garfield called this a "misapprehension," stating that to do so would "be a congestion of financial

President James A. Garfield. (Courtesy of Library of Congress)

power—at money centre—and would create great jealousy at the West. Collection and management of revenue should be kept as far apart as possible." Garfield met with Morton again the following day and reiterated that he would not "tolerate, or act upon any understanding that anything has been pledged to any party, state or person."[5] Garfield was a realist who understood the need to balance the geographic composition of his cabinet, but here he demonstrated that he could stand firm when necessary.

He returned to Ohio a few days later, and on December 1 the Electoral College voted 214–155, confirming his victory. No real doubt had existed, but it was now official: James Abram Garfield would be the twentieth president of the United States.

The trip to Washington exhausted Garfield, and he found no respite upon his return to Mentor. As winter descended on northeastern Ohio, office seekers continued to arrive in droves at Garfield's farm. "The personal aspects of the presidency are far from pleasant," he wrote. "I shall be compelled to live in great social isolation; almost everyone who comes to me wants something which he thinks I can and ought to give him, and this embitters the pleasure of friendship."[6]

On December 13 a delegation sent by Roscoe Conkling and Levi Morton arrived to prevail upon Garfield to appoint Morton secretary of the treasury. They insisted that Garfield had agreed to this deal in August, and Garfield continued to disagree. The president-elect admitted that he liked Morton and would be happy to have him in some high position—perhaps secretary of the navy or a prominent foreign minister—but Garfield held firm on his opinion that Morton or any New Yorker would be an unwise choice for the top treasury post. Morton's understanding was that he could select whichever cabinet position he wanted, including treasury. "I answered that I did not give him the option," Garfield wrote, "and by no implication tendered him the Treasury." Garfield also deftly invoked a federal conflict-of-interest statute that made Morton, a prominent financier, ineligible for the treasury job. The delegation was clearly unsatisfied when they left, but they told Garfield that they (and therefore Conkling) wanted to support his administration and make him likely to win a second term. In reply, Garfield told them in no uncertain terms that he would "not permit this four years to be used to secure the next for anybody."[7] The president-elect understood that any hope of support or cooperation from Conkling and the Stalwarts disappeared that evening along with his visitors. The freezing Ohio night was an apt metaphor for relations between Garfield and Conkling.

As the winter progressed and March 4 approached, Garfield stayed busy with office seekers, cabinet deliberations, preparations to move into the White House, and other tasks. He tried to take better care of his health, telling his diary at one point, "I have been dieting, carefully abstaining from tobacco, tea, coffee, potatoes, butter and grease of any kind."[8]

In January he sent his wife, Lucretia, to New York to buy dresses and other items she would need to fulfill her new social obligations as the nation's first lady. This trip had an ulterior motive as well: Garfield wanted his wife to relay any information or gossip she heard about the New York political scene. (Mrs. Garfield wisely kept a low profile during the trip, using the alias "Mrs. Greenfield" when checking into her New York hotel.) Garfield had heard little from Conkling, Morton, or the Stalwarts since the December meeting at his home, and he wanted to know what was happening in one of the nation's most important cities. Garfield was gloomier than usual with his wife gone for two weeks, and he despaired that the bad weather was preventing him from receiving her letters. "I want to learn what she has learned of N.Y. matters," he wrote on January 28. Three days later, he continued to lament "the prolonged absence of Crete [his nickname for Lucretia], when I so greatly need to consult her on several subjects about which she will bring me intelligence." When she finally arrived home later that evening, Garfield wrote, "My joy was full."[9]

While in New York, Lucretia had written to her husband, "Morton has been very ugly in his talk about you, using that expression that seems so gratifying to the Conkling clique—'That Ohio man' cannot be relied on to stand by his pledges." Mrs. Garfield also offered the president-elect her assessment and advice: "You will never have anything from those men [the Stalwarts] but their assured contempt until you fight them *dead*. You can put every one of them in his political graves . . . and that is the only place where they can be kept peaceable."[10]

Garfield also kept a close eye on Ohio politics during the winter of 1880–1881. His election to the presidency meant that Senator-elect Garfield would not go to the Senate after all, leaving his seat open. While he hoped to stay out of the wrangling over who the Ohio legislature should send in his place, Garfield naturally hoped to see another friendly and supportive face in the Senate. After determining that he would not retain fellow Ohioan John Sherman as treasury secretary (which Sherman blamed on the influence of Blaine), Garfield quickly determined that former senator Sherman's return to the Senate would be best for Garfield's administration, for Ohio, and for the Republican Party. "The Ohio Senatorship annoys me," he wrote in December 1880. "The defeat of Sherman leaves him where he can hardly accept anything else, and out of office he creates a dissatisfaction in Ohio, dangerous to the party peace."[11] Garfield also surely felt at least a modicum of guilt over obtaining the presidential nomination Sherman had so clearly craved.

Sherman indicated his interest in returning to the Senate, but he warned

Garfield, "If you can only restrain [Blaine's] immense activity and keep him from meddling with the other departments, you will have a brilliant secretary. If Blaine talks with you about the appointments in other Depts tell him you will confer with the head of that Dept."[12] As Garfield soon learned, Sherman's concerns were well founded: Blaine had every intention of advising the president-elect about appointments in other departments. But Garfield was pleased when the legislators in Columbus elected Sherman to return to the US Senate.

Another important job loomed over Garfield that winter, and it was one that confounded him: writing his inaugural address. Garfield was a powerful speaker and a gifted writer, so he wanted his speech to be magnificent. But uncharacteristically, he found himself procrastinating. Just before Christmas 1880, he read the inaugural addresses of all his presidential predecessors for inspiration. Nearly a month later, though, he told his diary, "I must begin to make special preparations for the inaugural. I have half a mind to make none." He finally began a draft on January 27 but felt "but little freedom in its composition. There are so many limitations." By February 10, he reported "some progress on the inaugural; but still feel unusual repugnance to writing." Less than a week before his inauguration: "I am greatly dissatisfied with the inaugural, which is still incomplete." Three days before the inauguration: "Last night I looked over the inaugural, and became so dissatisfied with it that I have resolved to rewrite it and made a beginning though very weary."[13]

Why did a writer and orator as skilled and accomplished as Garfield struggle with this particular speech? There were several reasons. First, as president-elect, Garfield was extremely busy. He had to prepare his Mentor, Ohio, property for his extended absence, pack clothes and books and other items to take to the White House, endure visits from family and friends, and, of course, deal with the seemingly endless flood of office seekers that continued to arrive at his home and that custom required him to see for at least a moment or two.

Garfield's physical and emotional health played a role as well. He suffered from regular headaches and chronic digestive troubles dating back to young adulthood. In early January 1881 he went to the dentist and had a wisdom tooth removed. "Face very sore and a dull headache," he wrote the next day.[14] He also moped for the two weeks in January that his wife was in New York. He was always morose when Lucretia was gone for more than a day or two.

Finally, the president-elect devoted hours each day to thinking about his

Garfield trying to tie enemies Blaine and Conkling together with patronage. (Courtesy of Library of Congress)

cabinet. He took dozens of meetings, read hundreds of letters and newspapers, and hosted visits from potential cabinet members, hoping to find the best people to serve in his "official family." He fretted over achieving geographic balance and keeping all the Republican factions happy. He worried about losing the support of Conkling and his cronies by not appointing Morton secretary of the treasury. He sought advice from Blaine, Sherman, and countless other allies, and many others shared their unsolicited opinions with him. His diaries and letters reflect how much time and effort Garfield put into his cabinet appointments. After long days spent having these types of conversations, it was surely hard to switch gears and write words worthy of an inaugural address.

On February 27, 1881, as his family prepared to spend their last night in the Mentor farmhouse, Garfield recorded in his diary: "This is the slate I carry to Washington, which will not be much changed. 1. Blaine, State. 2. [William] Windom, Treasury. 3. [Robert Todd] Lincoln [secretary of war]. 4. Morton, Navy. 5. Wayne MacVeagh, Att'y Gen. 6. [William] Hunt or [Don] Pardee, P.M.G. [postmaster general]."[15] Some of these men had already accepted their positions; others were merely waiting for a formal invitation from Garfield. But the president-elect had clearly established who would be part of his "official family." Garfield made no mention of the Department of the Interior, which was soon entrusted to Samuel J. Kirkwood.

Friday, March 4, 1881, dawned cold and snowy in Washington, DC. Close to noon, though, the weather cleared—just in time for Garfield's inauguration. As was customary, the president-elect went first to the Senate chamber, where he witnessed Chester A. Arthur, the New York Stalwart and Conkling acolyte, take the oath of office as vice president. Then it was on to the East Portico of the Capitol, where Frederick Douglass was among the invited guests. Garfield's final assessment of the inaugural speech over which he had struggled so greatly was brief: "Read my inaugural—slowly and fairly well—though I grew somewhat hoarse towards the close. Returning to the Executive Mansion, lunched with the family and then two-and-a-half hours on the reviewing stand."[16]

Lucretia Garfield had much more to say about the inauguration ceremony and her husband's speech (she noted that presidents-elect delivered their inaugural addresses before taking the presidential oath, not after): "The eyes of all that vast assembly were centered on the one majestic figure that now stood before them—the President-elect. . . . After a short pause the President elect stood out before the people and with the inspiration of the time and the occasion lifting him up into his fullest grandeur he became in the magnificence with which he pronounced his Inaugural almost superhuman."[17] After an inaugural ball and reception at the new Smithsonian Arts and Industries building (Garfield was a longtime Smithsonian regent), the Garfields returned to the White House and went to bed.

So, after all that hand-wringing, what words did Garfield finally decide were worthy of this moment in American history? He began his inaugural address by noting, "We stand today upon an eminence which overlooks a hundred years of national life—a century crowded with perils, but crowned with the triumphs of liberty and law." He reviewed the early nation's difficulties with self-government and paid deference to the founding fathers' wisdom in scrapping the Articles of Confederation in favor of the Constitution. Garfield also noted that "the supreme trial of this Constitution came at last under the tremendous pressure of civil war," stating that the Union emerged from that conflict "purified and made stronger." The argument about whether the federal government or state governments were supreme had been settled in favor of the former. "This decree," he said, "does not disturb the autonomy of the States nor interfere with their necessary rights of local self-government, but it does fix and establish the permanent supremacy of the Union."

Garfield boldly addressed civil rights, calling the abolition of slavery and the elevation of African Americans to citizenship "the most important political change we have known" since the Constitution's adoption in 1787. This change "liberated the master as well as the slave from a relation which wronged and enfeebled both," and it "freed us from the perpetual danger of war and dissolution." Acknowledging that many white Southerners were unhappy with citizenship and equal protection for black men, Garfield reminded Americans that "under our institutions there was no middle ground for the negro race between slavery and equal citizenship. There can be no permanent disfranchised peasantry in the United States," and the nation would not reach its full potential for greatness "so long as the law or its administration places the smallest obstacle in the pathway of any virtuous citizen."

Garfield also touched on the state of civil service reform, the nation's finances, agriculture, commerce, and religious freedom in his inaugural (although he did point out that "the Mormon Church . . . offends the moral sense of manhood by sanctioning polygamy"). He closed by stating that he would rely heavily on the wisdom and patriotism of Congress during his presidency and "upon our efforts to promote the welfare of this great people and their Government I reverently invoke the support and blessings of Almighty God."[18]

Garfield made many interesting and timely statements in his address, but the two most interesting were about the civil service and the relationship between the North and South, particularly as seen through the lens of the civil and political rights of African Americans.

Garfield had never been especially passionate one way or another about the civil service. He had not paid much attention to it during his long congressional service, and in fact, he had always been willing to try to secure a position for a friend or relative. However, many months of unsolicited visits and demands from office seekers had caused him to think differently about the civil service. After one particularly annoying visit in January 1881, he coldly remarked, "The questions of persons, and the value which each places upon his own merits as compared with the estimate which others place upon him, is the chief evil of choosing men for service."[19] Although Garfield was not yet a convert to sweeping civil service reform, he had at least thought about the issue and was willing to consider changes. Had he known that many more office seekers—including his future assassin Charles Guiteau—would monopolize his time as president and that civil service reform would play a role in his own death, Garfield surely would have made it a higher priority.

In Garfield's inaugural, the passages about race relations, the Civil War, and the future of black people are most compelling. Garfield could have chosen to ignore civil rights and race relations and concentrate on other issues: he was knowledgeable about fiscal issues, he cared deeply about education, and he wanted to reform and modernize the American naval fleet. But Garfield had fought in the Civil War as a Union general and then slugged it out in the House of Representatives during Reconstruction. Garfield once described himself as "cursed" by his ability to see both sides of every issue, and at various times he had been a Radical Republican, a moderate, and a conservative. But Reconstruction was over, and even many former Radicals believed the federal government had done all it could or should for African Americans. The temptation for Garfield to look forward, not backward, must have been great.

The Republican philosophies of equality and governmental activism to benefit all Americans had resonated with a young Garfield, and those attitudes stayed with him—even up to his inauguration as president. So to those who knew him then or those who study him now, it is no surprise

Assassin Charles Guiteau demanding "An Office or Your Life" from President Garfield. (Courtesy of Library of Congress)

"Heroes of the Colored Race," including James A. Garfield. (Courtesy of Library of Congress)

that Garfield reiterated his own and the government's commitment to civil rights and equality in his inaugural address. Though many in the Republican Party had moved on from the racial issues of the Civil War and Reconstruction eras and were looking for new alliances with financiers and industrialists, Garfield continued to believe that the government had not only the means but also the responsibility to promote equality and opportunity for all Americans.

Immediately upon taking office, President Garfield was inundated with office seekers. On the first full day of his presidency, the line of callers hoping for a moment of the president's time streamed out of the White House and onto Pennsylvania Avenue. He greeted thousands who had come to Washington for the inauguration at a morning reception, then met with several influential friends, including future president Benjamin Harrison. That evening, he learned the Senate had unanimously confirmed his entire cabinet.[20]

The new president quickly settled into a routine of rising, reading the newspapers and dictating letters, and eating breakfast with his family—

three of the Garfields' five children lived at the White House, while the other two were at boarding school in New Hampshire—before heading into the office to work. He met with members of Congress, greeted visiting foreign delegations, and held cabinet meetings. Then, of course, there were the conversations with office seekers. "The fountains of the population seem to have overflowed and Washington is inundated," he wrote four days after his inauguration. He did not mind meeting with well-wishers, but "the Spartan band of disciplined office hunters who drew paper on me as highway men draw pistols were the men with who[m] I had to wrestle like a Greek."[21] During one such meeting, Garfield chatted with a Southern Republican who rather sharply challenged the president, asking him whether he planned to run a "stalwart administration" and advising Garfield to give no patronage positions to Democrats. "I told him I declined to be lectured or have my Republicanism questioned," Garfield noted, "and he left rather sooner than he intended to."[22]

To handle all this work—managing his schedule, dealing with thousands of office seekers, and ensuring the smooth operation of the national government—Garfield had just seven clerks working for him, supervised by his private secretary Joseph Stanley-Brown. Stanley-Brown had served Garfield in a similar role in Mentor during the presidential campaign. After failing to convince John Hay, one of Lincoln's private secretaries (and a future ambassador to the United Kingdom and secretary of state), to return to the White House as his secretary, Garfield had given the job to Stanley-Brown. "Well, that is complimentary, to say the least, when all these other fellows have been first considered," Stanley-Brown said rather sharply upon being offered the job. Stanley-Brown accepted, though, and served Garfield and the country well. Had Garfield lived, he would have seen Stanley-Brown become his son-in-law in 1888, when the young man married Garfield's daughter Mollie.[23]

The new Garfield administration had thousands of patronage appointments to make. Few states had as many patronage jobs as New York—the very state that had put Garfield over the top in electoral votes. Of all the patronage jobs in that very important and wealthy state, none was more important than collector of the port of New York. More than half of the nation's customs duties came through that office, and the position was the nation's most coveted patronage post. For years, skilled politicians like Conkling had used such jobs to build power bases in their home states.

By getting friends, relatives, and colleagues appointed to these positions, Conkling and others created large webs of federal employees who were more loyal to their personal benefactors than to the public good. This system also generated income for the political parties, since those appointed to patronage jobs were expected to give the party a percentage of their income in what basically amounted to a kickback.

None had used this system more effectively than Conkling. In fact, he had appointed his protégé, Vice President Chester A. Arthur, to head the New York customhouse. Arthur had served in that position for nearly seven years—until President Hayes fired him in 1878 for turning a blind eye to corruption. This action, plus Hayes's desire for civil service reform, had fueled Conkling's hatred of the president. But with a new man in the White House—and one Grant had described as "not possessed of the backbone of an angleworm"—Conkling was confident that he and the Stalwarts could manipulate Garfield, end "snivel service reform," and call the shots from behind the scenes.

Conkling was not the only one eager to bend Garfield's ear (or his will) about New York patronage. Garfield's own postmaster general, Thomas James, was a New Yorker and a Conkling ally, and he pressured the president to appoint reliable Stalwarts whenever he could. Several members of the New York congressional delegation had lunch with Garfield at the White House and raised the issue, as did congressmen and senators from other states, either because they were Stalwarts or because they wanted to prevent a fight between Garfield and Conkling. Secretary of State Blaine, who was eager to exclude Stalwarts from as many posts as possible, also brought it up incessantly, often bickering with the president over appointees that Blaine thought were too close to Conkling. Just ten days into his presidency, Garfield was already tired of it. "I must resist," he wrote, "a very strong tendency to be dejected and unhappy at the prospect which is offered by the work before me. The contest between personal interests is very hateful to me . . . the contests of men about men I greatly dislike."[24]

In an effort to resolve the New York question and achieve rapprochement with Conkling, Garfield invited the senator to the White House on March 20. The meeting turned out to be the most cordial sit-down the two would ever have. Conkling pressed his case for the Stalwarts, and Garfield agreed to some of his suggestions. Garfield made it clear, however, that he also had to "recognize some of the men that supported me at Chicago." This was anathema to Conkling because many of those men had originally been pledged to Grant and had bolted for the Garfield bandwagon. Even so, Conkling was less combative than usual at this meeting. One name, though, made Conkling's blood boil: William H. Robertson, a New Yorker and one of the first to abandon Grant at the Chicago convention. Conkling suggested a remote foreign post for Robertson and some of the other "bolters," but Garfield refused, arguing that they did not deserve "exile, but a place in their own state."[25] As the hour grew late, Conkling asked the president what he planned to do about the collectorship of the port of New York, but Garfield deferred that question for another time.

Two days later, Garfield sent in several nominations. Most of them were friends of Conkling's, including Levi Morton as minister to France. Although Morton had not gotten the treasury post he wanted, the French consulship was one of the nation's most prestigious. Newspapers called these March 22 nominations a victory for Conkling, and reporters opined that Conkling had indeed intimidated and overwhelmed the new president and taken New York patronage out of Garfield's hands and back into his own. Really, what could one expect from a new and wholly accidental president?

That night, as Garfield enjoyed dinner with his wife and friends, Blaine rushed to the White House to complain about the New York nominations made earlier in the day. Blaine all but accused the president of selling out to Conkling and even threatened to resign from the cabinet. Garfield calmed him down and told him to come back later. Blaine returned at around 10:30 p.m. and stayed until midnight, and the two decided on a course of action. Lucretia Garfield noted in her diary what her husband had told her: "I have broken Blaine's heart with the appointments I have made today. . . . Perhaps I ought to have consulted Blaine before sending in some of those New York appointments." He also told the first lady about the plan he and Blaine had devised: "to send in another batch of appointments tomorrow which will very thoroughly antidote the first. These the President did not intend to send so soon, but . . . has concluded that *now* is the time."[26]

On Wednesday, March 23, Garfield did indeed send another set of appointments to the Senate for confirmation. That afternoon, as Vice President Arthur presided over the Senate, a clerk handed him a list of the new appointments. As historian Kenneth D. Ackerman writes, "When he got about halfway down the list, his heart jumped into his throat. His eyes stopped at one name that jumped off the page." Arthur had the clerk carry the list over to Senator Conkling, whose "face suddenly froze and turned crimson." Garfield had nominated William H. Robertson to be collector of the port of New York.[27]

To make room for Robertson at the New York customhouse, Garfield had initiated a series of moves, nearly all of which were sure to enrage Conkling and the Stalwarts. The current collector, Edwin Merritt, was to be moved to the consulship in London. Grant's confidant Adam Badeau, then consul general in London, would be moved to the same position in Copenhagen, Denmark. Grant's brother-in-law, Michael Cramer, would be moved from chargé d'affaires in Denmark to the same post in Switzerland. Nicholas Fish, the son of Hamilton Fish (Grant's longtime secretary of state) and current chargé d'affaires in Switzerland, was out of a job. Finally, in what Conkling surely saw as adding insult to injury, Garfield nominated William E. Chandler—the Half-Breed Republican who had managed Blaine's campaign at the 1880 convention—to be solicitor general of the United States.[28] Garfield had made all these moves without consulting Conkling or his junior Senate colleague Tom Platt, Vice President Arthur, or any of the New York Stalwarts. In Conkling's mind, this entire plan reeked of the influence of his nemesis James G. Blaine. "The war of the roses has now begun in good earnest," the *Boston Daily Advertiser* wrote the next day.[29]

At least a few of Garfield's cabinet members were close to Senator Conkling or outright Conkling loyalists, and over the next few days, they tried to dissuade the president from standing behind these appointments. Postmaster General Thomas James was particularly vocal about the Robertson nomination, and attorney general Wayne MacVeagh felt slighted by Chandler's nomination as solicitor general. Garfield seemed close to caving a few times, but he talked with Blaine and ultimately stood firm. "The President is authorized to nominate, and did so," he wrote. "A senator considers it a personal affront that he was not previously told of the purpose. I stand joyfully on that issue—let who will, fight me."[30]

Conkling was, as expected, furious over the nomination of Robertson, and he became even angrier when many of his colleagues, including New York governor Alonzo Cornell, encouraged him to drop the fight over the nomination to preserve party unity. Conkling refused. Instead, he argued that senatorial courtesy required the president to consult him before making any major appointments in Conkling's home state. Throughout much of April 1881, Conkling presented his case to fellow senators in an attempt to have the Robertson nomination rejected outright, thereby accomplishing two goals: retaining his control over the New York customhouse and embarrassing "that Ohio man" Garfield. The Senate went so far as to create a "Committee of Conciliation" to moderate between Conkling and the White House, but neither seemed inclined to budge. At one point, eager to see

Robertson's nomination put to a vote, Garfield withdrew every other nomination that had not yet been voted on.

Sensing that he was losing the battle—indeed, ninety-four New York newspapers had written editorials supporting Garfield's position, with just eighteen supporting Conkling's—the senator decided to take a drastic and dramatic step. On May 16 Vice President Arthur, who had been meeting regularly with Conkling and actively plotting against his own president, entered the Senate chamber and directed the clerk to read a message from Conkling: "Sir, Will you please announce to the Senate that my resignation as Senator of the United States from the State of New York has been forwarded to the governor of that State?" This was a bombshell. Then the clerk read a second message: "Sir, I have forwarded to the governor of the State of New York my resignation as Senator for the State of New York. Will you be pleased to announce the fact to the Senate? With great respect, your obedient servant, T[homas] C[ollier] Platt." Both of New York's senators had resigned and left Washington. They were headed to Albany, where they expected the New York legislature to immediately reappoint them, thereby strengthening their positions and weakening President Garfield's.[31]

Garfield saw this action for what it was: "a very weak attempt at the heroic . . . it will be received with guffaws of laughter. . . . Having done all I fairly could to avoid a fight, I now fight to the end." Indeed, later that month, Garfield reported to his diary, "Conkling received just one-third of the Republican votes of the two Houses at Albany, Platt 29—six less than Conkling. And this is the 'vindication' he appealed for."[32] The most intense political battle of Garfield's career was over. Conkling and Platt were gone from the Senate, giving the president a major victory just two and a half months into his administration. Presumably, he could now focus on other priorities, including modernizing the US Navy, organizing a conference of Latin American nations to be held in Washington in 1882, and continuing to improve the social, economic, and political standing of freedmen and -women in the South.

Throughout this tense political standoff during the early days of his presidency, Garfield's family watched nervously as First Lady Lucretia Garfield battled a nasty strain of malaria. Washington was infamous for its poor sanitary conditions, and the smell of sewage was pervasive, especially during the spring and summer months. Malaria was a common ailment, and the first lady developed a dangerous case of the disease in early May 1881.

Several times the family feared that her death was imminent, but after six weeks or so, she was sufficiently recovered to travel to the New Jersey shore for the restorative effects of the sea air. The president joined her there for several days in late June.

Ironically, former president Grant, still a strong Conkling ally and the author of at least one chastising letter to Garfield during the public squabble, was also at Elberon, New Jersey, that week, staying in a cottage owned by his son. The Grant cottage was across the street from the Elberon Hotel, where the Garfields stayed during their visit. Political protocol dictated that the former president pay a social call to the current president, but for several days the Garfields saw no sign of Grant. On June 24 Garfield recorded in his diary that he and his wife had gone for a carriage ride that evening, and "General Grant was standing in front of his son Jesse's cottage, and bowed, lifting his hat. This is his only courtesy to me since he came four days ago." Garfield added, "I do not think he can afford to show feeling in this way . . . he injures himself more than he does me." The next day, the Elberon Hotel held a reception for President Garfield and the first lady. Grant made a brief appearance, which Garfield noted was "a tardy recognition of respect due to the office he once held."[33]

Garfield departed Elberon and returned to Washington on June 27. His wife planned to stay for a few more days of exposure to the seashore's salt air and healthy climate. The two would reunite in five days, on July 2, when Mrs. Garfield would travel north and meet her husband for a trip to New England. They planned to stop at the president's alma mater, Williams College, where Garfield would make a speech, and then continue on to Maine for a vacation that would include a visit to the home of Secretary of State Blaine. After making a few other stops, they would eventually wind up at their Mentor, Ohio, farm, where they would spend part of August. It would be their first time back in Mentor since the start of Garfield's presidency. They had left the house and the farm in the care of Mrs. Garfield's father, Zeb Rudolph, and her brother, Joseph Rudolph. Garfield was eager to see his Mentor home again, and he had big plans for the property, where he and Lucretia intended to live in retirement after his presidency.

As President James A. Garfield rose on Saturday, July 2, 1881, he was in an unusually good mood. He played and sang with his children and looked forward to his reunion with his wife and their upcoming trip. His main headache—Conkling—was gone, and his handling of the Robertson nomination and the battle with Conkling had won rave reviews from the press and the public. He had invited Secretary of State Blaine to accompany

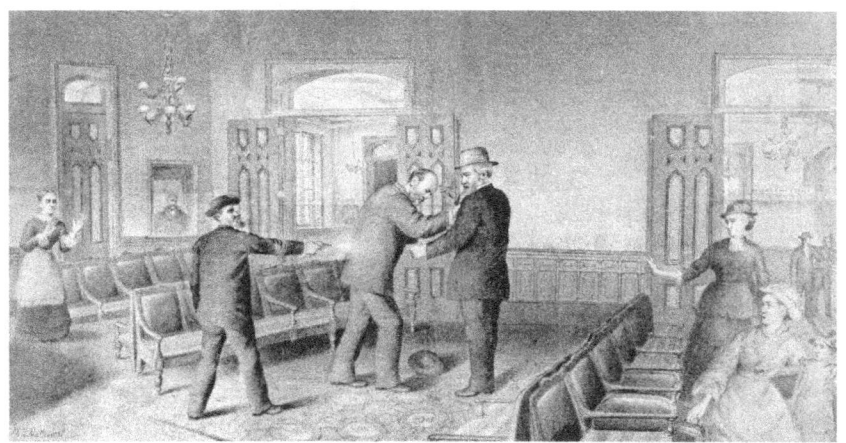

Charles Guiteau shot President Garfield at Washington's Baltimore and Potomac train station on July 2, 1881. Secretary of State James Blaine was at Garfield's side when Guiteau fired the gun. (Courtesy of Library of Congress)

him to the train station, and as the two rode together, they talked about the speech Garfield was planning to write for the Yorktown victory centennial in October. As he and Blaine stepped out of the carriage into the morning sun and walked toward the station, Garfield must have felt that his presidency was just beginning and that his best days as America's chief executive lay ahead.

CONCLUSION

James Garfield never got the chance to live up to his full potential as president. As he walked through Washington's Baltimore and Potomac train depot on the morning of July 2, 1881, a troubled drifter named Charles Guiteau approached and fired two bullets at Garfield. The first shot grazed the president's arm, but the second lodged in his back. As he struggled with a DC police officer, Guiteau told the crowd that had gathered, "I am a Stalwart, and Arthur will be president." Today, hulking Secret Service agents with earpieces and sunglasses are an obvious presence everywhere the president goes. It seems unbelievable that someone as disturbed as Guiteau was able to get within handgun-firing distance of Garfield, who walked into the train station that morning with no bodyguards or security.

As the investigation of Guiteau progressed, disturbing details emerged. The young man, who had tried and failed at several different careers, including law and the ministry, had stalked the president of the United States for weeks. As he told the crowd at the train station, Guiteau considered himself a Stalwart Republican—a Grant-Conkling-Arthur man. Guiteau had prepared a rambling speech in favor of the Grant ticket in 1880; when Garfield was nominated instead, he had simply crossed out Grant's name and inserted Garfield's. Guiteau had spent much of the presidential campaign hanging around Republican headquarters in New York. He had even given his speech a few times to confused crowds.

After Garfield's inauguration, Guiteau went to Washington to claim what he believed to be his rightful reward: a job in the new administration, preferably the American consulship to Vienna or Paris. He visited the White House many times, joining thousands of other office seekers. After the shooting, Garfield's personal secretary recalled seeing Guiteau at the White House at least fifteen times. After being told in no uncertain terms by Secretary of State James Blaine that he would not receive a consulship, Guiteau claimed that God spoke to him and told him to kill Garfield so that Arthur would be elevated to the presidency. "I had no ill will toward the President," Guiteau wrote after the shooting. "His death was a political necessity."[1]

But Garfield survived the shooting. He was carried back to the White House, where he endured horrendous medical care for the next two months. Dr. Willard Bliss, the primary physician caring for Garfield, did not believe in the existence of germs or the need to sanitize his hands or instruments before examining the president or probing his back wound in an effort to locate the bullet. Many European doctors had long since accepted Dr. Joseph Lister's method of antiseptic surgery, but just as many American physicians—including Bliss—had not. Bliss's unsanitary methods led to infection, which ravaged Garfield's body until his death on September 19, nearly eighty days after Guiteau's attack. When tried for murder, Guiteau told the jury, "I did not kill the President. The doctors did that. I merely shot him."[2] Today, Guiteau would almost surely be found not guilty by reason of insanity, but that argument did not work in the late nineteenth century. He was found guilty of murdering Garfield and hanged on June 30, 1882, just two days before the shooting's one-year anniversary.

In early September, Garfield was moved to the New Jersey seashore for his own comfort and in the hope that the sea air would rejuvenate his health. Shortly before his death, he asked his friend Almon Rockwell, "Do you think my name will have a place in human history?" Rockwell replied, "Yes, a grand one, but a grander place in human hearts."[3] It seemed to be an accurate prediction for a time: Garfield's funeral in Cleveland on September 26, 1881, was even larger than Abraham Lincoln's final ceremony in Springfield, Illinois. But over time, as Americans became more cynical about the Gilded Age, and as authors and historians either ignored the politicians of this period or reinforced the idea that they did nothing of note, Garfield and many of his contemporaries were all but forgotten.

This is unfortunate. All presidents of the United States, members of Congress, cabinet secretaries, and political appointees have a profound influence on American governmental policies and are worthy of thorough historical study and debate. Some may ultimately be found lacking and less consequential than others, but their places in history deserve examination

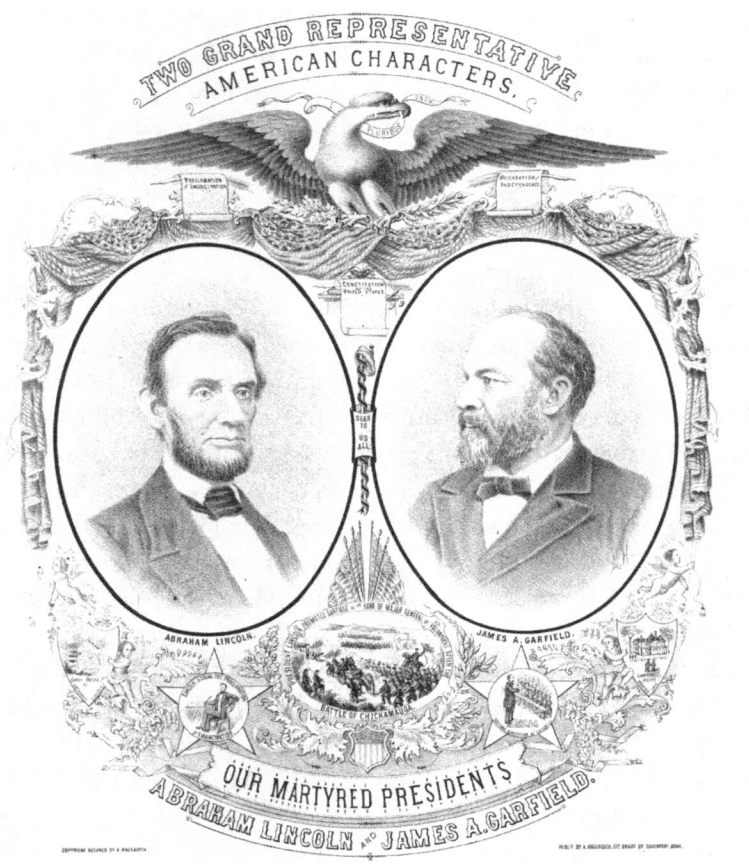

Two martyred presidents: Abraham Lincoln and James A. Garfield. (Courtesy of Library of Congress)

and interpretation by historians. In the case of James Garfield, the lack of scholarly interest in his life and his presidential potential has denied students of history the chance to honestly assess his impact, just as surely as Guiteau's bullets and Bliss's medical malpractice denied the American people the leadership of a man who could have been a fine president.

In 1880 James Garfield and Winfield Scott Hancock were the presidential nominees of two political parties in great transition. Garfield's Republicans were somewhat adrift, in search of new issues and alliances after two decades of focusing of the abolition of slavery, equality before the law, and the rights of freed black people. With Reconstruction over, the Republicans needed to identify new issues that would resonate with the American people if they wanted to hold on to the presidency and Congress. Many of Hancock's Democrats were just as concerned about the party's focus on the past; they wanted to distance themselves from secession but still find ways to reestablish white supremacy in the South and limit the freedoms and rights of black people. Nominating a decorated Union general seemed like the perfect way to demonstrate loyalty to the Union and negate the usual Republican "bloody shirt" campaign tactics.

The policy differences between the two parties—at least as enumerated in their 1880 platforms—seemed minimal. So perhaps it came down to which candidate and which party the voters believed had the greatest vision for America. Certainly Garfield, an elected official for nearly twenty years, had a longer track record for voters to assess. And despite his party's search for a new identity, Garfield maintained that the Republican Party had been founded on the idea of equality for all and should remain true to its roots. It is telling that Republicans at the 1880 nominating convention in Chicago chose Garfield to be their standard-bearer, not Grant or some other politician allied with the Conkling wing of the party. Just as telling is that American voters, albeit very narrowly, chose Garfield's vision for the country. They rejected the vision of the Democratic Party, which was still obsessed with returning power to white men in the South and minimizing black people's roles in civic life there.

Hancock, though certainly an honorable and accomplished man, had no real public identity for voters to consider and judge. He also maintained a lower profile during the campaign than did Garfield, who engaged in front-porch campaigning from his Ohio farmhouse. Because the Democratic Party did all of Hancock's campaigning for him, he was hamstrung by the overtly racist and reactionary vision his party espoused.

Despite the tradition of political parties doing the bulk of campaigning, Garfield was a fairly active participant in his own campaign. He ignored President Hayes's admonition to say nothing and look wise. Garfield, a seasoned politician, struck a near-perfect balance of active involvement in his own campaign while maintaining the appearance of little involvement. Hancock, in contrast, made few public appearances and spoke to few reporters.

Even so, the 1880 election was the closest popular-vote victory in American history. This demonstrates just how politically and geographically divided the American people were at the time—just as they are today. Ultimately, based on his past record of supporting the abolition of slavery and promoting freedom and equality, most reasonable readers will likely agree that the American people chose the right candidate in 1880. That James Garfield served only a few months in office—not nearly enough time to implement his vision for the nation's future—is one of the least understood but most significant tragedies in American political history.

NOTES

INTRODUCTION
1 Allan Peskin, "Presidents Anonymous," *Timeline*, October–November 1985, 22.
2 Thomas Wolfe, "From Death to Morning," in *The Complete Short Stories of Thomas Wolfe*, ed. Francis E. Skipp (New York: Francis E. Skipp, 1987).

CHAPTER 1. "HALF WAY BETWEEN GOD AND THE DEVIL"
1 "Rutherford B. Hayes 1876 Acceptance Speech," July 8, 1876, Rutherford B. Hayes Presidential Center, http://www.rbhayes.org/hayes/1876-acceptance-speech/.
2 Garfield diary, July 7 and 10, 1876, in *The Diary of James A. Garfield*, 4 vols., ed. Harry James Brown and Frederick D. Williams (East Lansing: Michigan State University Press, 1967–1981), 3:320–322.
3 Keith Ian Polakoff, *The Politics of Inertia: The Election of 1876 and the End of Reconstruction* (Baton Rouge: Louisiana State University Press, 1973), 106.
4 "Hayes 1876 Acceptance Speech."
5 Eric Foner, *Reconstruction: America's Unfinished Revolution, 1863–1877*, Francis Parkman Prize ed. (New York: History Book Club, 1988), 567.
6 "Republican Party Platform of 1876," June 14, 1876, Gerhard Peters and John T. Woolley, American Presidency Project, http://www.presidency.ucsb.edu/ws/?pid=29624.
7 Douglass and Hayes quoted in Michael A. Bellesiles, *1877: America's Year of Living Violently* (New York: New Press, 2010), 27–29.
8 Ingersoll quoted in Stanley P. Hirshson, *Farewell to the Bloody Shirt: Northern Republicans & the Southern Negro, 1877–1893*. (Bloomington: Indiana University Press, 1962), 23.
9 Letter to *Cincinnati Enquirer*, May 6, 1876, quoted in Michael F. Holt, *By One Vote: The Disputed Presidential Election of 1876* (Lawrence: University Press of Kansas, 2008), 101.
10 Holt, *By One Vote*, 101–103.
11 Holt, *By One Vote*, 110.
12 "1876 Democratic Party Platform," June 22, 1876, Peters and Woolley, American Presidency Project, http://www.presidency.ucsb.edu/ws/?pid=29581.
13 Rutherford B. Hayes to Carl Schurz, August 9, 1876, quoted in Lawrence

Grossman, *The Democratic Party and the Negro: Northern and National Politics, 1868–92* (Urbana: University of Illinois Press, 1976), 51.

14 John Bigelow quoted in Grossman, *Democratic Party and the Negro*, 51.
15 *The Campaign Text Book: Why the People Want a Change; The Republican Party Reviewed: Its Sins of Commission and Omission* (New York: Democratic National Committee, 1876), 246.
16 *Cincinnati Enquirer*, November 4, 1876, quoted in Grossman, *Democratic Party and the Negro*, 53.
17 Garfield and Hayes quoted in Charles W. Calhoun, *Conceiving a New Republic: The Republican Party and the Southern Question, 1869–1900* (Lawrence: University Press of Kansas, 2006), 104.
18 Holt, *By One Vote*, 28–32.
19 *Chicago Daily News*, November 8, 1876, quoted in Polakoff, *Politics of Inertia*, 200.
20 Hayes quoted in Hirshson, *Farewell to the Bloody Shirt*, 24–25.
21 Chandler quoted in Polakoff, *Politics of Inertia*, 203.
22 Hayes quoted in Polakoff, *Politics of Inertia*, 205.
23 Brown and Williams, *Diary of Garfield*, 3:379.
24 Brown and Williams, *Diary of Garfield*, 3:380.
25 Bigelow and Tilden, November 11, 1876, quoted in Polakoff, *Politics of Inertia*, 206–207.
26 Grant quoted in Calhoun, *Conceiving a New Republic*, 107.
27 Rutherford B. Hayes to Carl Schurz, November 13, 1876, quoted in Holt, *By One Vote*, 179.
28 Holt, *By One Vote*, 181.
29 Morton and Garfield quoted in Hirshson, *Farewell to the Bloody Shirt*, 23.
30 Palmer quoted in Polakoff, *Politics of Inertia*, 210.
31 Robert Granville Caldwell, *James A. Garfield: Party Chieftan* (New York: Dodd, Mead, 1931), 253.
32 Polakoff, *Politics of Inertia*, 212–213.
33 Polakoff, *Politics of Inertia*, 213–214.
34 Brown and Williams, *Diary of Garfield*, 3:391.
35 Wallace quoted in Polakoff, *Politics of Inertia*, 216.
36 C. Gibson to Samuel J. Tilden, November 23, 1876, quoted in Polakoff, *Politics of Inertia*, 222.
37 H. B. Stanton to Tilden, November 22, 1876; C. Gibson to Tilden, November 28, 1876, quoted in Holt, *By One Vote*, 204.
38 Hewitt quoted in Polakoff, *Politics of Inertia*, 273.
39 Brown and Williams, *Diary of Garfield*, 3:423–424, footnote.
40 Brown and Williams, *Diary of Garfield*, 3:420.
41 Garfield to Hayes, January 19, 1877, quoted in John M. Taylor, *Garfield of Ohio: The Available Man* (New York: W. W. Norton, 1970), 167.
42 Garfield to Hayes, quoted in Theodore Clarke Smith, *The Life and Letters of James Abram Garfield*, 2 vols. (New Haven, CT: Yale University Press, 1925), 1:630.

43 Brown and Williams, *Diary of Garfield*, 3:426.
44 Black quoted in Taylor, *Garfield of Ohio*, 169.
45 Brown and Williams, *Diary of Garfield*, 3:440–441.
46 D. J. Goodwin to Samuel J. Tilden, December 12, 1876; Leroy Pope Walker to Manton Marble, December 19, 1876, quoted in Holt, *By One Vote*, 236.
47 Cox to Hayes; Hayes to Cox; Hayes to Schurz, quoted in Calhoun, *Conceiving a New Republic*, 122–123.
48 Hayes to Douglass, quoted in Calhoun, *Conceiving a New Republic*, 123.
49 Lewis L. Gould, *Grand Old Party: A History of the Republicans* (New York: Random House, 2003), 75.
50 Brown and Williams, *Diary of Garfield*, 3:449–450.
51 C. Vann Woodward, *Reunion and Reaction: The Compromise of 1877 and the End of Reconstruction* (Boston: Little, Brown, 1951); Allan Peskin, "Was There a Compromise of 1877?" *Journal of American History* 60, 1 (June 1973): 63–75.
52 Allan Peskin, *Garfield* (Kent, OH: Kent State University Press, 1978), 418; Polakoff, *Politics of Inertia*, 313.
53 "Inaugural Address of Rutherford B. Hayes," March 5, 1877, Lillian Goldman Law Library, Yale University, http://avalon.law.yale.edu/19th_century/hayes.asp.
54 Garfield to Cox, quoted in Peskin, *Garfield*, 424.
55 Garfield to Lucretia, quoted in Peskin, *Garfield*, 424.
56 Hayes diary, quoted in Calhoun, *Conceiving a New Republic*, 142.
57 All quoted in Foner, *Reconstruction*, 582.
58 Foner, *Reconstruction*, 588.
59 Polakoff, *Politics of Inertia*, 319.
60 Comly quoted in Polakoff, *Politics of Inertia*, 319.
61 Stephens and Sherman quoted in Ari Hoogenboom, *The Presidency of Rutherford B. Hayes* (Lawrence: University Press of Kansas, 1988), 72.
62 All quoted in Hoogenboom, *Presidency of Hayes*, 72–73.

CHAPTER 2. "LET US NOT SHRINK NOW"

1 Garfield diary, January 2, 1879, in *The Diary of James A. Garfield*, 4 vols., ed. Harry James Brown and Frederick D. Williams (Lansing: Michigan State University Press, 1967–1981), 4:162.
2 Allan Peskin, *Garfield* (Kent, OH: Kent State University Press, 1978), 7.
3 Garfield diary, June 23, 1854, in Brown and Williams, *Diary of Garfield*, 1:248.
4 Garfield diary, November 2, 1855, in Brown and Williams, *Diary of Garfield*, 1:273.
5 Garfield to Lucretia Rudolph, June 15, 1856, quoted in Peskin, *Garfield*, 45.
6 Debbie Weinkamer, "James & Lucretia Garfield's Love Story," *The Garfield Observer: The Blog of James A. Garfield National Historic Site*, February 14, 2017, https://garfieldnps.wordpress.com/2017/02/14/james-lucretia-garfields-love-story/.
7 Peskin, *Garfield*, 70–71.
8 *Portage County Democrat*, September 12, 1860; *Ohio State Journal*, quoted in Peskin, *Garfield*, 77.

9   Garfield diary, November 6, 1860, in Brown and Williams, *Diary of Garfield*, 1:350.
10 Garfield to Lucretia, February 17, 1861, in *Crete and James: Personal Letters of Lucretia and James Garfield*, ed. John Shaw (Lansing: Michigan State University Press, 1994), 107.
11 Peskin, *Garfield*, 83.
12 Garfield to Burke A. Hinsdale, January 15, 1861, in *Garfield-Hinsdale Letters: Correspondence between James Abram Garfield and Burke Aaron Hinsdale*, ed. Mary L. Hinsdale (Ann Arbor: University of Michigan Press, 1949), 54–55.
13 Garfield to Hinsdale, in Hinsdale, *Garfield-Hinsdale Letters*, 55.
14 Garfield to Harry Rhodes, April 14, 1861, in Theodore Clarke Smith, *The Life and Letters of James Abram Garfield*, 2 vols. (New Haven, CT: Yale University Press, 1925), 1:160.
15 Garfield to Harry Rhodes, May 1, 1862, in Smith, *Life and Letters*, 1:211–212.
16 Peskin, *Garfield*, 233.
17 Garfield to Lucretia, June 14, 1862, in Shaw, *Crete and James*, 142.
18 Garfield quoted in Peskin, *Garfield*, 153.
19 Peskin, *Garfield*, 139.
20 Garfield to Harry Rhodes, May 1, 1862, in *The Wild Life of the Army: Civil War Letters of James A. Garfield*, ed. Frederick D. Williams (Lansing: Michigan State University Press, 1964), 89.
21 Garfield quoted in Smith, *Life and Letters*, 1:355–356.
22 Garfield quoted in Benson J. Lossing, *A Biography of James A. Garfield: Late President of the United States* (Chicago: Henry S. Goodspeed, 1882), 303.
23 Garfield, "The Constitutional Amendment Banning Slavery," in *Works of James Abram Garfield*, 2 vols., ed. Burke A. Hinsdale (Boston: James R. Osgood, 1883), 1:84.
24 Garfield quoted in Alan Gephardt, "'The Most Important Political Change We Have Known': James A. Garfield, Slavery, and Justice in the Civil War Era, Part II," *The Garfield Observer: The Blog of James A. Garfield National Historic Site*, February 15, 2013, https://garfieldnps.wordpress.com/2013/02/15/the-most-important-political-change-we-have-known-james-a-garfield-slavery-and-justice-in-the-civil-war-era-part-ii/.
25 Hinsdale, *Works of Garfield*, 1:85–94.
26 Garfield to David Swaim, quoted in Gephardt, "'The Most Important Political Change We Have Known.'"
27 Peskin, *Garfield*, 252.
28 Garfield to Hinsdale, in Hinsdale, *Garfield-Hinsdale Letters*, 88.
29 "Garfield's 1868 Decoration Day Oration," in Daniel J. Vermilya, *James Garfield in the Civil War: For Ohio and the Union* (Charleston, SC: History Press, 2015), 183–187.
30 Peskin, *Garfield*, 241–242.
31 Garfield to Hinsdale, in Hinsdale, *Garfield-Hinsdale Letters*, 135.
32 Todd Arrington, "The Impeachment of Andrew Johnson," We're History, March 13, 2018, http://werehistory.org/the-impeachment-of-andrew-johnson/.

33 Peskin, *Garfield*, 309.
34 Peskin, *Garfield*, 310.
35 Garfield quoted in Peskin, *Garfield*, 319–320.
36 Brown and Williams, *Diary of Garfield*, 2:146.
37 Garfield to Hinsdale, in Hinsdale, *Garfield-Hinsdale Letters*, 268.
38 Garfield to Hinsdale, January 7, 1875, in Hinsdale, *Garfield-Hinsdale Letters*, 309.
39 Garfield, February 4, 1875, in *Congressional Record*, House of Representatives, 43rd Congress, 2nd session, 1005.
40 Peskin, *Garfield*, 396–397.
41 Peskin, *Garfield*, 397–398.
42 Garfield quoted in Peskin, *Garfield*, 401.
43 L. Q. C. Lamar, "Speech on the Policy of the Republican Party and the Political Situation in the South," August 2, 1876, in Edward Mayes, *Lucius Q. C. Lamar: His Life, Times, and Speeches, 1825–1893* (Nashville: Publishing House of the Methodist Episcopal Church South, 1895), 286–288.
44 Garfield, "The Democratic Party and the Government," August 4, 1876, in Hinsdale, *Works of Garfield*, 2:353–387.
45 *New Orleans Democrat*, April 22, 1877.
46 Peskin, *Garfield*, 426.
47 Garfield, "Ought the Negro to Be Disfranchised? Ought He to Have Been Enfranchised?" *North American Review* 128, 268 (March 1879): 244–250.
48 Garfield to Hinsdale, January 30, 1879, in Hinsdale, *Garfield-Hinsdale Letters*, 398.
49 Alan Gephardt and Joan Kapsch, "The 1879 'Government Shutdown,' Part I," in *The Garfield Observer: The Blog of James A. Garfield National Historic Site*, https://garfieldnps.wordpress.com/2016/10/28/the-1879-government-shutdown-part-i/.
50 Hayes quoted in Ari Hoogenboom, *The Presidency of Rutherford B. Hayes* (Lawrence: University Press of Kansas, 1988), 75.
51 Hayes quoted in Gephardt and Kapsch, "The 1879 'Government Shutdown,' Part I."
52 Garfield, "Revolution in Congress," in Hinsdale, *Works of Garfield*, 2:655–678.
53 Conkling and Blaine quoted in Alan Gephardt and Joan Kapsch, "The 1879 'Government Shutdown,' Part II," in *The Garfield Observer: The Blog of James A. Garfield National Historic Site*. https://garfieldnps.wordpress.com/2016/11/10/the-1879-government-shutdown-part-ii/.
54 Peskin, *Garfield*, 442.
55 Garfield quoted in Gephardt and Kapsch, "The 1879 'Government Shutdown,' Part II."
56 Garfield quoted in Smith, *Life and Letters*, 2:687.
57 Peskin, *Garfield*, 442–443.
58 Peskin, *Garfield*, 440.
59 Peskin, *Garfield*, 451.
60 Peskin, *Garfield*, 451–454.

CHAPTER 3. "ANTAGONISMS AND CONTROVERSIES"

1. Garfield diary, July 1, 1879, in *The Diary of James A. Garfield*, 4 vols., ed. Harry James Brown and Frederick D. Williams (Lansing: Michigan State University Press, 1967–1981), 4:258.
2. Allan Peskin, *Garfield* (Kent, OH: Kent State University Press, 1978), 454.
3. *New York Times*, September 27, 1877.
4. Peskin, *Garfield*, 452. Peskin notes that Conkling would have made a fascinating test subject a little later in history as the field of psychiatry advanced: "Even an age as yet uninstructed by Freud could not help being fascinated by Conkling's dread of being touched, his predilection for lavender ink and canary waistcoats, his blond spitcurl, and his strutting, aggressive show of masculinity."
5. In a February 2017 interview on the NBC News program *Today*, former president George W. Bush called this power "addictive" and "corrosive." Grant was certainly not the first or the last former president to miss it and want it back.
6. Julia Dent Grant quoted in Kenneth D. Ackerman, *Dark Horse: The Surprise Election and Political Murder of President James A. Garfield* (Falls Church, VA: Viral History Press, 2011), 40.
7. Grant and Adams quoted in Ackerman, *Dark Horse*, 37.
8. Grant quoted in Ackerman, *Dark Horse*, 39.
9. Davis quoted in *New York Times*, October 2, 1879.
10. *New York Times*, February 10, 1880.
11. Blaine quoted in Ackerman, *Dark Horse*, 12.
12. Heather Cox Richardson, *To Make Men Free: A History of the Republican Party* (New York: Basic Books, 2014), 74.
13. Conkling quoted in Ackerman, *Dark Horse*, 13.
14. Herbert J. Clancy, S.J., *The Presidential Election of 1880* (Chicago: Loyola University Press, 1958), 32–33.
15. Chandler quoted in Clancy, *Presidential Election of 1880*, 33.
16. Blaine and Bruce quoted in Philip Chin, "The Path to the Chinese Exclusion Act, 1868 to 1882," http://www.chineseamericanheroes.org/history/; Nicholas Patler, "A Black Vice President in the Gilded Age? Senator Blanche Kelso Bruce and the National Republican Convention of 1880," *Journal of Mississippi History*, July 2013, 105–139.
17. Garfield quoted in Theodore Clarke Smith, *The Life and Letters of James Abram Garfield*, 2 vols. (New Haven, CT: Yale University Press, 1925), 2:677.
18. Garfield diary, February 24, 1879, in Brown and Williams, *Diary of Garfield*, 4:187.
19. Rutherford B. Hayes, "Veto Message, March 1, 1879," University of California–Santa Barbara, American Presidency Project, http://www.presidency.ucsb.edu/ws/?pid=68652.
20. Brown and Williams, *Diary of Garfield*, 4:187.
21. A. N. Cole to John Sherman, quoted in Clancy, *Presidential Election of 1880*, 35.
22. Brown and Williams, *Diary of Garfield*, 4:329.
23. Brown and Williams, *Diary of Garfield*, 4:315–316.

24 Garfield and Henry quoted in Peskin, *Garfield*, 445; Brown and Williams, *Diary of Garfield*, 4:316.
25 Peskin, *Garfield*, 446.
26 Brown and Williams, *Diary of Garfield*, 4:346–347.
27 Brown and Williams, *Diary of Garfield*, 4:356.
28 Garfield quoted in Smith, *Life and Letters*, 2:949.
29 Garfield quoted in Smith, *Life and Letters*, 2:949; L. Sheldon to Garfield, quoted in Peskin, *Garfield*, 455.
30 Nichol quoted in Peskin, *Garfield*, 456.
31 Brown and Williams, *Diary of Garfield*, 4:369–370.
32 Foster quoted in Clancy, *Presidential Election of 1880*, 37.
33 Brown and Williams, *Diary of Garfield*, 4:405.
34 Stan M. Haynes, *President-Making in the Gilded Age: The Nominating Conventions of 1876–1900* (Jefferson, NC: McFarland, 2016), 45.
35 Sheldon quoted in Peskin, *Garfield*, 458.
36 Hinsdale to Garfield, quoted in *Garfield-Hinsdale Letters: Correspondence between James Abram Garfield and Burke Aaron Hinsdale*, ed. Mary L. Hinsdale (Ann Arbor: University of Michigan Press, 1949), 450–451; Barker quoted in Peskin, *Garfield*, 459.
37 Peskin, *Garfield*, 459.
38 Brown and Williams, *Diary of Garfield*, 4:422.
39 Brown and Williams, *Diary of Garfield*, 4:423.
40 Smith, *Life and Letters*, 2:957–958.
41 Brown and Williams, *Diary of Garfield*, 4:424.
42 Adam Badeau, *Grant in Peace: From Appomattox to Mount McGregor* (Freeport, NY: Books for Libraries Press, 1971), 319–320.
43 *Washington Post*, June 1, 1880.
44 Conkling and Jewell quoted in Ackerman, *Dark Horse*, 40–41.
45 *Chicago Tribune* and Logan's son quoted in Ackerman, *Dark Horse*, 42.
46 Julia Dent Grant, *The Personal Memoirs of Julia Dent Grant*, ed. John Y. Simon (Carbondale: Southern Illinois University Press, 1975), 321.
47 Brown and Williams, *Diary of Garfield*, 4:424.
48 Garfield to Lucretia Garfield, quoted in *Crete and James: Personal Letters of Lucretia and James Garfield*, ed. John Shaw (Lansing: Michigan State University Press, 1994), 368.
49 Garfield to Lucretia Garfield, quoted in Shaw, *Crete and James*, 368.
50 *Chicago Tribune*, May 30, 1880.
51 Sherman quoted in Ackerman, *Dark Horse*, 47.
52 Peskin, *Garfield*, 461.
53 *Baltimore Sun*, June 1, 1880, quoted in Haynes, *President-Making in the Gilded Age*, 49–50.
54 Brown and Williams, *Diary of Garfield*, 4:425.
55 *Proceedings of the Republican National Convention, Held at Chicago, Illinois, Wednesday–Tuesday, June 2–8, 1880* (Chicago: Jno. B. Jeffery Printing House, 1881), 5.

56 *Proceedings of the Republican National Convention*, 17–18.
57 Haynes, *President-Making in the Gilded Age*, 52.
58 *Proceedings of the Republican National Convention*, 34–37.
59 Wharton Barker, "The Secret History of Garfield's Nomination," *Pearson's Magazine*, May 1916, 435–443.
60 Peskin, *Garfield*, 464–465.
61 Barker, "Secret History of Garfield's Nomination," 441.
62 Ackerman, *Dark Horse*, 71.
63 Peskin, *Garfield*, 463–464.
64 Peskin, *Garfield*, 465.
65 Haynes, *President-Making in the Gilded Age*, 54.
66 *Proceedings of the Republican National Convention*, 163–165.
67 Republican Party Platform of 1880, Gerhard Peters and John T. Woolley, American Presidency Project, https://www.presidency.ucsb.edu/documents/republican-party-platform-1880.

CHAPTER 4. "IF ANY OUTSIDER IS TAKEN, I HOPE IT WILL BE GARFIELD"

1 Wharton Barker, "The Secret History of Garfield's Nomination," *Pearson's Magazine*, May 1916, 440.
2 Unnamed Ohio delegate and Bateman quoted in Allan Peskin, *Garfield* (Kent, OH: Kent State University Press, 1978), 462–463.
3 Herbert J. Clancy, S.J., *The Presidential Election of 1880* (Chicago: Loyola University Press, 1958), 97.
4 *Proceedings of the Republican National Convention, Held at Chicago, Illinois, Wednesday–Tuesday, June 2–8, 1880* (Chicago: Jno. B. Jeffery Printing House, 1881), 175–177.
5 *Proceedings of the Republican National Convention*, 177–179.
6 *Proceedings of the Republican National Convention*, 179.
7 *Proceedings of the Republican National Convention*, 179–182.
8 Kenneth D. Ackerman, *Dark Horse: The Surprise Election and Political Murder of President James A. Garfield* (Falls Church, VA: Viral History Press, 2011), 74.
9 Stan M. Haynes, *President-Making in the Gilded Age: The Nominating Conventions of 1876–1900* (Jefferson, NC: McFarland, 2016), 57.
10 Ackerman, *Dark Horse*, 75.
11 Garfield to Lucretia Garfield, quoted in *Crete and James: Personal Letters of Lucretia and James Garfield*, ed. John Shaw (Lansing: Michigan State University Press, 1994), 376.
12 *Proceedings of the Republican National Convention*, 184.
13 Garfield to Lucretia Garfield, quoted in Shaw, *Crete and James*, 376.
14 *Proceedings of the Republican National Convention*, 184.
15 *Proceedings of the Republican National Convention*, 184–185.
16 *Proceedings of the Republican National Convention*, 186.
17 *Proceedings of the Republican National Convention*, 185.
18 *Proceedings of the Republican National Convention*, 186.

19 *Proceedings of the Republican National Convention,* 188.
20 Ingersoll quoted in *Washington Evening Star,* June 6, 1880.
21 Murat Halstead to Sherman, quoted in Ackerman, *Dark Horse,* 76–77.
22 Lucretia to Garfield and Garfield to Lucretia, quoted in Shaw, *Crete and James,* 375–376.
23 *New York Times,* June 8, 1880.
24 Coan to Garfield, quoted in Ackerman, *Dark Horse,* 81.
25 *Proceedings of the Republican National Convention,* 197–251.
26 Ackerman, *Dark Horse,* 88–89.
27 Ackerman, *Dark Horse,* 90.
28 *Proceedings of the Republican National Convention,* 261.
29 *Cleveland Herald,* June 12, 1880.
30 *Proceedings of the Republican National Convention,* 269.
31 George F. Hoar, *Autobiography of Seventy Years* (New York: Charles Scribner's Sons, 1903), 396–397.
32 Ackerman, *Dark Horse,* 93; Peskin, *Garfield,* 475.
33 Ackerman, *Dark Horse,* 94.
34 Ackerman, *Dark Horse,* 94; John Sherman, *John Sherman's Recollections of Forty Years in the House, Senate and Cabinet* (Chicago: Werner, 1895), 612.
35 Ackerman, *Dark Horse,* 95.
36 *Proceedings of the Republican National Convention,* 270–276.
37 *Cleveland Herald,* June 9, 1880; Peskin, *Garfield,* 476.
38 *Proceedings of the Republican National Convention,* 277.
39 Shaw, *Crete and James,* 377.
40 Recent scholarship indicates that the idea of vice-presidential candidates providing any real geographic advantage has been grossly overstated. See Christopher J. Devine and Kyle C. Kopko, *The VP Advantage: How Running Mates Influence Home State Voting in Presidential Elections* (Manchester, UK: Manchester University Press, 2016).
41 Peskin, *Garfield,* 480–481.
42 Peskin, *Garfield,* 481.
43 Ackerman, *Dark Horse,* 104; Sherman, *Recollections of Forty Years,* 614–615.
44 James G. Blaine, *Twenty Years of Congress: From Lincoln to Garfield, with a Review of the Events which Led to the Political Revolution of 1860,* 2 vols. (Norwich, CT: Henry Bill Publishing, 1884–1886), 666.

CHAPTER 5. "THE MOST INFAMOUS MAN IN AMERICA"

1 Frank P. Vazzano, "The Louisiana Question Resurrected: The Potter Commission and the Election of 1876," *Louisiana History: The Journal of the Louisiana Historical Association* 16, 1 (Winter 1975): 39–57.
2 Stan M. Haynes, *President-Making in the Gilded Age: The Nominating Conventions of 1876–1900* (Jefferson, NC: McFarland, 2016), 65–66.
3 Tilden and Whitney quoted in Herbert J. Clancy, S.J., *The Presidential Election of 1880* (Chicago: Loyola University Press, 1958), 76.
4 *Atlanta Constitution,* June 9, 1880.

5   McGlacklin quoted in Clancy, *Presidential Election of 1880*, 79.
6   Patience Essah, *A House Divided: Slavery and Emancipation in Delaware, 1863–1865* (Charlottesville: University Press of Virginia, 1996), 5–8.
7   Edward Spencer, *An Outline of the Public Life and Services of Thomas F. Bayard, Senator of the United States from the State of Delaware, 1869–1880* (New York: D. Appleton, 1880), 17–18.
8   David M. Jordan, *Winfield Scott Hancock: A Soldier's Life* (Bloomington: Indiana University Press, 1988), 44.
9   Ulysses S. Grant, *Personal Memoirs of Ulysses S. Grant*, vol. 2 (New York: Charles L. Webster, 1886), 539–540.
10 Hancock to Almira Hancock, quoted in Jordan, *Winfield Scott Hancock*, 201.
11 *New Orleans Times*, August 29, 1867.
12 *The Civil Record of Major-General Winfield S. Hancock: During His Administration in Louisiana and Texas*, 1880, YA Pamphlet Collection, Library of Congress, Washington, DC.
13 Hancock to Almira Hancock, quoted in Jordan, *Winfield Scott Hancock*, 204.
14 Andrew Johnson, "Special Message," December 18, 1867, Gerhard Peters and John T. Woolley, American Presidency Project, http://www.presidency.ucsb.edu/ws/?pid=72153.
15 Speech of James A. Garfield, January 17, 1868, in *Congressional Globe: House of Representatives, 40th Congress, 2nd Session*, 594; Garfield to Hinsdale, quoted in Allan Peskin, *Garfield* (Kent, OH: Kent State University Press, 1978), 284.
16 *New Orleans Times*, December 6–7, 1867.
17 *New Orleans Republican*, January 8, 1868; Lionel Sheldon to James A. Garfield, quoted in Peskin, *Garfield*, 284.
18 Hancock quoted in Jordan, *Winfield Scott Hancock*, 207.
19 All quoted in Jordan, *Winfield Scott Hancock*, 208.
20 *New Orleans Commercial Bulletin*, January 13, 1868.
21 Jordan, *Winfield Scott Hancock*, 208.
22 *New Orleans Daily Picayune*, February 9, 1868.
23 *New Orleans Times*, February 12, 1868.
24 "Mr. Tilden's Letter," in *Official Proceedings of the National Democratic Convention, Held in Cincinnati, O., June 22d, 23d, and 24th, 1880* (Dayton, OH: Daily Journal Book and Job Rooms, 1882), 103–107.
25 *New York Sun*, June 21, 1880.
26 Speech of George Hoadly, in *Official Proceedings of the National Democratic Convention*, 3–7.
27 *Official Proceedings of the National Democratic Convention*, 70.
28 Clancy, *Presidential Election of 1880*, 132–133.
29 *Official Proceedings of the National Democratic Convention*, 77.
30 *Official Proceedings of the National Democratic Convention*, 86–87.
31 *New York Times*, June 24, 1880.
32 *Official Proceedings of the National Democratic Convention*, 108–112; Clancy, *Presidential Election of 1880*, 140.
33 Henry L. Bryan quoted in Clancy, *Presidential Election of 1880*, 141.

34 "The 1880 Democratic Party Platform," Peters and Woolley, American Presidency Project, https://www.presidency.ucsb.edu/documents/1880-democratic-party-platform.
35 *New York Times*, July 20, 1880.

CHAPTER 6. "INDEFATIGABLE AGITATORS"

1 Herbert J. Clancy, S.J., *The Presidential Election of 1880* (Chicago: Loyola University Press, 1958), 163.
2 James B. Weaver, letter of acceptance, July 3, 1880, in Edward McPherson, *A Hand-Book of Politics for 1880: Being a Record of Important Political Action, National and State, from July 1, 1878 to July 1, 1880* (Washington, DC: James J. Chapman, 1880), 196–198.
3 *New York Times*, June 12, 1880.
4 Mark A. Lause, *The Civil War's Last Campaign: James B. Weaver, the Greenback-Labor Party, and the Politics of Race and Section* (Lanham, MD: University Press of America, 2001), 206–208.
5 Frank L. Byrne, *Prophet of Prohibition: Neal Dow and His Crusade* (Madison: State Historical Society of Wisconsin, 1961), 114.
6 David C. Rankin, *Diary of a Christian Soldier: Rufus Kinsey and the Civil War* (Cambridge: Cambridge University Press, 2004).

CHAPTER 7. "THOSE GREAT QUESTIONS OF NATIONAL WELL-BEING"

1 *Boston Herald*, June 8, 1880; *Chicago Tribune*, June 9, 1880.
2 *New York Times*, June 10, 1880.
3 Allan Peskin, *Garfield* (Kent, OH: Kent State University Press, 1978), 482.
4 Hayes to Garfield, quoted in Peskin, *Garfield*, 482.
5 Reid to Garfield, quoted in Kenneth D. Ackerman, *Dark Horse: The Surprise Election and Political Murder of President James A. Garfield* (Falls Church, VA: Viral History Press, 2011), 127.
6 Garfield diary, September 26, 1876, in *The Diary of James A. Garfield*, 4 vols., ed. Harry James Brown and Frederick D. Williams (Lansing: Michigan State University Press, 1967–1981), 3:357.
7 Lucretia Garfield to James Garfield, June 15, 1880, in *Crete and James: Personal Letters of Lucretia and James Garfield*, ed. John Shaw (Lansing: Michigan State University Press, 1994), 377–378.
8 *New York Sun*, June 25, 1880; *New York Herald*, June 25, 1880; *Philadelphia Inquirer*, June 25, 1880.
9 *Philadelphia Inquirer*, June 25, 1880.
10 Johnston to Hancock, quoted in David M. Jordan, *Winfield Scott Hancock: A Soldier's Life* (Bloomington: Indiana University Press, 1988), 284.
11 *Philadelphia Press*, June 25, 1880; *St. Louis Globe Democrat*, June 25, 1880; *Harper's Weekly*, July 10, 1880.
12 *Philadelphia Inquirer*, June 25, 1880.
13 *New York Times*, June 30, 1880; *New York Sun*, June 30, 1880.
14 *Washington Evening Star*, June 15–18, 1880; *Washington Post*, June 15–18, 1880.

15 Garfield quoted in Ackerman, *Dark Horse*, 132; David M. Jordan, *Roscoe Conkling of New York: Voice of the Senate* (Ithaca, NY: Cornell University Press, 1971), 347.
16 Ackerman, *Dark Horse*, 132–135.
17 Peskin, *Garfield*, 486–487.
18 Peskin, *Garfield*, 483–484.
19 Peskin, *Garfield*, 484.
20 Ackerman, *Dark Horse*, 127.
21 Almira Russell Hancock, *Reminiscences of Winfield Scott Hancock* (New York: Charles L. Webster, 1887), 172.
22 Herbert J. Clancy, S.J., *The Presidential Election of 1880* (Chicago: Loyola University Press, 1958), 209.
23 James A. Garfield, "Letter Accepting the Presidential Nomination," July 12, 1880, Gerhard Peters and John T. Woolley, American Presidency Project, http://www.presidency.ucsb.edu/ws/?pid=76221; Ackerman, *Dark Horse*, 154–155.
24 Ackerman, *Dark Horse*, 155.
25 Peskin, *Garfield*, 484; *Nation*, July 22, 1880.
26 Garfield to Hinsdale, July 25, 1880, in *Garfield-Hinsdale Letters: Correspondence between James Abram Garfield and Burke Aaron Hinsdale*, ed. Mary L. Hinsdale (Ann Arbor: University of Michigan Press, 1949), 454–455.
27 "Gen. Hancock's Letter of Acceptance, July 29, 1880," in Democratic National Committee, *The Campaign Text-book: Why the People Want a Change* (New York: Democratic National Committee, 1880), 4–6.
28 *New York Times*, August 2, 1880.
29 Jordan, *Winfield Scott Hancock*, 289–290.
30 "Hon. Wm. H. English's Letter of Acceptance, July 30, 1880," in Democratic National Committee, *Campaign Text-book*, 6–8.
31 Thomas C. Reeves, *Gentleman Boss: The Life and Times of Chester Alan Arthur* (Newtown, CT: American Political Biography Press, 1975), 189.
32 Dorsey quoted in Peskin, *Garfield*, 487.
33 Brown and Williams, *Diary of Garfield*, 4:429–430.
34 Garfield diary, August 3–4, 1880, in Brown and Williams, *Diary of Garfield*, 4:433–435.
35 Garfield diary, August 5, 1880, in Brown and Williams, *Diary of Garfield*, 4:435.
36 *New York Times*, August 6, 1880.
37 Garfield diary, August 6, 1880, in Brown and Williams, *Diary of Garfield*, 4:436–437.
38 James A. Garfield, "Speech of Gen. Jas. A. Garfield Delivered to the 'Boys in Blue,' New York, August 6, New York, 1880," https://www.loc.gov/item/rbpe.12900200/.
39 Garfield diary, August 7–9, 1880, in Brown and Williams, *Diary of Garfield*, 4:437–439.
40 *Nation*, July 3, 1880.
41 Spencer quoted in Clancy, *Presidential Election of 1880*, 211–212.

42 Black quoted in *New York Commercial Advertiser,* September 25, 1880; Garfield diary, October 6, 1880, in Brown and Williams, *Diary of Garfield,* 4:465.
43 Clancy, *Presidential Election of 1880,* 213–214.
44 *The Democratic Campaign Text Book for 1880* (New York: John Polhemus Press, 1880), 265.
45 Peskin, *Garfield,* 377.
46 Peskin, *Garfield,* 491–492.
47 Jordan, *Winfield Scott Hancock,* 293.
48 *Paterson (NJ) Daily Guardian,* October 8, 1880.
49 Brown and Williams, *Diary of Garfield,* 4:445.
50 James A. Garfield, *Garfield: His Speeches at Home, 1880* (Oneonta, NY: C. S. Carpenter, 1880), 9–21.
51 Douglass quoted in Candice Millard, *Destiny of the Republic: A Tale of Madness, Medicine and the Murder of a President* (New York: Doubleday, 2011), 62.
52 Brown and Williams, *Diary of Garfield,* 4:450.
53 eskin, *Garfield,* 492–493.
54 Garfield diary, September 28, 1880, in Brown and Williams, *Diary of Garfield,* 4:461–462.
55 Brown and Williams, *Diary of Garfield,* 4:462, n. 286.
56 Garfield diary, September 30, 1880, in Brown and Williams, *Diary of Garfield,* 4:463, n. 287.
57 Clancy, *Presidential Election of 1880,* 218–219.
58 *New York Times,* October 14, 1880; *New York Sun,* October 18, 1880.
59 Dana quoted in Jordan, *Winfield Scott Hancock,* 299.
60 Garfield diary, October 20, 1880, in Brown and Williams, *Diary of Garfield,* 4:471.
61 Brown and Williams, *Diary of Garfield,* 4:473; Joan Kapsch, "An 1880 October Surprise," in *The Garfield Observer: The Blog of James A. Garfield National Historic Site,* October 19, 2012, https://garfieldnps.wordpress.com/2012/10/19/an-1880-october-surprise/.
62 *Paterson (NJ) Daily Guardian,* November 3, 1880.
63 Hancock, *Reminiscences of Winfield Scott Hancock,* 172.
64 Peskin, *Garfield,* 510–513.

CHAPTER 8. "THE PERSONAL ASPECTS OF THE PRESIDENCY ARE FAR FROM PLEASANT"

1 Garfield diary, December 31, 1880, in *The Diary of James A. Garfield,* 4 vols., ed. Harry James Brown and Frederick D. Williams (Lansing: Michigan State University Press, 1967–1981), 4:519.
2 Allan Peskin, *Garfield* (Kent, OH: Kent State University Press, 1978), 514–515.
3 H. Wayne Morgan, *From Hayes to McKinley: National Party Politics, 1877–1896* (Syracuse, NY: Syracuse University Press, 1969), 13.
4 Garfield diary, November 27, 1880, in Brown and Williams, *Diary of Garfield,* 4:496–498.
5 Garfield diary, November 27, 1880, in Brown and Williams, *Diary of Garfield,* 4:495.

6   Garfield diary, December 11, 1880, in Brown and Williams, *Diary of Garfield*, 4:505.
7   Brown and Williams, *Diary of Garfield*, 4:506–507.
8   Garfield diary, December 7, 1880, in Brown and Williams, *Diary of Garfield*, 4:503.}
9   Brown and Williams, *Diary of Garfield*, 4:535–537.
10 Lucretia Garfield to James Garfield, January 21, 1881, in *Crete and James: Personal Letters of Lucretia and James Garfield*, ed. John Shaw (Lansing: Michigan State University Press, 1994), 380–381; see also Kenneth D. Ackerman, *Dark Horse: The Surprise Election and Political Murder of President James A. Garfield* (Falls Church, VA: Viral History Press, 2011), 209.
11 Garfield diary, December 7, 1880, in Brown and Williams, *Diary of Garfield*, 4:503.
12 John Sherman to Garfield, January 23, 1881, in Theodore Clarke Smith, *The Life and Letters of James Abram Garfield*, 2 vols. (New Haven, CT: Yale University Press, 1925), 2:1148.
13 Garfield diary, December 1880–March 1881, in Brown and Williams, *Diary of Garfield*, 4:511–552.
14 Garfield diary, January 3, 1881, in Brown and Williams, *Diary of Garfield*, 4:520–521.
15 Brown and Williams, *Diary of Garfield*, 4:550.
16 Garfield diary, March 4, 1881, in Brown and Williams, *Diary of Garfield*, 4:553.
17 Lucretia Garfield diary, March 4, 1881, in Brown and Williams, *Diary of Garfield*, 4:629.
18 James A. Garfield, "Inaugural Address," March 4, 1881, Gerhard Peters and John T. Woolley, American Presidency Project, http://www.presidency.ucsb.edu/ws/?pid=25823.
19 Garfield diary, January 13, 1881, in Brown and Williams, *Diary of Garfield*, 4:525.
20 Ackerman, *Dark Horse*, 273–274.
21 Garfield diary, March 8, 1881, in Brown and Williams, *Diary of Garfield*, 4:555.
22 Garfield diary, March 9, 1881, in Brown and Williams, *Diary of Garfield*, 4:557.
23 Stanley-Brown quoted in Ackerman, *Dark Horse*, 245.
24 Garfield diary, March 14, 1881, in Brown and Williams, *Diary of Garfield*, 4:558.
25 Garfield diary, March 20, 1881, in Brown and Williams, *Diary of Garfield*, 4:561.
26 Lucretia Garfield diary, March 22, 1881, in Brown and Williams, *Diary of Garfield*, 4:631–632.
27 Ackerman, *Dark Horse*, 259.
28 Ackerman, *Dark Horse*, 260–261; Garfield diary, March 23, 1881, in Brown and Williams, *Diary of Garfield*, 4:562–563.
29 *Boston Daily Advertiser*, March 24, 1881.
30 Garfield diary, March 27, 1881, in Brown and Williams, *Diary of Garfield*, 4:565.
31 Ackerman, *Dark Horse*, 316–345; Peskin, *Garfield*, 543–572.
32 Garfield diary, May 16 and 31, 1880, in Brown and Williams, *Diary of Garfield*, 4:593, 602.

33 Garfield diary, June 24–25, 1881, in Brown and Williams, *Diary of Garfield*, 4:613–616.

CONCLUSION

1 Guiteau quoted in Kenneth D. Ackerman, *Dark Horse: The Surprise Election and Political Murder of President James A. Garfield* (Falls Church, VA: Viral History Press, 2011), 331.
2 Guiteau quoted in Ackerman, *Dark Horse*, 392.
3 Allan Peskin, *Garfield* (Kent, OH: Kent State University Press, 1978), 611.

BIBLIOGRAPHIC ESSAY

This book is based on published primary sources and secondary sources. The availability of online materials, the interlibrary loan system, and local repositories near my home in the Cleveland, Ohio, area made accessing these sources—and therefore writing this book—much easier.

James A. Garfield is the primary historical figure in this book, and source material on his life and various careers is plentiful. This may surprise people who think of Garfield as an accidental president who served only briefly before his assassination. However, scholars have done a lot of respectable work to make Garfield's papers and diaries accessible. Decades ago, Harry James Brown and Frederick D. Williams edited and published four volumes of Garfield's diaries as *The Diary of James A. Garfield* (Lansing: Michigan State University Press, 1967–1981). Williams also edited selected Civil War letters written by Garfield; see Frederick D. Williams, ed., *The Wild Life of the Army: Civil War Letters of James A. Garfield* (Lansing: Michigan State University Press, 1964). For insight into Garfield's marriage and home life, see John Shaw, ed., *Crete and James: Personal Letters of Lucretia and James Garfield* (Lansing: Michigan State University Press, 1994).

Several of Garfield's friends and associates published works about him after his death in 1881. Some of these are collections of their correspondence with Garfield, and others are compilations of notable speeches. See Burke A. Hinsdale, ed., *Works of James A. Garfield*, 2 vols. (Boston: James R. Osgood, 1883), and Mary L. Hinsdale, ed., *Garfield-Hinsdale Letters: Correspondence between James Abram Garfield and Burke Aaron Hinsdale* (Ann Arbor: University of Michigan Press, 1949). Garfield's widow, Lucretia Rudolph Garfield, selected Theodore Clarke Smith as her husband's official biographer. See Theodore Clarke Smith, *The Life and Letters of James Abram Garfield*, 2 vols. (New Haven, CT: Yale University Press, 1925).

Anyone interested in the dramatic 1880 Republican convention that nominated Garfield for president can read the official record: *Proceedings of the Republican National Convention, Held at Chicago, Illinois, Wednesday–Tuesday, June 2–8, 1880* (Chicago: Jno. B. Jeffrey Printing House, 1881). The Democratic convention that nominated Winfield Scott Hancock also published official proceedings: *Official Proceedings of the National Democratic Convention, Held in Cincinnati, O., June 22d, 23d, and 24th, 1880* (Dayton, OH: Daily Journals Book and Job Rooms, 1882).

For those interested in Garfield's years in the House of Representatives, his speeches make fascinating reading. They can be accessed through the Library of Congress at https://memory.loc.gov/ammem/amlaw/lwcg.html. The Library of

Congress recently made Garfield's official papers available online as well (though not soon enough for the writing of this book). They can be accessed at https://www.loc.gov/collections/james-a-garfield-papers/about-this-collection. This availability will serve future Garfield scholars well.

The University of California–Santa Barbara's American Presidency Project is an excellent online repository for presidential speeches, executive orders, and more. I found items such as inaugural addresses and nomination acceptance letters through this valuable site: https://www.presidency.ucsb.edu/.

Newspapers covered the Garfield-Hancock election and remain important resources to understand what the public was reading and learning about the candidates. I consulted papers from different parts of the country and those affiliated with both Republican and Democratic perspectives. Important newspapers for this work included the *Atlanta Constitution, Baltimore Sun, Boston Herald, Chicago Daily News, Cleveland Herald, Harper's Weekly, New Orleans Daily Picayune, New York Herald, New York Times, Philadelphia Inquirer, St. Louis Globe-Democrat, Washington Evening Star*, and *Washington Post*.

I benefited greatly from several excellent secondary sources about Garfield. The definitive academic biography, published more than forty years ago but still fresh and informative, is Allan Peskin, *Garfield* (Kent, OH: Kent State University Press, 1978). For a more recent take that focuses on Garfield's 1880 nomination and election and his brief presidency, see Kenneth D. Ackerman, *Dark Horse: The Surprise Election and Political Murder of President James A. Garfield* (Falls Church, VA: Viral History Press, 2011). The book that is most responsible for the resurgence of interest in Garfield is Candice Millard, *Destiny of the Republic: A Tale of Madness, Medicine and the Murder of a President* (New York: Doubleday, 2011). In 2016 Millard's book was adapted into an excellent PBS American Experience documentary entitled *Murder of a President*. Garfield's Civil War experience is well documented in Daniel J. Vermilya, *James Garfield and the Civil War: For Ohio and the Union* (Charleston: SC: History Press, 2015).

The last major work on the 1880 election was published more than sixty years ago but still proved valuable. See Herbert J. Clancy, S.J., *The Presidential Election of 1880* (Chicago: Loyola University Press, 1958). The only compilation of Garfield's "front porch" campaign speeches is *Garfield: His Speeches at Home* (New York: C. S. Carpenter, 1880). For the views of other important Republicans of the period, see George F. Hoar, *Autobiography of Seventy Years* (New York: Charles Scribner's Sons, 1903); James G. Blaine, *Twenty Years of Congress: From Lincoln to Garfield, with a Review of the Events which Led to the Political Revolution of 1860*, 2 vols. (Norwich, CT: Henry Bill Publishing, 1884–1886); and John Sherman, *John Sherman's Recollections of Forty Years in the House, Senate, and Cabinet* (Chicago: Werner, 1895). For details about the roots and evolution of the Republican Party, the most authoritative book available is Heather Cox Richardson, *To Make Men Free: A History of the Republican Party* (New York: Basic Books, 2014). The online blog of the James A. Garfield National Historic Site proved informative as well: available at http://garfieldnps.wordpress.com

Understanding the 1876 election and the Reconstruction era is critical to making sense of the 1880 election. The best account of the disputed Hayes-Tilden contest and its resolution is Michael F. Holt, *By One Vote: The Disputed Presidential Election of 1876* (Lawrence: University Press of Kansas, 2008). Other books that were useful in understanding the 1876 election, Reconstruction, and the personalities, attitudes, and viewpoints of the Republican and Democratic Parties were Keith Ian Polakoff, *The Politics of Inertia: The Election of 1876 and the End of Reconstruction* (Baton Rouge: Louisiana State University Press, 1973); Charles W. Calhoun, *Conceiving a New Republic: The Republican Party and the Southern Question, 1869–1900* (Lawrence: University Press of Kansas, 2008); Eric Foner, *Reconstruction: America's Unfinished Revolution*, Francis Parkman Prize ed. (New York: History Book Club, 1988); Michael Bellesiles, *1877: America's Year of Living Violently* (New York: New Press, 2010); Lawrence Grossman, *The Democratic Party and the Negro: Northern and National Politics, 1868–92* (Urbana: University of Illinois Press, 1976); C. Vann Woodward, *Reunion and Reaction: The Compromise of 1877 and the End of Reconstruction* (Boston: Little, Brown, 1951); Stanley P. Hirshon, *Farewell to the Bloody Shirt: Northern Republicans and the Southern Negro, 1877–1893* (Bloomington: Indiana University Press, 1962); and Richard White, *The Republic for which It Stands: The United States during Reconstruction and the Gilded Age, 1865–1896* (New York: Oxford University Press, 2017).

For research on the Democratic campaign of 1880, I consulted sources about Winfield Scott Hancock and the Democratic Party. See Almira Russell Hancock, *Reminiscences of Winfield Scott Hancock* (New York: Charles L. Webster, 1887). *The Campaign Text-book for 1880: Why the People Want a Change* (New York: Democratic National Committee, 1880) clarified the Democrats' approach to the 1880 election. I also reviewed Ulysses S. Grant, *Personal Memoirs of U. S. Grant* (New York: Charles L. Webster, 1886), to learn more about Grant's attitude toward his former subordinate. Edward Spencer's *An Outline of the Public Services of Thomas F. Bayard, Senator of the United States from the State of Delaware, 1869–1880* (New York: D. Appleton, 1880) provided insight on Bayard and his interest in the Democratic presidential nomination in 1880. I found various Democratic documents and speeches online through the Library of Congress and the American Presidency Project website run by the University of California–Santa Barbara. Secondary literature I consulted about Hancock and the Democrats included David M. Jordan, *Winfield Scott Hancock: A Soldier's Life* (Bloomington: Indiana University Press, 1988), and Glenn Tucker, *Hancock the Superb* (Seattle: Morningside Press, 1980).

For information on the 1880 candidates from outside the two major parties, see Mark A. Lause, *The Civil War's Last Campaign: James B. Weaver, the Greenback-Labor Party, and the Politics of Race and Section* (Lanham, MD: University Press of America, 2001), and Robert B. Mitchell, *Skirmisher: The Life, Times, and Political Career of James B. Weaver* (Roseville, MN: Edinborough Press, 2008). For the Prohibition Party candidate, see Frank L. Byrne, *Prophet of Prohibition: Neal Dow and His Crusade* (Madison: State Historical Society of Wisconsin, 1961).

INDEX

Numbers in italics refer to pages with figures.

Abbott, Josiah G., 20
Ackerman, Kenneth D., 140, 177–178
Adams, Henry, 25, 56
African Americans
    Garfield's presidential campaign and, 151–152
    Garfield's private view of, 39
    New Orleans aldermen controversy and, 108–109
    See also black suffrage; civil rights; Southern black voters
American (Know-Nothing) Party, 148
American Anti-Mason Party, 125–126
Ames, Oakes, 43
Anderson, Robert, 34–35
Arlington House, 40
Arlington National Cemetery, 40
Army of the Cumberland, 36–38
Army of the Potomac, 103
Arthur, Chester A.
    Roscoe Conkling and, 54, 175–176
    Garfield's patronage appointments as president and, 175–176, 177–178, 179
    Rutherford Hayes and, 54, 143, 176
    letter of acceptance, 143–144
    oath of office as vice president, 170
    selected as Garfield's running mate, 94–95
Atlanta Constitution, 99–100

Badeau, Adam, 67, 69, 178
Baker, George, 136–137
Baker, Joshua, 108
Baltimore Sun, 147
banking reform, 42
Barker, James M., 76
Barker, Wharton, 64, 65–66, 74, 78
Barnum, William H., 113, 132, 138
Bascom, William, 33
Bateman, Warner, 79, 91
Bayard, James A., Jr., 100
Bayard, Richard A., 100
Bayard, Thomas F.
    attack on Garfield in the presidential campaign, 147
    balloting at the Democratic National Convention and, 115, 116
    contender for the Democratic presidential nomination, 10, 100–101
    electoral commission of 1877 and, 20
    Winfield Hancock's presidential campaign and, 138, 155
    nominated at the Democratic National Convention, 114
big business, alignment of the Republican Party with, 26, 146
Bigelow, John, 14
Black, Jeremiah S., 19, 20, 21, 99, 147
black Civil War veterans, 151–152
black suffrage
    Garfield's *North American Review* piece on, 47–48
    Winfield Hancock's position on, 142
Blaine, James G.
    balloting at the Republican National Convention and, 87, 88, 89, 90, 91–92
    civil service reform and, 136
    Roscoe Conkling and, 58, 136
    federal appropriations crisis of 1879 and, 49–50

Blaine, James G., *continued*
   fusionist crisis in Maine and, 58–59
   Garfield's assassination and, 181
   Garfield's cabinet appointments and, 164
   Garfield's campaign and Maine's 1880 congressional elections, 152–153
   Garfield's patronage appointments as president and, 175–176, 177–178
   Charles Guiteau and, 183
   nomination at the Republican National Convention, 79–80
   nonattendance at Republican National Convention, 67
   North American Review article on black suffrage and, 47, 48
   presidential election of 1876 and, 44, 45
   pursuit of the 1880 Republican presidential candidacy, 58–59, 61, 66
   reaction to Garfield's nomination, 95–96
   relationship with Garfield, 48
   significance of the presidential election of 1880 and, 2
   unit rule fight at the Republican National Convention and, 70
Blair, Montgomery, 47
Bliss, Willard, 183
Boston Daily Advertiser, 178
Boston Herald, 127
Bradley, Joseph P., 20
Bristow, Benjamin, 44, 45
Bruce, Blanche K., 59, 94
Butler, Benjamin, 120–121, 125

cabinet appointments, by Garfield, 162–165, 166, 168, 170
Cameron, Donald
   balloting at the Republican National Convention and, 87
   Grant's pursuit of the Republican presidential candidacy and, 54, 55, 57
   official convening of the Republican National Convention, 72
   Stalwart Republicans and, 54
   unit rule fight at the Republican National Convention and, 69, 70, 71
   See also Triumvirate
Campbell, Archibald W., 73–74
Casenave, Gadane, 15
Cassoday, John B., 90
Catholic Herald, 148–149
Catholics, 148–149
Chaffee, Jerome, 71
Chambers, Barzillai J., 122, 123, 124
Chandler, William E.
   James Blaine's candidacy and, 59, 69, 79
   Garfield's patronage appointments and, 178
   Garfield's presidential campaign and, 136
   presidential election of 1876 and, 13
   reaction to the selection of Chester Arthur as vice presidential candidate, 94–95
   selection of Republican Party national leadership in 1880 and, 133, 134
   as temporary chairman of the Republican National Convention, 71
Chandler, Zachariah, 8
Chase, Salmon P., 32
Chernow, Ron, 2, 43
Chicago Tribune, 25, 68, 69, 127
Chicago Weekly Tribune, 120
Chickamauga, battle of, 37–38, 148
Chinese Exclusion Act, 59–61
Chinese immigration policy
   William English's position on, 143
   Stephen Field and, 114
   Garfield, Rutherford Hayes, and the Chinese Exclusion Act, 59–61
   Garfield and the Morey letter hoax, 157–158
   Garfield's position on in his letter of acceptance, 139
   Greenback Party and, 123
   presidential campaign of 1880 and, 134
   Republican national platform on, 77
Cincinnati Enquirer, 10, 12

civil rights
    Garfield and, 4, 39, 44, 140, 145–146, 171, 172, 174
    Winfield Hancock's position on, 142
    Rutherford Hayes and, 7–8, 23, 25–26
Civil Rights Bill (1875), 44
civil service reform
    absence from the 1880 Republican national platform, 76–77
    James Blaine and, 136
    Roscoe Conkling's opposition to, 7, 54, 175–176
    Garfield's assassination and, 4
    Garfield's policy disputes with Hayes over, 46
    Garfield's views on, 7, 24, 42, 139, 141, 172
    Rutherford Hayes and, 7, 8, 23–24, 46, 136
    Republican presidential campaign of 1880 and, 134, 136
Civil War
    Thomas Bayard and, 100–101
    Neal Dow and, 125
    Garfield's response to Southern secession and the start of, 34–35
    Garfield's service in, 35–38, 148
    Winfield Hancock and, 103–104, 110–112
    John Phelps and, 125–126
    William Rosecrans and, 148
    James Baird Weaver and, 121
Clancy, Herbert J., 116
Clifford, Nathan, 20
Coan, Titas, 88
Cole, A. N., 61
Colfax, Schuyler, 38, 43, 149
Colorado, 12–13, 23
Comly, James M., 26
Committee of Conciliation, 178
Congress
    Credit Mobilier scandal and, 43–44
    early voting congressional elections and the 1880 presidential campaign, 152–155, 156
    electoral crisis of 1876 and, 18–23
    federal appropriations crisis of 1879 and Garfield's rise to national prominence, 48–50

Garfield's career in the House, 36, 38, 41, 42–43, 44, 45–48, 49, 50
Garfield's pursuit of a seat in the Senate, 52, 54, 61–63
Greenback Party and, 120
Conkling, Roscoe
    1880 presidential election results and, 159
    Chester A. Arthur and, 54, 176
    balloting at the Republican National Convention and, 87–88, 89, 92
    James Blaine and, 58, 136
    conflict between Stalwart and Half-Breed Republicans and, 72–73
    conflict with Garfield at the Republican National Convention, 74, 75, 79
    conflict with Garfield over patronage appointments, 175–180
    Credit Mobilier scandal and, 43
    federal appropriations crisis of 1879 and, 49–50
    Garfield's cabinet appointments and, 164, 166, 167
    Garfield's nomination at the Republican National Convention and, 93
    Garfield's presidential campaign and, 133, 134, 139, 144, 145, 153–155
    Grant's pursuit of the Republican presidential candidacy and, 54, 55, 57, 61, 68–69
    Rutherford Hayes and, 7, 21, 54
    nomination of Grant at the Republican National Convention, 68–69, 80–82
    opposition to civil service reform, 7, 54, 176
    presidential election of 1876 and, 44–45
    selection of Garfield's running mate and, 94
    selection of Republican Party national leadership in 1880 and, 133
    Stalwart Republicans and, 54
    unit rule fight at the Republican National Convention and, 68–69, 70–71, 73–74
    See also Triumvirate

INDEX 209

Contraction Act (1866), 119
Cooper, Peter, 120
Cornell, Alonzo, 178
Couch, Darius, 103
Cox, Jacob D., 21, 24, 32–33, 35, 46
Cox, Samuel, 38
Cramer, Michael, 178
Credit Mobilier scandal, 43–44, 127, 149
currency reform, 42, 102, 118–120
Curtin, Andrew, 14
Curtis, George William, 143

Daily Alta Californian, 148
Dana, Charles A., 113, 156
Davis, David, 20
Davis, George S., 57
Davis, Henry Winter, 38
Davis, Jefferson, 126
Dawes, Henry, 38
Decoration Day, 40
DeGolyer McClelland Company, 149
DeGolyer Pavement scandal, 127, 149
De La Matyr, Gilbert, 120–121
Delaware Guard, 100
Democratic Campaign Text Book for 1880, 149
Democratic National Committee, 132, 138
Democratic National Convention (1880)
    balloting and selection of Winfield Hancock, 115–116
    George Hoadly and the opening of, 113–114
    nomination of candidates, 114–115
    party platform, 116–117
    Samuel Tilden's uncertain status as a candidate and, 112–113
Democratic Party
    1880 National Convention, 112–117
    Thomas Bayard and, 100–101
    campaign attacks on Garfield, 147–149
    electoral crisis of 1876, 13–23
    favorite-son contenders for the 1880 nomination, 100–102
    federal appropriations crisis of 1879 and, 48–50
    Stephen Field and, 101–102
    fusionist crisis in Maine and, 58–59
    Winfield Hancock and the presidential election of 1880, 102–103 (*see also* Hancock, Winfield Scott)
    Thomas Hendricks, 102
    L. Q. C. Lamar's defense of in the 1876 presidential campaign, 45–46
    midterm elections of 1878, 26, 27–28, 29
    party platform in 1876, 11
    party platform of 1880, 116–117
    Potter investigation of the 1876 presidential election and, 26–27, 97–98
    presidential campaign of 1880 and early voting congressional elections, 152–153, 156
    presidential campaign of 1880 and the need to unify party factions, 137–138
    presidential election of 1876 and, 2–3, 10–11
    Reconstruction politics in Louisiana and, 44
    Republican tactic of "waving the bloody shirt" and the presidential election of 1876, 9–10, 11
    significance of the presidential election of 1880, 2–3, 185
    Southern black vote and the presidential election of 1876, 11–12
    Samuel Tilden and the presidential election of 1880 (*see* Tilden, Samuel J.)
    voter intimidation and Garfield's attack on, 28
Dennison, William, 92
Department of the Atlantic, 102, 110, 112, 132, 147
Destiny of the Republic (Millard), 2
Disciples of Christ, 30, 31
district representation, 70
Dorsey, Stephen W., 134, 144
Dougherty, Daniel, 115
Douglass, Frederick, 8, 21, 152
Dow, Neal, 124–125
Drake, E. F., 80
Durant, Thomas, 43

Edmunds, George F., 20, 70, 72, 86, 88, 89
Eighteenth Amendment, 125
Elberon Hotel, 180

electoral votes
  crisis of 1876, 13–23
  Garfield's strategy, 136–137
  Garfield's victory, 160, 165–166
Elkins, Stephen, 91
Elliott, Robert B., 85–86
English, William H., 116, 132, 143, 156
Evarts, William, 60

federal appropriations crisis of 1879, 48–50
Field, Cyrus West, 101
Field, David Dudley, 101
Field, Stephen J., 20, 101–102, 114
Fifth Military District, 104–109
Fish, Nicholas, 178
Fisk Jubilee Singers, 146, 155
Fisk University, 146
Flanagan, Webster, 76
Flanders, Benjamin Franklin, 108
Florida
  1880 presidential election results and, 159
  electoral crisis of 1876 and, 13, 14, 16, 17, 20, 22
Foner, Eric, 8, 26
Forbes, John, 133–134
Fort Sumter, 34–35
Forty-Second Ohio Volunteers, 35
Foster, Charles, 64, 66, 79, 128, 133
Fourteenth Amendment, 142
Free Will Baptist Geauga Seminary, 30
Freylinghuysen, Frederick, 20
"From Death to Morning" (Wolfe), 1
Frye, William P., 80
fusionist crisis, 58–59

Galveston News, 28
Garcelon, Alonzo, 59
Garfield, Abram, 30
Garfield, Eliza, 30, 31, 128
Garfield, Eliza Arabella, 33, 38
Garfield, James A.
  1880 presidential election results and, 159–160
  assassination of, 4, 181, 182–183
  astuteness as a politician, 40
  attack on the Democratic Party and voter intimidation, 28
  James Blaine and, 66, 136
  cabinet appointments and other activities as president-elect, 162–170
  children of, 33, 38
  Chinese Exclusion Act and, 59–61
  civil rights and, 4, 39, 44, 140, 145–146, 171, 172, 174
  civil service reform and (*see* civil service reform)
  Civil War experience, 35–38, 148
  congressional career, 36, 38, 41, 42–43, 44, 45–48, 49, 50
  Roscoe Conkling and (*see* Conkling, Roscoe)
  Credit Mobilier scandal and, 43–44, 127, 149
  daily routine as president, 174–175
  Decoration Day of 1868 and, 40
  DeGolyer Pavement scandal and, 127, 149
  early life and education, 30–31
  early political career, 31–34
  electoral crisis of 1876 and, 13–14, 15, 16, 18–19, 20, 22
  federal appropriations crisis of 1879 and, 49, 50
  funeral of, 183
  hard money stance, 42, 119
  Rutherford Hayes's presidential nomination in 1876 and, 45
  health concerns, 166, 168
  inauguration and inaugural address, 170–174
  Andrew Johnson and, 41
  letter of acceptance, 138–141
  marriage to Lucretia Rudolph, 31
  Mentor home, 128–129 (*see also* Mentor, OH, home of Garfield)
  midterm elections of 1878 and, 27, 29
  modern lack of knowledge about, 1
  Morey letter hoax and, 157–158
  North American Review piece on black suffrage, 47–48
  opposition to slavery, 31, 33–34, 35–36
  policy disputes with Rutherford Hayes, 24, 46–47
  presidential campaign of 1880 and (*see* presidential campaign of 1880)

INDEX 211

Garfield, James A., *continued*
   private view of African Americans, 39
   pursuit of Ohio's US Senate seat, 52, 54, 61–63
   Radical Republicans and, 39–40, 41
   relationship with James Blaine, 48
   relationship with Grant, 41–42, 180
   Republican contenders for the presidential election of 1876 and, 44–45
   Republican National Convention of 1880 (*see* Republican National Convention)
   Republican reactions to the nomination of, 95–96
   response to Winfield Hancock's command of the Fifth Military District, 106–107
   response to Rutherford Hayes's 1876 letter of acceptance, 7
   response to Southern secession and the Civil War, 34–35
   rise to national prominence in 1879, 29, 49, 50–51, 52
   role in choosing Republican Party leadership in 1880, 133–134
   William Rosecrans and, 147–148
   John Sherman's pursuit of the 1880 Republican presidential candidacy and, 52, 53–54, 61–62, 63–64, 65–66, 67
   significance of the presidential election of 1880 and, 2, 3, 4, 5, 183–186
   support for Rutherford Hayes in the 1876 presidential campaign, 45–46
   on Tilden and the presidential election of 1876, 12
   view of Lincoln, 34, 36
   view of Reconstruction politics in Louisiana, 44
   view on being elected president, 161–162
Garfield, Lucretia (nèe Rudolph)
   1880 presidential campaign and, 129–130, 137
   1881 trip to New York City, 166–167
   children of, 33
   family of, 30
   on Garfield's inauguration, 170–171
   letter to Garfield during the Republican National Convention, 86–87
   malaria and, 179
   marriage to Garfield, 31, 33
Garfield, Mollie, 175
"Garfield's ride," 38, 148
Gastinel, Arthur, 108
General Orders No. 40, 105–106
Gilded Age, modern reexamination of, 1–2
Glass Palace, 72
Godkin, E. L., 141
gold standard, 42, 118, 119
Gould, Jay, 145
Grant (Chernow), 2
Grant, Julia, 55, 69
Grant, Ulysses S.
   assessments of the presidency of, 43
   balloting at the Republican National Convention and, 87, 88, 89, 90, 91, 92
   William Bascom and, 33
   civil service reform and, 7
   criticism of Winfield Hancock as a presidential candidate, 142–143
   electoral crisis of 1876 and, 13, 14, 18, 19
   Garfield's presidential campaign and, 153–155
   on Winfield Hancock in the Civil War, 103–104
   Winfield Hancock's command of the Fifth Military District and, 104, 109
   Rutherford Hayes and, 21
   modern reexaminations of, 2
   nomination at the Republican National Convention, 68–69, 80–82
   paper money policy, 119
   presidential election of 1868 and, 41
   presidential election of 1876 and, 6, 7, 9
   pursuit of the 1880 Republican presidential candidacy, 54, 55–58, 61, 67–69
   reaction to Garfield's nomination, 95

Reconstruction and, 25, 44
relationship with Garfield, 41–42, 179–180
scandals and the presidency of, 43–44, 54, 149
Stalwart Republicans and, 54, 55, 57–58
unit rule fight by supporters of at the Republican National Convention and, 68–69, 70–71, 73–74
view of Rutherford Hayes, 55
wavering Republican support for in 1880, 68, 69
James Baird Weaver and, 121
world tour following the presidency of, 55, 56
Gray, George, 114
Greeley, Horace, 111
Greenback Party
convention and nomination of James Weaver, 120–122
formation of, 27, 120
fusionist crisis in Maine and, 58
members in Congress, 120
national platform, 122–123
overview and significance of, 5
paper currency issue and, 118–120
potential for influence on the 1880 presidential election, 126
presidential campaign and, 123–124
presidential election results, 124
greenbacks, 42, 102, 118–120
Guiteau, Charles, 172, 173, 181, 182–183

Hale, Eugene, 72, 73, 133
Half-Breed Republicans
friction with the Stalwart Republicans, 72–73, 134, 136
opposition to Grant's nomination, 76, 93
selection of Republican Party national leadership in 1880 and, 133
support for James Blaine, 61
Hamburg Massacre, 11
Hampton, Wade, 47, 115
Hancock, Almira, 137, 139, 159
Hancock, Russell, 132
Hancock, Winfield Scott
1880 presidential election results and, 159

Civil War experience, 103–104, 110–112
command of the Department of the Atlantic, 102, 110, 112, 132, 147
command of the Fifth Military District during Reconstruction, 104–109
contender for the 1880 Democratic nomination, 102–103
Democratic National Committee and, 132
electoral crisis of 1876 and, 21
General Orders No. 40, 105–106
letter of acceptance, 141–142
Mexican-American War and, 103
New Orleans aldermen controversy and, 108–109
nomination and selection at the 1880 Democratic National Convention, 115–116
political assets in 1880, 110–112
presidential ambitions prior to 1880, 109–110
presidential campaign of 1880 and (see presidential campaign of 1880)
presidential election of 1876 and, 10, 103
Republican reactions to the nomination of, 130–132
significance of the presidential election of 1880 and, 2, 3–4, 5, 184, 185
tariff gaffe and, 150, 155–156
view of Reconstruction, 105
Hancock, Winfield Scott, II, 132
hard money policy. *See* gold standard
Harper's Weekly, 130
Harrison, Benjamin, 91, 144, 174
Hay, John, 162, 175
Hayes, Rutherford B.
acceptance letter for the Republican nomination in 1876, 6–8
Henry Adams's description of, 56
advice to Garfield on the 1880 presidential campaign, 128
alignment of the Republican Party with big business, 26
Chester A. Arthur and, 54, 143, 176
Chinese Exclusion Act and, 59–61
civil rights and, 23, 25–26

INDEX 213

Hayes, Rutherford B., *continued*
    civil service reform and, 23–24, 136
    Roscoe Conkling and, 54
    electoral crisis of 1876, 13–21
    "ending" of Reconstruction and,
        25–26
    federal appropriations crisis of 1879,
        48–50
    Garfield's policy disputes with, 24,
        46–47
    Garfield's view of in 1876, 45
    Grant's view of, 55
    midterm elections of 1878 and, 27, 28
    presidency of, 23–28
    presidential election of 1876 and, 2, 45
    Republican National Convention of
        1876 and, 87
    response to Garfield's letter of
        acceptance, 141
    response to the 1880 Republican
        National Convention, 95
    John Sherman's pursuit of the 1880
        Republican presidential candidacy
        and, 65
    the South and sectional reconciliation,
        24–26, 28
    Stalwart Republicans and, 55
Haynes, Stan M., 73
Hendricks, Thomas A., 10, 11, 47, 114–115
Henry, Charles, 62
Hewitt, Abram, 13, 14
Hinsdale, Burke, 40, 50, 65, 107, 141
Hoadly, George, 113–114
Hoar, George F., 19, 72, 73, 74, 90–91,
    93
Holman, William, 38
Holt, Michael F., 11
home rule, 116
Hook, George A., 79
Hopkins, Mark, 38
Hunton, Eppa, 20

impeachment, 40–41
Independent Party, 120
Indiana, 156, 159
Ingersoll, Robert, 10, 75, 79, 86

James, Thomas, 176, 178
Jewell, Marshall, 68, 133–134, 143

Johnson, Andrew, 40–41, 104, 105, 106,
    109
Johnston, Joseph E., 130
Jones, George, 57
Jones, John, 92
Joy, James F., 79
Julian, George W., 14

Kelly, John, 114, 156
Key, David M., 46
Kirkwood, Samuel J., 121, 170
Ku Klux Klan, 2

Lamar, L. Q. C., 45–46, 47
"Lawnfield," 150
Lee, Robert E., 40
letters of acceptance
    by Chester A. Arthur, 143–144
    by William English, 143
    by Garfield, 138–141
    by Winfield Hancock, 141–142
Lincoln, Abraham
    Stephen Field and, 102
    Garfield's career in Congress and, 38
    Garfield's view of, 34, 36
    preliminary Emancipation
        Proclamation, 36
    presidential election of 1860 and, 110
    Republican National Convention of
        1860 and, 87
    William Rosecrans and, 148
    view of African Americans, 39
Lincoln, Robert Todd, 164
Lister, Joseph, 183
Logan, John
    balloting at the Republican National
        Convention and, 87
    Decoration Day and, 40
    Garfield's cabinet appointments and,
        164
    Garfield's nomination at the
        Republican National Convention
        and, 93
    Garfield's presidential campaign and,
        154–155
    Grant's pursuit of the 1880
        Republican presidential candidacy
        and, 54, 55, 57, 69
    opposition to civil service reform, 7

selection of Republican Party national
leadership in 1880 and, 133, 134
Stalwart Republicans and, 54
unit rule fight at the Republican
National Convention and, 69, 70
See also Triumvirate
Louisiana
1880 presidential election results and,
159
electoral crisis of 1876 and, 13–14,
15–16, 17, 22
Winfield Hancock's command of the
Fifth Military District, 104–109
Reconstruction politics in, 44

MacVeagh, Wayne, 74, 164, 178
Maine, 58–59, 152–153
Manning, Daniel, 98, 112–113
Matthews, Stanley, 54
McClellan, George B., 101, 103, 110
McCormick, Richard, 133
McElrath, J. E., 114
McGlacklin, A. C., 100
Meade, George Gordon, 109–110
Mentor, OH, home of Garfield
description of, 128–129
Garfield's campaigning from home,
127–128, 129–130, 150–152, 154–155
Garfield's planned return to in August
1881, 180–181
Merritt, Edwin, 178
Mexican-American War, 103
midterm elections of 1878, 26, 27–28, 29
military commissions, 107
Millard, Candice, 2
Miller, Samuel F., 20
Moore, A. C., 74
Morey, H. L., 158
Morey letter hoax, 157–158
Morrill, Justin, 38
Morrison, William, 102
Morton, Levi P., 154–155, 164–165, 166,
167, 177
Morton, Oliver P., 15, 20, 44–45

Nation, 25, 141
New, John C., 144
New Orleans aldermen controversy,
108–109

New Orleans Commercial Bulletin, 108
New Orleans Daily Picayune, 109
New Orleans Democrat, 46
New Orleans Republican, 107
New Orleans Times, 105, 109
New York City
Lucretia Garfield's 1881 trip to,
166–167
Garfield's campaign trip to, 144–146
New York Herald, 56
New York state
1880 presidential election results and,
159
Garfield's conflict with Roscoe
Conkling over patronage
appointments, 175–180
Garfield's electoral strategy and, 137
Winfield Hancock's presidential
campaign and, 138
importance in the presidential election
of 1880, 156–157
Samuel Tilden and, 10
New York Sun, 43, 113
New York Times, 57, 115, 116, 117, 124, 142,
145, 155, 156
New York Tribune, 27, 128
New York Truth, 149, 158
Nichol, Thomas, 50–51, 64
Nicholls, Francis T., 15
North American Review, 47–48

Ohio
congressional election of 1880, 156
Garfield's early life and education, 30
Garfield's early political career, 31–34
Garfield's presidential campaign and,
153–155
Garfield's pursuit of US Senate seat,
52, 54, 61–63
John Sherman as US senator, 167–168
Oregon, 13, 14, 17

Palmer, John M., 15
Panic of 1873, 119
Payne, Henry B., 20, 98
Peckham, Rufus W., 115
Pelton, William T., 27, 98
Pendleton, George, 38
Peskin, Allan, 22, 50, 62, 66, 75, 136

INDEX 215

Phelps, John W., 125–126
Philadelphia Inquirer, 112
Philadelphia Press, 130
Phillips, Wendell, 47
Pixley, F. M., 80
Platt, Thomas, 133, 178, 179
Polakoff, Keith Ian, 26
Pomeroy, Samuel C., 125, 126
Potter, Clarkson N., 26–27, 97
Potter Committee, 26–27, 97–98
presidential campaign of 1880
    Democratic attacks on Garfield, 147–149
    Garfield and campaigning from home, 127–128, 129–130, 150–152
    Garfield and the Chinese immigration issue, 134
    Garfield and the civil service reform issue, 134, 136
    Garfield and the Morey letter hoax, 157–158
    Garfield's campaign trip to New York City, 144–146
    Garfield's electoral strategy, 136–137
    Garfield's relationship with Roscoe Conkling and, 133, 134
    Garfield's role in choosing Republican Party leadership and, 133–134
    Garfield's support from John Sherman, 132–133
    Winfield Hancock and campaigning by Democratic surrogates, 147–149
    Winfield Hancock and campaigning from home, 130, 132, 137
    Winfield Hancock's need to unify Democratic factions, 137–138
    Winfield Hancock's tariff gaffe and, 150, 155–156
    impact of early-voting congressional elections on, 152–155, 156
    letters of acceptance by the candidates and their running mates, 138–143
    overview and significance of, 3–4
    Republican attacks on Winfield Hancock, 142–143, 149–150
    role of the tariff and economic issues in, 155–156
presidential election of 1860, 110
presidential election of 1868, 41, 54, 109
presidential election of 1872, 54

presidential election of 1876
    Colorado's statehood and, 12–13
    Democratic Party and, 2–3, 10–11
    electoral crisis, 13–23
    Garfield's support of Hayes in the national campaign, 45–46
    Winfield Hancock and, 103, 110
    Rutherford Hayes's letter accepting the Republican nomination, 6–8
    Thomas Hendricks and, 102
    the Potter Committee investigation and, 26–27, 97–98
    presidential election of 1880 and, 6
    Republican contenders for, 44–45
    Republican Party and "waving the bloody shirt," 9–10, 11
    Republican platform, 8
presidential election of 1880
    James Blaine's pursuit of the Republican candidacy, 58–59, 61, 66
    Democratic National Convention, 112–117
    election results, 158–160, 165–166
    favorite-son Democratic contenders, 100–102
    Grant's pursuit of the Republican candidacy, 54–58, 61, 67–69
    historical significance of, 2–5, 184–186
    importance of New York in, 156–157
    presidential election of 1876 and, 6
    Republican National Convention and (*see* Republican National Convention)
    John Sherman's pursuit of the Republican candidacy, 52–54, 61–62, 63–64, 65–66, 67
    third-party candidates, 118–126
    Samuel Tilden's indecision about entering the 1880 race, 97–100
    Union military veterans and, 3
    See also Garfield, James A.; Hancock, Winfield Scott; presidential campaign of 1880
Prohibition Party, 124–125

racial violence, 11
Radical Republicans
    alliance with big business, 146
    Garfield and, 39–40, 41

response to Winfield Hancock's command of the Fifth Military District, 106–108
Rainey, Joseph H., 28
Randall, Samuel J., 22, 27, 38, 46, 115
Reconstruction
    Garfield's policy disputes with Hayes, 46–47
    Grant and the scaling down of, 25
    Winfield Hancock's command of the Fifth Military District and, 104–109
    Winfield Hancock's view of, 105
    Rutherford Hayes and the "ending" of, 25–26
    Rutherford Hayes and the presidential election of 1876, 7–8
    modern reexamination of, 1–2
    politics in Louisiana and, 44
Redeemers, 26
Reid, Whitelaw, 128, 145
Republican National Committee, 133–134, 144–145, 158
Republican National Convention (1876), 8
Republican National Convention (1880)
    balloting and selection of Garfield, 87–93
    concern of Sherman's supporters about Garfield, 78–79, 86
    Roscoe Conkling and the nomination of Grant, 68–69, 80–82
    credentials issue, 75
    emergence of Garfield as a compromise candidate, 74–75, 86–87
    friction between the Stalwart and Half-Breed factions, 72–73
    Garfield and the unit rule fight, 68–72, 73–74, 75–76
    Garfield as head of the Committee on Rules, 72, 75–76
    Garfield's conflicts with Roscoe Conkling at, 74, 75, 79
    Garfield's role of supporting John Sherman at, 69, 70, 78–79
    Garfield's speech nominating John Sherman, 82–85, 86
    nomination of James Blaine, 79–80
    nomination of William Windom, 80
    nominations of George Edmunds and Elihu Washington, 86
    official convening of, 72
    party platform, 76–77
    practice of candidates not attending, 67
    Jerry Rusk and, 50
    seconding speeches for John Sherman, 85–86
    selection of Chester Arthur as Garfield's running mate, 94–95
    staged applause and, 78
Republican Party
    alignment with big business, 26, 146
    James Blaine's pursuit of the 1880 presidential candidacy, 58–59, 61, 66
    campaign attacks on Winfield Hancock, 142–143, 149–150
    Colorado's statehood and the presidential election of 1876, 12–13
    contenders for the presidential election of 1876, 44–45
    electoral crisis of 1876, 13–23
    federal appropriations crisis of 1879, 48–50
    Garfield's campaign and the early-voting congressional elections, 152–153, 156
    Garfield's rise to national prominence in 1879, 29, 49, 50–51, 52
    Garfield's role in choosing party leadership in 1880, 133–134
    Grant's pursuit of the 1880 Republican presidential candidacy, 54–58, 61, 67–69
    the Rutherford Hayes presidency, 23–28
    Rutherford Hayes's acceptance letter for the presidential nomination in 1876, 6–8
    historical significance of Garfield and the 1880 election, 2, 184–186
    midterm elections of 1878, 27, 28, 29
    National Convention of 1880 (*see* Republican National Convention)
    party platform in 1876, 8
    party platform in 1880, 76–77

Republican Party, *continued*
   reactions to Garfield's nomination, 95–96
   reactions to Winfield Hancock's Democratic nomination, 130–132
   Reconstruction politics in Louisiana and, 44
   response to Winfield Hancock's command of the Fifth Military District, 106–108
   John Sherman's pursuit of the 1880 Republican presidential candidacy, 52–54, 61–62, 63–64, 65–66, 67
   Warren rally for Garfield, 154–155
   wavering support for Grant's candidacy in 1880, 68, 69
   "waving the bloody shirt" and the presidential election of 1876, 9–10, 11
   James Baird Weaver and, 121
   See also Half-Breed Republicans; Stalwart Republicans
returning boards, 13, 15
Reunion and Reconstruction (Woodward), 22
"Revolution in Congress" (Garfield speech), 49, 52, 153
Richardson, Heather Cox, 2
Richardson, Israel B., 103
Robertson, William H., 177, 178–179
Rockwell, Almon, 183
Rosecrans, William S., 37–38, 147–148
Rudolph, Joseph, 180
Rudolph, Lucretia, 30, 31
Rudolph, Zeb, 30, 180
Rusk, Jeremiah ("Jerry"), 50–51

Sacramento Daily News, 153
San Francisco Call, 148
Schurz, Carl, 14, 21, 131, 140, 141, 160, 163–164
secession, 34
Seward, William Henry, 110, 145
Seymour, Horatio, 41, 109, 111
Sheldon, Lionel, 65
Sheridan, Philip H., 90, 104, 105, 107, 108, 109
Sherman, Ellen, 148–149

Sherman, John
   balloting at the Republican National Convention and, 87, 88, 89, 90, 91, 92
   Garfield as a supporter of in 1880, 52, 53–54, 61–62, 63–64, 65–66, 67
   Garfield's role of supporting at the Republican National Convention, 69, 70, 78–79
   Garfield's speech nominating at the Republican National Convention, 82–85, 86
   lack of appeal as a presidential candidate, 65
   on the Potter Committee investigation, 27
   pursuit of the 1880 Republican presidential candidacy, 52–54, 61–62, 63–64, 65–66, 67
   reaction to Garfield's nomination, 95–96
   reaction to the selection of Chester Arthur as vice presidential candidate, 94
   seconding speeches for at the Republican National Convention, 85–86
   as secretary of the treasury, 24, 29
   significance of the presidential election of 1880 and, 2
   support for Garfield in the 1880 presidential campaign, 132–133
   unit rule fight at the Republican National Convention and, 71
   as a US senator following Garfield's election, 167
   warning to Garfield about James Blaine's meddling, 168
Sherman, William Tecumseh, 88, 130
Simonton, James W., 158
slavery, Garfield's opposition to, 31, 33–34, 35–36
Smith, Theodore Clark, 67
soft money policy. *See* greenbacks
South
   electoral crisis of 1876, 13–23
   Garfield on post-Reconstruction conditions and civil rights in, 140

Winfield Hancock's command of the
  Fifth Military District, 104–109
Rutherford Hayes and sectional
  reconciliation, 24–26, 28
Rutherford Hayes and the presidential
  election of 1876, 7–8
L. Q. C. Lamar's defense of in the
  1876 presidential campaign, 45–46
popularity of Winfield Hancock in, 110
presidential election of 1880 and, 3, 159
Republican withdrawal from and the
  return of white supremacy, 140
secession and the start of the Civil
  War, 34–35
South Carolina
  1880 presidential election results and,
    159
  black voters and midterm elections of
    1878, 28
  Decoration Day and, 40
  electoral crisis of 1876 and, 13, 14, 16,
    17, 22
  Hamburg Massacre and the
    presidential election of 1876, 11
Southern black voters
  Democrats and the presidential
    election of 1876, 11–12
  electoral crisis of 1876 and, 14–15
  Hamburg Massacre and, 11
  the Rutherford Hayes presidency and,
    25
  midterm elections of 1878 and, 28
Specie Resumption Act (1875), 119
Spencer, Edward, 147
Stalwart Republicans
  absence of civil service reform in the
    1880 Republican national platform
    and, 76–77
  friction with the Half-Breed faction,
    72–73, 134, 136
  Garfield's cabinet appointments and,
    164–165, 166
  Garfield's conflict with Roscoe
    Conkling over patronage
    appointments, 175–180
  Garfield's presidential campaign and,
    139
  the Grant presidency and, 54, 55
  Grant's pursuit of the 1880

  Republican presidential candidacy
    and, 54, 55, 57–58, 61
  reaction to Garfield's nomination
    at the Republican National
    Convention, 93
  selection of Garfield's running mate
    and, 94
  selection of Republican Party national
    leadership in 1880 and, 133, 134
  unit rule fight at the Republican
    National Convention and, 68–72,
    73–74, 75–76
Stanley-Brown, Joseph, 155, 175
Stanton, Edwin, 104
Stephens, Alexander, 27, 47
Stevens, Thaddeus, 38
Stevenson, John W., 114
St. Louis Globe Democrat, 130
Strong, William, 20
"Suffrage and Slavery" (Garfield address),
  39

Taft, Alphonso, 62
tariff, 150, 155–156
Texas, 28, 107
Thayer, John M., 106
Thirteenth Amendment, 38
Thomas, George H., 104, 148
Thompson, Henry Adams, 124, 125
Three Hundred and Six Guard, 93
Thurman, Allen G., 11, 20, 102, 114
Tilden, Samuel J.
  electoral crisis of 1876, 13–21
  Winfield Hancock's presidential
    campaign and, 138
  health issues, 98
  George Hoadly's opening speech at
    the 1880 Democratic National
    Convention and, 113, 114
  indecision about entering the 1880
    presidential race, 97–100, 112–113
  the Potter Committee investigation
    and, 27, 97–98
  presidential election of 1876 and, 2–3,
    10, 11, 12
  significance of the presidential
    election of 1880 and, 2–3
  withdrawal from the 1880 Democratic
    presidential race, 115, 116

INDEX 219

To Make Men Free (Richardson), 2
Train, George Francis, 43
Triumvirate
    absence of civil service reform in the 1880 Republican national platform and, 77
    balloting at the 1880 Republican National Convention and, 87
    members of, 54
    unit rule fight at the Republican National Convention and, 68–69, 70–71, 73–74
    See also Cameron, Donald; Conkling, Roscoe; Logan, John
Trumbull, Lyman, 14
Tweed Ring, 10

Union Pacific Railroad, 43
unit rule, 68–72, 73–74, 75–76
US Supreme Court, Stephen Field and, 102

Voorhees, Daniel, 38, 114–115
voter fraud/intimidation
    electoral crisis of 1876 and, 14–15
    midterm elections of 1878 and, 28
    Reconstruction politics in Louisiana and, 44
voter registration, 108

Walker, Leroy Pope, 21
Wallace, Lew, 16
Wallace, William, 132
Warren rally, 154–155
Washburne, Elihu, 38, 70, 86, 87, 88, 89
Washington, George, 55
Washington Evening Star, 86
Washington National Republican, 28
Washington Post, 67–68
"waving the bloody shirt," 9–10, 11, 110, 132
Weaver, James Baird, 5, 121–122, 123–124
Weed, Smith M., 98
Weed, Thurlow, 145
Wells, J. Madison, 15
Western Reserve, 30
Western Reserve Eclectic Institute, 30, 31
West Virginia, 73–74
Wheeler, William, 6
white supremacy
    Democratic desire for home rule and, 116
    Winfield Hancock's command of the Fifth Military District and, 104–109
    L. Q. C. Lamar's defense of in the 1876 presidential campaign and, 45–46
    Republican withdrawal from the South and, 140
Whitney, William C., 99
Williams College, 31, 101
Wilson, Henry, 149
Windom, William, 70, 80, 88, 89
Winkler, E. C., 85
Wolfe, Thomas, 1
Wood, Fernando, 38
Woodward, C. Vann, 22
Wormley, James, 22
Wormley's Hotel meeting, 22, 24

Young, John Russell, 56, 67–68

www.ingramcontent.com/pod-product-compliance
Lightning Source LLC
Chambersburg PA
CBHW070802230426
43665CB00017B/2461